Anna's War

By Penny Altmann

Anna's War
©2018 by Penny Altmann

Dedication

To my husband David, who stole my heart
and our five children,
Marc, Louise, Tamara, Charity and Luc.

But most of all to my sister Tina
who left us far too early
and who I miss more than words can say.

Endorsement

"This is Penny Altmann's first published novel; however she has honed her work for many years, quietly writing for her own pleasure and that of family and close friends. She is a highly creative and talented artist, who at last has decided to let the rest of the world know about her hidden talents.

Anna's War is a beautiful and compelling love story involving an intercontinental plot, which has all the twists and turns you would expect from a seasoned writer, based in war torn London and Normandy, with secrets even the main character's family don't know. Tantalisingly Altmann holds her readers in the suspense of what happens in the war as well as the romance between a young couple in a more innocent age. I am happy to have discovered her, and highly recommend her as a thoroughly good read – definitely a book to add to your library."

International Business, Lifestyle & Legacy Strategist; Author of *Colour Your Legacy, Paint the Canvas of Your Perfect Life.*

"What a tangled web we weave when first we practice to deceive."

– Sir Walter Scott
1771-1832

Prologue

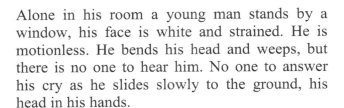

Alone in his room a young man stands by a window, his face is white and strained. He is motionless. He bends his head and weeps, but there is no one to hear him. No one to answer his cry as he slides slowly to the ground, his head in his hands.

Alone in a different part of town in another room, a young woman stands silently by a window. She too bends her head and weeps, but there is no one to hear her. No one to answer her cries. Hot tears stream down her face as she too falls silently to the ground.

Chapter 1

Anna

It was five o'clock and almost dark, tea and buttered toast lay ready on a small table by the fire. Mama was playing cards with the girls. I was trying to draw but I had felt restless all day and couldn't concentrate on anything. It was like I was waiting for something to happen. I couldn't put my finger on it, but something niggled at me making me fractious.

Earlier I had walked into town. The overnight bombings had ceased and again London lay devastated. We had been lucky, our street had hardly been touched, yet behind us a whole row of houses had been razed to the ground. One house still stood, if precariously, its façade gone leaving a shell where the fireplace appeared to hang in mid-air, a piece of wall barely holding it up, the flowered wallpaper incongruous in the burnt out desolation surrounding it. Seeing it made me shiver. Mary had lived there with her two younger sisters and parents. That night she had been out with a crowd of us. The rest of the family were hiding in the cellar when the bomb struck. Mary is my best friend; we had grown up together, gone to the same school, danced with the same boys and even kissed the same ones.

Seeing her so heartbroken was terrible. Why do the worst things always happen to the nicest people? I kicked at some blackened bricks lying in the road, the pain was excruciating, and a hot knife shot up from my toe into my head. 'Damn. Damn. Damn!' I was so angry, angry at how all this misery had destroyed Mary and her family's life. 'God I hate you, how can I believe in someone that would let this happen? I will never ever pray to you again, never, ever.' I was shouting by now and an old man passing by looked nervously out of the corner of his eye, scurrying past his cane hitting the pavement urgently.

Opposite was the church. The churchyard now full of new graves, some already with their stones engraved but mostly there were just dark mounds of black earth scattered with wilted flowers. The church had remained virtually untouched, just the spire stood, bent at a strange angle with a gaping hole in the side. Inside it was icy cold, so cold I could see my breath. A few candles burned at the altar, fresh flowers stiffly arranged in their vases stood as if to attention. I looked up above the altar where a crucifix hung. How can I pray to you I thought angrily; if I did pray it wouldn't change a thing, nothing would, would it? Oh how pointless it all seemed. Once I had believed that there was a God that loved us, but how could I believe that now; if there was a God he was a God of wrath, a God of evil, not the God of love I had been brought up to worship. Suddenly I felt very tired and wanted to be home. It was getting dark, so I left the sad cold church and walked slowly down the road. My nose was running, and tears slipped down my face, I wiped my nose on my sleeve and thought how Mama would have scolded me. My toe throbbed where I had kicked the bricks, it was almost pleasurable, and I welcomed the pain; I needed something to concentrate on other than the wretched war and how it ripped the heart out of ordinary people like us.

Sitting around the fire with Mama and the girls made me more settled somehow. The tea was hot and sweet and the buttered toast delicious. I started to feel a bit better. We had been so lucky, our house had missed the terrible bombings and maybe I should thank God for that. We were all safe, Mama, Papa, me and the girls, but I still felt dreadfully sad and didn't feel much like being thankful about anything. I was enjoying sketching the little group now and I was pleased with the result. I was looking forward to finishing it and transferring it to pastel paper, hopefully it would go into my exhibition, fingers crossed I thought. I was at my happiest with a pencil in my hand.

The old wall clock chimed five times, it's deep, rich sound always so comforting, especially now in such a dark world. At the same time I heard the front door bell. 'I'll go,' I jumped up and turned the light on in the porch, the red and green of the stained glass door threw lozenges of light across the black and white tiled floor. Suddenly remembering there was a black out I turned it off immediately leaving George standing on the doorstep in the dark. 'Come in, I thought you would be at the surgery with your father.' I took his hand, 'Come on, it's freezing out there.'

'I can't stay,' his voice sounded harsh and broken.

'George, what's wrong, you look awful, please come in.'

He looked at me, he still had hold of my hand, 'It's Jack, Anna,' his hand was squeezing mine so tight.

'Oh my God.' I felt sick.

His face was so sad. 'There was a telegram earlier, it just said *missing in action*. That's all, nothing else.'

I thought I was going to faint. I could feel my teeth chattering. He put his arm around me.

'I don't know any more than that, nobody does. Come on,' he said shutting the front door and then he was leading *me* into the living room.

Mama and the girls were still playing cards, they all looked up as we walked in. The firelight throwing a golden light around them, reminded me in a strange unreal way of a Caravaggio's chiaroscuro, the light casting dark shadows across the little lamp lit scene. How could I notice something so trivial at such a terrible time? How strange the mind was. The sight of my family looking so peaceful broke my heart, how quickly things changed. *Dear God*, I thought, *give me strength to cope with all this please.*

'Oh George, how lovely come and sit down, there's some tea and toast waiting to be eaten,' Mama patted the chair next to her. 'Come and get warm you look frozen,' she looked questioningly at each of us. 'What's wrong? You both look frightful.'

'It's Jack, Evelyn.' I could feel his nails digging into my palm. 'He's missing in action.' Giving a dry sob he let go of my hand and sunk down onto a chair. 'My dear boy,' Mama stood up and put her arms around him. 'Your poor mother, how is she?'

'Pretty bad but Father gave her something to calm her, I don't think she's taken it in really, none of us have, it's such a shock.' He shook his head. 'Such a bloody awful shock.'

After George left I went up to my room, I felt sick, so tired I could hardly drag my feet up the stairs. Lying on my bed I thought it can't be true, it is all a terrible mistake, it has to be, I won't let it be true, I won't. I wanted to die. I felt frightened, frightened of what may have happened to Jack, my mind making up deadly scenarios, scaring myself half to death. I got up and walked over to the window, the light was pale and washed out, like me, I thought, colourless. I felt I could fly my body felt so light and insubstantial. Jack, Jack, Jack, that is all I could think. My head whirled with the words, with the sorrow of it all. It was an indescribable almost unbearable pain that I could hardly bear.

That night, I lay there with my hands straight at my side, in my white nightgown, my shroud; I am dead too I thought. A great weight seemed to press me down through the bed, through the floor, through the earth, down and down until my limbs were like stone, so heavy I knew I could not and did not want to move. I lay like that until the walls, covered in pink, white and crimson roses turned to silver as the green light from the moon slanted across my bed

I had met Jack when I was ten years old, his family had moved in just across the river and were to come to dinner that night. There were twin boys of fourteen and we were to behave ourselves and not tease them. They were the only children and probably not used to big families. We were told we could stay up and eat with everyone if we behaved. My little sisters were too young to really understand and just clapped their chubby hands together and twirled around. Bertie turned a double somersault with joy at the idea of having some boys to play with. I was intrigued, never having met twins before and thought it all tremendously exciting

That evening I fell in love with the boy with green eyes and curly black hair. To me he looked just like a gypsy from one of my books. His brother looked identical, but Jack's smile was different, well to me it was; it lit up his face somehow. Both the boys were very polite and shook hands with us which made me feel very grown up. Their mother was French and their father a doctor who was to take over the practice in town. The boys fascinated me. I spent most of the evening gazing in wonder at these beautiful people. I got confused who was who but when Jack smiled I knew which one was which, well I thought I did.

Chapter 2

One year earlier, September 3^{rd,} 1939

Anna's father, Teddy Cooper sat glumly by his wireless. At precisely 11-15 am on the BBC there was to be an announcement by Neville Chamberlain. With Teddy were his wife Evelyn, Anna, her elder brother Bertie, who leaning against the fireplace was trying to be extremely nonchalant about the whole thing, shooting his cuffs while puffing hard on a cigarette; finally their two younger sisters, Elizabeth and Victoria, both giggling with their hands across their mouths, too young to comprehend what was about to happen. It was as though the very air was clenched while everyone held their breath and waited. Then from the wireless came the sombre voice of Neville Chamberlain.

'This morning the British Ambassador in Berlin handed the German government a final note, stating that, unless we heard from them by eleven o'clock that they were prepared at once to withdraw their troops from Poland, a state of war would exist between us. I have to tell you now, that no such undertaking has been received, consequently this country is at war with Germany.'

There was a sudden intake of breath and then silence, only the steady ticking of the grandfather clock could be heard. Teddy bent down and turned the wireless off, he was holding his wife's hand very tightly. Evelyn looked across at Bertie there was pain in her eyes. The thought of her son who now would be torn away from her to fight was almost too much to bear. Please don't let me lose him too she prayed as the memories of her dead babies flashed across her mind.

Across the other side of town in another house, in another drawing room the same scene was being set, but here there were just four people playing their parts. Ernest and Nell with their sons, Jack and George. They too were listening to the wireless, which, encased in a rather magnificent piece of mahogany furniture with the soft light from the coal fire dancing across its highly polished surface, gave a feeling of warmth and security to the little group.

If you were watching them you would want to join them. To sit and enjoy the heat from the fire and sip your tea from the fine china cups and be included in their company, which even at a time like this seemed remarkably calm and easy.

After the sombre news, silence lay heavily like a blanket wrapped around them. Ernest leant over and turned the wireless off. He looked at his wife and his sons. 'Well,' he took a huge intake of breath and sighed deeply. 'There we are, we knew it would be bad news.' He rubbed his hands across his eyes. 'I think a large G & T would be an extremely sensible idea. One of you boys can sort it out I need to make a few phone calls.'

'Listen!' George jumped up and looked out of the window, 'it's a bloody siren!'

Outside the streets were deserted, the sky grey and heavy with unshed rain.

'I'm sure it's just a practice or something.'

'Bloody hope so.' Jack looked at his father hopefully.

'Definitely, it has to be a try-out, listen it's stopped. That's a relief.'

'Good heavens.' Helen sat down heavily on the sofa. 'This all seems so unreal somehow. I can't imagine what will happen to us all.'

She started to cry.

'It's okay mother,' said the boys, 'it will be alright, please don't cry, you never cry.'

'Well I am now, if I can't cry when war is being declared when can I? You know, that Gin and Tonic would be most welcome even if it is so early in the day. Drastic times mean drastic measures.' She laughed, 'I'm okay boys, just shocked.'

Ernest smiled across at her, 'I think we all are.'

'Now what happens?' Helen sighed, 'I suppose you boys will be called up.'

'I think you will find you boys are exempt for the time being. According to Teddy, who has the ear of the PM, anyone - doctors, surgeons and people in an important and necessary role in the community - will be called up once the majority are enlisted. That is if the need for more men becomes imperative. Unless of course you are a pacifist then you would probably land up in jail.'

George roared with laughter and Jack smiled rather wanly.

'Well,' sighed Nell, 'that is a bit of relief, a stay of execution as they say. Oh God, what a dreadful mess this all is.' She laughed slightly hysterically raising her glass. 'God bless you both, my darlings.'

'And may Hitler go to Hell,' they said in unison. Their glasses clinked, and Nell's heart lurched suddenly at the thought of what could happen to their sons. What would the future bring? She would have to be strong, something she wasn't very good at she pondered, but I am sure I will learn.

Putting the phone down Ernest watched his family and felt alarmed that more than likely his sons would be dragged into this ghastly war. They say war brings people closer together, he grunted to himself. It seems to me it will tear us all apart.

Chapter 3

'Well I guess we will be called up; I wonder how long we will have to wait? Jack, are you listening, what the hell are you doing?'

'Nothing, I'm listening and yes I know we will be called up. Bloody hell, the thought of it, another fucking war. Britain's still recovering from the last one. It's crazy.'

'I don't think it would be all that bad actually,' George replied. 'It will be a bit of excitement to blunt the boredom, an adventure I suppose.'

'You suppose wrong George it will be a sodding mess and you well know it. Look at the last one.'

'But this is different.'

'No, it's not, it will be even worse this time. Look at all the killing machines we have now.'

'Well we don't have a choice, so we will have to get on with it and bite the bullet as they say. Literally.'

'Not funny George. You like excitement and to you it is as you said, an adventure, but to me it is a nightmare. Leaving work just when things are starting to make sense. It horrifies me to think all our work will come to nothing. We, I, were just starting to find some clues to it all, the thought of letting it all go to waste is horrendous. The rest of the team will be called up of course and then I will be, so the whole bloody research department will fold, and we are so near with it all.. I hate the thought of having to let it all fizzle out. It is such a big step in understanding the Brain, the Mind whatever it's called. So there you go. That is why I am dubious about enlisting.'

'Bit of a pacifist, Jack?' George laughed. 'They'll bang you up in the Tower or shoot you, you know that don't you?'

'Oh, fuck off George, that's not the slightest bit funny.'

'Well if that is what you have decided to do, it will be hard for Mother and Father to understand, and what the hell will Anna think of you?'

'She will think I am a coward probably and she would be right. Anyway, they won't take you with your heart murmur, so you will be out of it and can carry on being a GP with Father.'

'You're right. Bloody, bloody hell, I never thought of that, but it's only an innocent murmur, you know; Father knows. Anyway, look at Grandfather, he has the same problem and he is ninety and still rides a bicycle.'

'Makes no difference, you will be turned down, it's ironical if you think about it. Here you are desperate to do bloody deeds and here I am terrified by it all. It's really quite funny.'

George stared at Jack. 'Of course, there's your answer, we will change places, you stay here, and I will go in your place.'

'What on earth are you going on about? Don't be ridiculous. You're insane!'

'Why am I? We are identical twins, really identical; no would know the difference. We can go to be enlisted together as ourselves, when I am turned down you will become me and stay here, and I will ride away like a knight on a white charger. Remember when we were at school and you would do my detention for me in exchange for me letting you read my comic first. We did it four or five times and no one was any the wiser.'

'For God's sake, that was when we were children. We are grown men now and we are talking about war, not playing games at school. Are you quite mad? Mother and Father would know straight away and what about Anna? She'd guess, she knows me better than anyone.'

'In the biblical sense, Jack?'

'No unfortunately not, just waiting, more's the pity, but I'm working on it.'

'How do you know they will boot me out, you don't know for sure. This war has never happened before!'

'Well I guarantee I am right,' said Jack. 'And I still think it's a stupid idea, far too dangerous. What if we were found out, I can't let you go. What sort of brother do you think I am?'

'*My* brother, and I told you, it is nothing. I can live with it, you know all about it. The medical board will say no but you will be me so that will be fine!'

'I guess so, but I would still have to give up the research. I will have to be you, a GP. How on earth can I do a job like that?'

'Easy peasy, you are a trained doctor, it's only a matter of holding people's hands and listening to their woes. Father is the mainstay of the surgery, he does all the serious stuff, and the nurse will never know the difference. She's so weird anyway so she will be no problem. Also, think about it, you can work in your lab when you can. It will be a doddle I just know, best thing I have ever thought up, sheer genius.'

'Oh do shut up. I really don't think it will work. Say something awful happens to you, then what am I going to feel like? A shit, that's what. No, it's a non-starter I will just have, as you said, to bite the bullet and get on with it.'

'Nothing will happen to me, they're not going to put me on the front line, just think about it. We can't do anything now anyway. Wait until we hear from the hierarchy. I think it's a brilliant idea.'

Chapter 4

At the same time the boys were discussing their plan, Anna was lying on her bed trying to come to terms with Chamberlain's broadcast. It didn't seem possible. It couldn't be happening, not to her. Anna Cooper, eighteen years old; it was too scary to contemplate. She was terrified, what would happen to her, and what about Bertie, he would be called up. She felt tears pricking behind her eyes. It was all too terrible. And both Jack and George will be called up of course. Jack will go away - he may even be killed. She felt tears slide down her face and into her ears.

She sat up abruptly. This is ridiculous, I have to be grown up about this. Mama will be in a state and Father will be trying to organise everyone and get some kind of order into the chaos. 'My German ancestry,' he would laugh. His grandfather had been German, married an English girl and moved to Britain with her. Anna could barely remember either of them, they had died when she was still a child, yet there were of course photos of them everywhere. He was very handsome, she was tiny, rather like a little bird. How ironic Anna

thought that we are yet again fighting the Germans.

She sighed and got off the bed feeling exhausted. Hopefully it will all be over in a few months and maybe the boys won't be called up at all. She looked at herself in the dressing table mirror. Her hair was a wild tangle of black curls her grey eyes were tired. She looked like she felt; a mess. 'Time to go downstairs,' she sighed again. 'I ought to go and see how everyone is after this morning. I bet the twins are worried about it all. Oh, how glad I'm a girl,' she smiled to herself. 'I am really rather pleased I wasn't born a boy.'

Evelyn was in the kitchen by herself. She looked up when Anna walked in. She saw that her mother had been crying. 'Oh Mama.' She put her arms around her. She couldn't remember the last time she had seen her cry. Evelyn looked at her daughter and smiled through her tears. 'I knew there was a chance that war would be on the cards but somehow I never quite believed it and now it has happened. You know I just can't bear the thought of losing Bertie to this wretched war, maybe to die, oh God it is so dreadful.' She started to cry again. 'But I am not alone, think of all the other mothers in the same situation. Look at poor Nell, both the boys will leave her, it is all too terrible.'

She held tightly to Anna's hand and kissed her gently on the cheek. 'I thank God I have you and the girls to keep me sane and your father will be strong as usual, so let's have a cup of tea and go and sit by the fire. I will bring in the

Simmel cake too, and we will spoil ourselves. I think we deserve it, don't you?' She smiled.

Evelyn had married Teddy Cooper when she was just eighteen. She had fallen immediately, desperately in love with this tall handsome stranger who courted her outrageously with presents, flowers, invitations to dinner, theatres, operas; anything that was 'the thing' at the time. It seemed as if she was in a crazy whirlwind of such euphoria and was borne along with it all as if in a heady dream. She could hardly believe that someone like Teddy Cooper could be courting her like this, swearing that he adored her and couldn't live a moment more without her.

They had met at Ada Foster's Dancing School in London. He had asked her to dance, making her stomach lurch. It was her second week at the school and she had been feeling shy and awkward and really had far too few lessons to be any good at all. She felt too tall, as usual. Then instead of some horribly short man, here was this gloriously tall Adonis who was standing with his hand outstretched. She took it and her life changed for ever.

They had married three months later much to everyone's incredulity. Her parents were charmed by Teddy, even more so when they knew of his wealth. They were really rather glad to get their only daughter off their hands, as young as she was. Their life would be so less complicated without her and they had a lot of travelling planned. They loved Evelyn deeply, but children were never really quite in their scheme of things and her arrival had been rather bewildering to them both and still seemed to be at times.

Exactly nine months after they were married Evelyn gave birth to Bertie. Sitting with Teddy in the evenings curled up at his feet they would listen to the wireless, smoke their cigarettes and talk of their tiny son asleep upstairs and wonder what the future might bring. He would twist his fingers through her thick dark hair while she leant against his knees, and he would kiss her throat whispering words of love. Then winding her arms around his neck he would take her upstairs.

Shortly after, Evelyn gave birth to twin boys. Born at home, so early that they could do nothing but die. There in her arms, swaddled in their white shawls she held them close to her like broken dolls and felt as though her heart would burst. She had never known such agony, such helplessness. Teddy had tried to stroke her hair, but she pushed him away sobbing that he couldn't understand; how could he? They were her babies and they were dead, and she wished she was dead too.

For weeks after the twins' death she had laid upstairs in her bed and would see no one. Only Bertie who would come and look at her questioningly, far too young to know what was going on. She wanted nothing but sleep. At twenty-one she felt her life was over.

Slowly Evelyn returned to her family and friends, but things were different. She would turn her back when Edward came to bed; see the hurt in his eyes when he watched her brushing her hair, getting dressed, all the things she used to love doing when she knew he was looking. There would be that wonderful surge of passion but now it was all so different. She would feel his eyes forever on her and catch sight of him so forlorn she wanted to weep. For Evelyn there could be no more babies, how could she carry inside her something so wonderful, so precious and yet take that awful chance that again she may go through the terrible agony of never being able to love, only to mourn.

Sometimes she would awake from idyllic dreams of her baby boys, of them running towards her, with golden curls bouncing against their rosy cheeks. Kneeling down to feel their kisses like butterflies on her face she would hold them close and smell their sweet scent. She

would awaken with tears on her face and all the next day she would feel exhausted with such overwhelming sadness that she wondered how she could bear it, but she told no one, it was her sorrow and that sorrow she embraced.

Yet, even so when time had healed her deepest wounds Anna was born then six years later Victoria, a surprise baby as was Elizabeth, born two years after. 'We were very irresponsible,' Evelyn laughed, 'but so glad we were!' Both were beautiful healthy girls, she loved them without question but her '*lost boys*' as she secretly called them were never far from her thoughts.

Now there were different sorrows, different worries. Her children were grown, and she was happy, not with that blissfulness that came with youth but with a kind of acceptance that her life was what it was, and she must accept it. The loss of her baby boys faded into the distance but the love of them was enclosed within her like a secret that she treasured.

Chapter 5

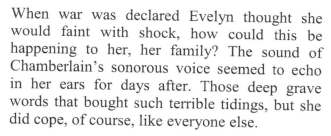

When war was declared Evelyn thought she
would faint with shock, how could this be
happening to her, her family? The sound of
Chamberlain's sonorous voice seemed to echo
in her ears for days after. Those deep grave
words that bought such terrible tidings, but she
did cope, of course, like everyone else.

At the start of the war Churchill had suggested
that middle aged men who had served in the last
war should form their own army which became
to be known as the Home Guard. There was one
requisite, that they were capable of firing a rifle
or shotgun, which, according to Teddy he was a
dab hand at, as he informed Evelyn and the
children. Bertie's eyes lit up at the idea of
getting his hands on a gun, at twenty he was still
very much a boy, he gave one the impression of
someone trying too hard to grow up and yet not
really wanting to.

Taking his family into the garden Teddy started
shooting at a target with his old WW1 gun he
had stashed away, never thinking it would be
needed again. Evelyn was appalled and insisted
he stopped immediately, Victoria and Elizabeth
clapped their hands with glee, and watched as
Anna had a go, much to Evelyn's horror, Bertie

tried too and made a real mess of it, feeling rather embarrassed he laughed, 'Not sure how good I'm going to be fighting the Nazi's, I don't seem to have a very good eye!'

'Oh, for goodness sake Teddy, put the wretched thing away it terrifies me, and yes you were very good dear,' Evelyn gave a weak smile. 'Let's hope you never have to use it!'

A couple of weeks later Bertie enlisted and decided on the Navy, much to Evelyn's relief, as somehow him being at sea seemed much more favourable than on the ground running around with a gun.

When Bertie left by train she felt as if her heart would break. To her he was no more than a child, yet deemed old enough to go and fight for his country and more than likely to die while doing it. She had cried and ached with love for him, but her hands were tied; she could do nothing, she was helpless. He was like all those other sons, being torn brutally from their families. All she could do now was pray he would come back to them all.

The night before he left she had been sitting with him on his bed, helping to sort out his clothes; the thought of him leaving horrified her. She started to talk too quickly and erratically, trying hard to hide her fear of the entire situation; the sheer misery she felt inside of having to watch him go and maybe never see him again was unbearable.

She thought of the day he had left for boarding school, the terrible feeling of despair inside her all that day, seeing him look so grown up at ten, too young to leave. But it was the school his father had been at and his father before him, so it was a tradition too dear to Teddy's heart to change it.

'Do you think you will be warm enough? I hope they give you some warmer clothes once you are there. I am sure you will make lots of friends, you always do. Remember when you left for boarding school, how worried you were because you knew no one and cried, then by half term you made good friends and spent the holiday with one of them instead of coming home. I was quite bereft you know,' she laughed. 'And now you are off again only ten years older; you won't forget to write will you, just to let us know you are okay, Father said the letters would be censored but just to hear from you will be nice...'

Her voice trailed off, she knew she was talking utter rubbish. She thought she would break into pieces, she could feel the tears threatening but she had promised herself she wouldn't cry. She would just scream instead. 'Don't go, please don't go, you may die, how will I live without you, I can't bear it, I can't.' But of course she did nothing of the sort and did what all *'good'* mothers do, pretend it didn't matter. She hid her face as she started to sort, fold and arrange his small amount of clothes on the bed. Bertie had hugged her and laughed, 'Mother I'll be okay really, please don't worry, and I'll be back before you know it. She had smiled and swallowed the tears that were promising to choke her.

'Yes I know, I will be fine, probably it will be better once we have all said goodbye and anyway I always hate goodbyes of any sort, she patted the small pile ofclothes on the bed as if it was a small animal, then packing it all carefully into the little brown leather case and clicking the catches she patted the case itself. 'I am just going to make some tea will you have some?'

'Good idea Mother, I will be right there, just need to make sure everything is tickety-boo here and I have all my papers sorted out and all that sort of thing. I'll join you in a sec.'

As she walked towards the door he reached out and grabbed her hand. 'I will be okay, I promise, I do love you, I know I never say it, but well you know,' he shrugged.

He was her child again and her heart ached for him,

'I will miss you all dreadfully.'

She saw his eyes fill with tears as he turned away; of course, she thought, he was scared too. She smiled at him, 'and we will miss you too my darling, just stay safe and whatever you do don't die!'

They both laughed and in the midst of her sadness she was glad that she had made such a stupid remark while this dreadful drama was unfolding in front of them all.

The whole family had been there to see him off. Paddington Station was full to bursting, with children being sent to the country, and young men to their units. Victoria and Elizabeth, in their best navy blue wool coats, the collars trimmed with velvet, their hair tied back in tight pigtails with scarlet ribbons, stood transfixed by the deafening noise of carriage doors slamming, whistles blowing and the incessant river of voices as porters shouted above the noise, while a multitude of people boarded the trains that hissed and threw out their evil smoke into the already sulphurous air.

Anna and her mother stood silently. Both in their new cloche hats with tiny white spotted veils just skimming their eyebrows, making Anna feel rather mysterious and exotic. Evelyn, waiting for the goodbyes that would arrive any minute, was again holding back the tears that were due to spill over any second now.

Everywhere there were families weeping and clutching their loved ones as if they would disappear never to be seen again. Evelyn clung on to Teddy, as if he too would suddenly vanish along with them.

Bertie stood proud in his naval uniform; straightening his back and tilting his head he felt immortal, invincible. He had no intention of dying - he would return a hero.

Then suddenly over a loudspeaker came orders for his unit to board the train, grabbing his small suitcase and looking far less confident than he felt before, he kissed his mother and his sisters goodbye. Evelyn with tears finally falling held him so tight as if she would never let him go.

Teddy took his son's hand in both of his and squeezed it, Bertie looked at him and threw his arms around him. 'Goodbye Father, look after the girls and Mother, won't you? He could feel his voice trembling, 'time to go.'

Evelyn, clinging tightly to Teddy's hand watched as their only son boarded the train and was then swallowed up by men jostling and pushing their way on board. Pulling down the corridor window he shouted above the racket. 'Don't worry Mother, I'll be fine, bye girls, bye Father.' As the train pulled away they all stood there waving and waving until it disappeared out of sight.

'Right,' said Teddy. 'Tea at Claridges, definitely, I can't let my beautiful girls miss being seen in their new hats.'

'Yes, yes Daddy.' The two little girls jumped up and down clapping their hands, pigtails flying around their heads. Bertie's farewell fading into the distance.

Evelyn looked at Anna. 'Come on,' she laughed, 'let's show them how hats should be worn!'

Wiping their eyes and holding their heads high, hands clasping each other's, while Teddy held up the rear with two very excited little girls in tow, they walked towards the row of black taxi cabs glistening in the rain. To Evelyn they were like a line of black hearses, ready to whisk her family away. She shivered and clasped Anna's hand tighter as if she too may suddenly disappear as Bertie had.

Chapter 6

Six months later

Jack and George were ensconced in the local pub one Sunday morning. Sitting in a corner away from the crowd with their pints of bitter, they planned their deception.

'So this is what we will do,' George talked in a hushed voice. 'When we volunteer we go in together, dress alike, not that anyone will really be looking at us, otherwise I can't see a problem. Everyone says it's all very quick and easy. We have a medical and then the usual rigmarole of birth certificates etc. We just need to be really organised.'

'Fuck George, are you sure we should do this, it sounds nerve wracking to me. Are you positive we won't be found out? Somehow I can't see me being much good at pretending to be you,'

'Of course you will be, there's nothing to do really - just remember to answer when someone calls you George! I think it is a bloody good idea, and no one will be any the wiser I guarantee it.'

'Okay.' Jack said looking extremely sceptical. 'Let's go through it again, alright.'

A week later the twins sat in the town hall. The place was crowded with young men, all looking extremely nervous and puffing furiously on cigarettes, each engrossed in their own thoughts. No one was talking. One by one they went into a separate room and came out looking far happier and smiling. One or two, put their thumbs up, saying, 'no problem chaps, easy as pie.'

'Well,' said George. 'Here we are, do hope I go in first, how I hate this wretched waiting.'

'We have only been here ten minutes for goodness sake, anyway I think this is all crazy – I'm really not sure if I want to go ahead with this.'

'Well there's nothing to do yet. Bertie said it was a doddle when he enlisted for the Navy, so can't see there will be much different for us joining the RAF, so stop worrying. Anyway, it's obvious I will be rejected, and you won't be. There's nothing to it. For heaven's sake, have another fag and stop looking as if you are going to the guillotine.'

A large man with a huge moustache shouted across the room. 'You lot next.' He read out a list of names one of them George's.

'Good luck old chap,' Jack squeezed his elbow, gave a rather weak smile trying to look as though he was enjoying the whole situation.

Twenty minutes later George emerged smiling and sat down next to Jack. 'No problems, brother, just a bit of a parade and then a bit of paperwork.'

'So? Jack almost growled, 'what happened?'

'Well, not a lot really. Except we had to parade up and down the room in single file while stark bollock naked in front of a load of officers. Then we had to stop, turn to the right while the inspecting officer looked at our private bits, then if he thought we looked free from anything remotely unpleasant he waved us on and that was it. Rather ghastly actually, and bloody cold too. I will be rejected of course, I saw they had all the info on my *innocent heart murmur,* but even so I have to go to another part of the building for a medical which seems a waste of time considering they know I won't be joining up.'

The moustached man shouted again, and Jack and others walked hesitatingly towards the door. 'In here lads.' Moustache smiled, showing large yellow teeth, his fat pink lips smirking. 'There is a room over there where you will all need to undress and wait until you are called.' He closed the door softly behind him.

Chapter 7

A week later

'So there you go Jack, I have been rejected and you are the chosen one. Now we have to start turning into each other! God, I need a stiff drink.'

They found a bar in a nearby hotel which was a bit seedy but convenient.

'Well we are halfway there Jack, here's to us.' Clinking glasses they sunk into the patched padded seats and lit up the inevitable cigarettes. There was silence as they both inhaled deeply before knocking back their large whiskies.

'Now things are on a roll Jack, we have to really get this so right.'

'Not sure about all this,' sighed Jack scratching his head. 'It all seems so wrong somehow. Such deception. You with a bloody heart murmur joining up it all seems absurd to me. They'll probably put us in prison if the authorities find out. We have to stop it now before it's too late. I am serious George.'

'I'm serious too Jack. It will be okay, you know my heart murmur is innocent, which is not dangerous. Remember Father talking to us about it when they found out I had the problem? You are a medical man anyway, so you know it is nothing.'

'What about Anna though? She would murder me if she knew, or probably never talk to me again and Mother and Father I am sure they will guess something is up, they're not stupid, and we are their children.'

'They won't know, why should they? Anyway I plan to write a letter to them saying it was all my idea; which you will keep in case anything does happen to me. But it won't, before you interrupt. Now listen, I have just realised that you part your hair on the left and I on the right, so we have to change that immediately.' And he starts to play with Jack's hair.

'Hey, leave off, people will think we are a couple of pansies.'

'Oh give us a kiss then.'

'Sod off.'

'Seriously Jack, it's what you wanted; you can carry on with your research. As you said that is more important than anything. If I really thought it wouldn't work I would say, I think it will be a doddle.'

'Huh, don't think that is the right word somehow George.'

'Righty ho, we have a month at least before I leave for training apparently, so we have to sort things out. Give it a try just give it a try, okay?'

'If I do, it doesn't mean anything is definite as long as you get that into your head, alright?'

'Okey dokey. So first things first, I am going to wash my hair then part it on the other side it really hurt when it was dry when I tried, so I guess if it is wet it will be okay.'

'You are joking of course. Good grief if anyone could hear this conversation.'

So the deception began.

Five weeks later George left for Uxbridge where he was given his uniform and a white canvas kit bag which would travel everywhere with him. They gave him his RAF number and best of all a wad of five one pound notes. Payment in advance. Riches for a young man who had done nothing to earn it. Well not yet, but he would, without doubt, earn every penny. After about six weeks he left for Scotland and his training to become a pilot in His Majesty's Royal Airforce began.

Chapter 8

Jack

There were a few phone calls from George but no information as everything was all apparently top secret. When he came home on leave he would talk excitedly how he was learning to fly a Tiger Moth. How he was soon to be upgraded to Spitfires which he said was quite amazing. He told me that later he was actually more nervous than he thought he would be now he was starting the 'real stuff.'

I told him that things seemed to be okay with Anna but how I felt like a first class shit! 'God help me', I said, 'if she ever found out. I am sure she is telling me things she would never have done to my face, it actually is quite uncomfortable at times.' George laughed and said he bet I loved it and was certain my head was definitely bigger since he had left.

Anna had joined us boys earlier in the day and had clung onto George like a limpet. 'God I missed you, how am I going to cope when you go away to fight? I can't bear it.' She looked at him her grey eyes full of tears

Poor George, I thought as I witnessed them with their arms entwined. He does look so uncomfortable, poor chap. What I want to know is what happens when he kisses her? Surely then she'll suspect something. Also the thought of George snogging her is not what I want to think about somehow.

The day George went back to his unit, he said he felt like nothing on earth leaving me in such a quagmire, and when Mother wept that she would miss him and told him to stay safe he said he nearly blurted out that he was really George and wished none of his had stupid idea had come to fruition. I felt bad for him and forever guilty.

When he left it was as though part of me went with him and my conscious was killing me. What have I done, what have I done? The words kept repeating in my head over and over until I thought I would go half-crazy with it all.

Being with Anna was so hard. She talked continuously of me, Jack. Saying how much she missed me and loved me. She really did think I was George as everyone else seemed to, which really surprised me. I was so sure someone would come up and whisper. *'I know who you really are.'* I would wake at night convinced he or she was outside the door ready to pounce and unmask me. My dreams were confused, and I would wake wondering who I actually was and if I was going slightly mad.

I walked around on tenterhooks for days after George left. Mother and Father seemed completely unaware of anything untoward. We really have fooled them I thought, feeling dreadful at the thought of all the deceiving we were doing. It was as though I was spiralling into chaos, gathering momentum day by day.

Working in the surgery was strange for the first few days. George had left screeds of information on patients and their foibles, writing that – somehow *they* seemed more important than their maladies - A lot of the women had sons or husbands who had joined up, so I had the feeling the earache and headache and any ache was an excuse to talk. I often wondered what they would have thought if they had known who I really was. The nurse was rather strange as George had said. She came across as a real dizzy blonde with lots of permed hair and very red lipstick, but even so she appeared to be efficient enough and the patients seemed to like her. She was perfectly at ease with me and did flutter her eyelashes from time to time, which was obviously meant for George.

Father seemed oblivious to most things, except for his dedication as a doctor. I felt such admiration for him. He always had time to talk to his patients however worn out and tired he was. I never let my guard down, but it was exhausting, and sleepless nights weren't helping as well as worrying about how my research was progressing. I would go to my lab most evenings after surgery and then work until late. I told Mother and Father I was with friends, luckily no one questioned me.

I remember the first time I had met the man who had held out a hand of friendship to me when I was confused with what path to take. I was up at Oxford with George. He was reading medicine. I was reading science and pathology, I had no idea what I wanted to do no real passion, unlike George, who had always wanted to be a doctor like father. I sort of followed suit but was more interested in research and thought maybe I would follow that route.

I first met Howard Florey, an unassuming Australian, both a pharmacologist and pathologist, when he was carrying out clinical trials at the Radcliffe Infirmary, treating a postman who had severe septicaemia. The man had an eye removed as he was in such agony and was slowly dying. Florey's team treated him with doses of penicillin and he started to recover but the penicillin ran out. They tried the radical process of recycling his urine, but he relapsed and died. It was a huge downer for the team, so they changed their treatment to children as only small amounts needed to be used. But Florey said he never forgot the poor postman from Wolvercote and how he had, he felt, let him down in the worst possible way.

I had been fascinated before I met Florey, by Fleming, who just after the First World War, it was said, had been experimenting with bacteria when a tear fell from his eye onto a culture plate. I would invent stories that Fleming was crying from unrequited love, telling Florey this had us both inventing stories that were completely off the wall. We then agreed that we both had the same stupid sense of humour which we agreed was a good start.

Fleming was reported as saying that he realised afterwards that there must be a substance in the tear which killed the bacteria, but left the white blood cells untouched -he called it Lysozome - This was the beginning of the discovery of penicillin which became probably the most important drug ever discovered.

Fleming had always been applauded for his discovery but in all fairness it was Florey along with his research team that turned it into a useful drug after earlier research was abandoned as being too difficult to manufacture. I had no idea that I would ever have anything to do with this miracle drug, I was one lucky man.

Florey had gathered a team of scientists at Oxford University in the mid thirties. I met him when I was a student and we became good friends. I mentioned how confused I was about choosing a path in life and said how fascinated I was by his trials into penicillin. 'Come and be an onlooker and see how we do it.' Florey laughed. So I did.

I then realised that research was the way to go. I had found my passion at last. The work on penicillin was the most exciting thing I had ever known. So my new life began. I worked alongside his new team, as Florey had decided that working alone was far too big a task for one man. Watching the experiments on mice opened my eyes to the wonders of this unassuming Australian genius. Eight mice were used, all given a fatal dose of streptococci bacteria; four were injected with penicillin, they survived; the other four died. This was hugely significant at the time and pointed the way to the manufacturing of penicillin which was used on the troops in America and England, saving thousands of men dying from infected wounds and amputation. But it was still very early days and the trials were just beginning and no one had any real idea of what the future held.

The team treated a four year old child, who scratching her arm on a rose thorn had developed severe septicaemia and there was a strong possibility that the arm would be amputated as she was slowly dying. It was a terrible sight to see, an appalling waste of a young life. Then Florey injected the child with small amounts of penicillin and I watched in amazement as the young child recovered completely with no side effects whatsoever.

It made me so determined to see what difference, if any, I could make so I nicked a few bedpans and grew cultures and filtered them through parachute silk to see what I could achieve. It was one long tedious job, but I loved every second of it.

No drug companies in Britain wanted anything to do with Florey so he and a colleague Chain, in desperation flew to the US in a blacked out plane. A complete act of madness but there was no point in staying in England where there would be no help in securing government help. Once in America they finally managed to manufacture large amounts of penicillin therefore saving thousands of lives on and off the battlefield.

I had hoped Florey would ask me to go too but he said he couldn't take the responsibility of such a dangerous trip; but before he left he asked me if I would be willing to do some lab work for him while he was gone and that is how the story started and how a young boy called Jack O'Brien became, along with others, a pioneer in the discovery of penicillin.

I wasn't supposed to have anything to do with this research as Britain had washed it hands of anything to do with it while the war was on and there was concern that the penicillin may fall into German hands which would be disastrous. *'Better to let the bastards die rather than getting their paws on it, we need it for our troops,'* were the government's words. Cruel to be sure but we were at war and things were different now. So I worked in my lab secretly. The only person outside the team who knew was George, another secret, another deception.

Chapter 9

Anna

Missing Jack is awful, I think of him all the time and wish he would write but he said everything is censored so it's a bit pointless, but happily he did manage to call from a phone box near his base, but the reception was dreadful and I could hardly hear what he was saying. Then when he did come home it all seemed so wrong. He didn't seem the same Jack that went away. He said he was nervous about the days ahead when he would be flying into enemy territory and hoped he could live up to the expectations that was expected of him. Also the fact that so many young men were dying in the skies, some on their very first mission made him feel very vulnerable and very immortal but otherwise he admitted he was enjoying the training on the Spitfire.

He couldn't really give us any information about his work. Top secret he said tapping his nose and laughing. All we knew was that he had been training in Scotland. The first day back he spent mainly with his family but that evening our lot met up with his and we had a big dinner together at our house. Even Victoria and Elizabeth were allowed to stay up for a while and were fascinated by Jack's uniform. They were wide eyed and tried his hat on and sat on his knee. It was lovely to see, and I daydreamed of us being married with our children loving him in the same way. I felt like crying but smiled at the three of them instead, while my heart ached for my man.

Being with Jack on that last day was lovely but hateful at the same time. I didn't know if I would ever see him again, what if he died? He could die we all knew that, but it was never mentioned. There was just a lot of laughter and love that day but even so the elephant loomed darkly in the corner of the room.

I dragged Jack away for a walk even though I felt somehow he would rather have stayed with everyone, but I needed to be with him for a short while. We held hands and he talked of what he was going to be doing, the little bit that he was allowed to tell me. He said not to worry as he wasn't going to be a fighter or a bomber pilot so was not to be involved in any fighting.

He was to fly over France as a reconnaissance photographer and would be photographing railway lines and shipyards. Monitoring German troop movements and generally finding out the lay of the land. He said it was nowhere near dangerous unless he got shot down!

We walked for a bit down by the river and watched the swans some with their cygnets nestling amongst their feathers. It was a beautiful evening and it all seemed so perfect. The air was still and night was edging its way in with purple clouds gathering above the hill in the distance. I just wanted it to stay like that forever. I turned to Jack and looked up at him, 'Kiss me Jack.' He looked almost shy. 'Don't you want to?' I frowned at him. He laughed and hugged me close and kissed me. Oh how strange it felt, not Jack's kiss at all, it was a chaste kiss. Maybe he was just preoccupied with what was to come, so I put it down to that. Feeling a little peeved I slipped my arm through his and suggested we walked back as he would be leaving soon to catch his train.

I told him how I was painting a lot and wanted to get an exhibition going, if I could, as it was keeping my mind of everything, especially you I said trying to be casual about it all, without much luck.

After he'd left everyone was very subdued. His mother was very quiet and tearful, and my heart ached for her. She hugged me and kissed my cheek. 'Take care darling girl and make sure you come and see me as soon as you can, we will both miss Jack, but we must just pray he stays safe. By the way good luck with the training,' and she laughed, 'rather you than me!'

Along with many other women I had joined the WVS. I had to wait a bit for the uniform, but I was so proud when it finally arrived and I could wear it. The dress was blue serge, a bit itchy to be honest with a badge saying WVS Civil

Defence and the name of the area I was dispatched to; along with a rather snazzy hat with a brim and a silver badge plus a canvas bag with everything and anything in it, or so it seemed.

I was to drive ambulances. But I think maybe the powers to be rather wish I wasn't. The first time I went out with a driver I was useless. I stalled the engine time after time, nearly ran into a bus and generally made a complete hash of the whole thing. When we stopped I was trembling all over and I rather think the poor chap sitting next to me was in even a worse state. In a shaky voice he informed me that if the patient hadn't been dead when we started he certainly was now!

'Oh dear, then I am no good?' He gave a weak smile, sighed, patted my knee and said. 'You will improve I am sure, let's try again.'

When I told Mary what he had said about the patient she had hysterics and we laughed until the tears poured down our cheeks.

So I tried again and again and again, but my poor patient instructor never gave up. I would have done had I been teaching him. I was appalling but now I am perfect. I drive everywhere and feel confident that I am doing a serious job however small it may seem in the scheme of things.

I remember September 7th 1940 being one of the most terrible of days. It was reported in the news that Hitler had sent in planes to bomb London, in order to destroy the moral of the British people, but without success. It was definitely the steely determination of the British that we would never be overpowered, especially by a little twerp called Adolf Hitler.

That day was a day in hell. Afterwards it was claimed that there had been 348 German bombers escorted by 617 fighter planes planning to destroy our beautiful city. It was frightening and overwhelming. It went on for fifty seven days in a row. Then the night bombing began as well, which somehow seemed even more appalling. A school being used as an air raid shelter was destroyed and nearly 500 people lost their lives. It was like living a nightmare. I was in the midst of all this, driving the injured to hospital. It was terrifying and the smell of burning flesh and fire clogged your mind. The dreadful destruction was heart-breaking, it seemed never ending. I would stand by with my ambulance and watch while victims were dragged from the wreckage of their homes. When someone was found alive it was like a gift from heaven. I will never ever forget it and no one who was there during those terrible days will either.

It all ended on May 11th 1941, but London had been broken and its people would never be the same again. So many families lost their lives. So many children died. It is always the innocent that suffer of course, taking their little broken bodies out of the rubble of their homes was the worst thing I have ever witnessed and the men that dug and toiled night after night were angels in disguise, as were the firemen who fought the dreadful blazes with all their strength to distinguish the fires, often or not with little effect as the fires built themselves into huge infernos engulfing everything within sight. It left me with a sense of sheer terror. I don't think I can be a very brave person. I felt so useless standing their while others worked through the nightmare. I asked if I could help but they told me it as far too dangerous. They didn't actually say for a girl but I somehow got the message.

When the ambulance was full of the injured someone would bang the roof and off I went. I had another girl with me sometimes but usually I was alone but I must say I did feel better when there was someone else with me. Somehow it didn't seem quite so frightful when there were two of us.

So many of us WVS women were being killed during the Blitz while providing food and drink around the clock to those who were fighting the fires and those made homeless by the bombing. Being in the middle of all this was terrifying.

One of the saddest parts of my job was moving children who were being evacuated out of London. Seeing the despair on the mothers' faces was heartrending and I thanked God that my little sisters were still at home with us. Whether it was a good thing, who was to say, but Mama was adamant that they stayed. I think after losing her twin boys has made us children even more special than normal.

Because of the blackout the whole of London seemed plunged into darkness so early. There were no lights from houses no street lights even bicycles had no lights. Father said it was a nightmare cycling after dark. He was enjoying the Home Guard and I think he felt happy that he was doing something however small, to help.

So the air raids went on and on and the fires grew fiercer and more people died. The RAF had aircraft circling around and around defending the skies. It was all so unreal. I just wanted it to be over and life back to normal as we all did.

Huge barrage balloons were tethered to the ground by steel wires, ostensibly to try and stop the enemy aircraft getting too near, but it appeared to me that nothing would stop them in their determination to destroy everything it their sight.

Mary who is a nurse in the local hospital, says it is forever overflowing with casualties since the Blitz. The worst thing she said was when the children were bought in, some to die before they could be treated.

'It is unbearable,' she cried and we held each other tight and wept for our city and its people.

One night sitting on my bed drinking hot chocolate Mary asked if I was missing Jack. 'Dreadfully' I said. 'I think the worst thing is I don't know where he is and there is no contact at all. I keep expecting a telegram to arrive saying he is dead.' I started to cry, there were a lot of tears shed during those years mostly by the women who were left to keep their families together, a task that was insurmountable somehow.

'Do you think you will marry Jack?'

'I hope so,' I laughed. 'He was always saying we should get married before he went to war. I must say I was very tempted but it seemed wrong to rush into it but how I wish we had. Maybe it wouldn't be so hard without him if I was Mrs. Jack O'Brien. I might even be having his baby!'

'Have you, you know, done anything yet?'

'No, but wish we had. I think I was terrified of actually getting pregnant, but now I wish I was. What about you, have you done anything with Henry?'

'No not really. I have a feeling he wants to, he is nearly thirty so obviously has had girlfriends before. I never ask about them, I'm not sure I actually want to know. But if I tell you something promise to keep it a secret.'

'Of course.'

'Well he has asked to marry me and I just had to tell you, that's why I wanted to stay the night. I was so excited I am not sure I could have kept it to myself if I had stayed home.'

'Oh Mary, I threw my arms around her sending hot chocolate everywhere. 'Oh God quick pass me something, anything will do.' My pyjamas were the first things to hand. After a great palaver we managed to get most of the mess up and then we stood on the bed and jumped up and down like a couple of kids.

'That is so exciting, when?'

'Well Henry thinks it should be soon in case we both get blown up! But I am not sure, I do love him but we have only known each other for six months, it seems so quick.'

'I know but it is under extraordinary circumstances with this wretched war. I think you should do it straight away and I will be maid of honour of course. What's it like being in love with a vicar, does he preach to you and ask why you don't go to church?'

'Don't be daft, he's not like that, you know he isn't. He never questions me that is why I think I love him, he is such fun to be with. I actually read one of his sermons the other day and it was hilarious. I am sure that's why the church is full. Mother said there were so many people there last Sunday that some were standing up at the back. He is really so unlike the stereotype of a vicar, he smokes, drinks and kisses extremely well. She hugged herself, I think I am so lucky and maybe I will do what you say and marry him straight away, what am I waiting for anyway.'

We laughed and hugged and shared the last of my chocolate and talked of weddings and what to wear and how wonderful everything was; and for those few hours, it really was.

Three weeks later Mary and Henry tied the knot, married in a registry office. Then a blessing by the vicar in the next parish. Robert, her father gave her away, a proud man as he walked her down the aisle. I was maid of honour; her sisters were bridesmaids and Henry's brother the best man. It was all such a wonderful day, a little bit of light and happiness in a dark, dark world.

Mary wore a lovely white lace dress her mother made from material she had hidden away. She had unpicked her own wedding dress and wrapped it in tissue waiting, she said, for when the first daughter got married. Mary looked so beautiful, with white flowers in her hair. The lace dress was amazing with long sleeves, a sweetheart neckline embroidered with pearls and a skirt of tulle overlaid with lace and tiny crystals and more pearls. Over it all that she wore a little white fur bolero and with white roses in her bouquet she looked the perfect bride.

The girls and I were dressed in pale blue silk. All made by Mary's mother, we had yellow and white flowers in our hair and white muffs to keep our hands warm.

I felt beautiful for a change. Henry wore a dinner suit and looked splendid. There were friends and family dancing until the early hours. The reception was held in the vicarage where blackout curtains were strictly drawn, with candles everywhere instead of lights, making it a little bit of heaven at a hellish time.

Chapter 10

George

Today I flew solo. Changing to a Spitfire from my training planes was exhilarating if terrifying. I really felt in control now and soon I would be doing what I was trained for, a reconnaissance photographer. With my camera built in to the nose of my plane I would fly across occupied France, over the Normandy and Brittany fields photographing marshalling yards, tank and troop movements. It was exhausting but I came back with enough information for the bomber pilots to do their dangerous work.

Waiting for them to return after night sorties was a terrible time. One late evening a squadron of twelve planes went out. Only four returned. It was the worst casualty list we had had. It was a sombre time for everyone. I lost so many friends it was dreadful. The comradeship had become very strong. I suppose because we were all in the same boat, even though I knew my job was such a doddle compared to the bomber and fighter pilots. I had huge admiration for them, some so young I am sure they weren't even shaving yet. There was so much death around us that it became matter of fact, making it even more appalling,

6 months later

One early morning I was to photograph the dry docks of St. Naziare in the heart of Brittany. There was a lot of movement around the area and my orders were to take as many close ups of the docks that I could without getting shot at. That was said with tongue in cheek but I knew it was a chance I had to take. It was a cold misty morning in March, ice was on the runway and snow lay in white patches on the fields. The night before I had hardly slept and was up before dawn, with the engineers checking and re checking the camera and making sure everything was in the right place. The ground crew shouted *good luck and see you later*. Their usual words to every pilot but even so we all knew some of us would never return.

Everything went smoothly, the sun had come out and the skies were clear. Slowly but surely I flew towards my target. The landscape below me was beautiful, untouched it seemed by human hand. The fields laid out like a painting but lurking amongst that beauty was the ugliness of an occupied land. Around lay the inevitable farmw dotted with tiny white shapes of sheep and darker ones of cows. It was a pastoral vision.

I flew across the sea the sun shining like tiny diamonds on the waves, it was all so beautiful. St. Nazaire came into view. I flew over at 3,000 feet taking as many photos as possible, then I made another passing run at the same altitude in the opposite direction. I managed to get more photographs than I thought possible. Then flying up to 7,000 feet I turned around and flew back to the base, thanking God that I had been lucky yet again.

Two days later I was to fly over St. Nazaire once more, but this would be a night job. I had been instructed to fly lower this time, as some of the earlier photos were too indistinct to verify exactly what was going on.

It was about 3.00 am when I took the last photo flying as low as I could. Suddenly I felt the whole plane shudder and move erratically. My first thought was my God I have been hit and how right I was. I looked down to see red fire from ominous guns pointing up at the sky. Suddenly, there was a massive explosion and then a strong smell of burning. I turned around to look out the back, only to see the tail was one huge ball of fire. The smell of something scorching was overpowering. It was my seat, red hot. The undercarriage must have been hit. I pulled back on the controls to try and take her up again, but they were not responding. Nothing seemed to be working.

The plane started to fall as huge tracer fire criss-crossed the skies. I had to get out. Fuck, fuck, fuck. Undoing my straps I did the best thing I could think of, I turned the plane upside down. Not quite sure how I did it, but I did. Then I fell out into the sky and I hurtled at a terrifying pace towards the earth. All at once my beautiful parachute opened and rocked me gently in its arms. As I looked upwards I watched as my poor burning Spitfire spiralled towards the ground then exploded into a thousand pieces. It was terrible, I had really got to love that plane. And all those photos that would never be seen. That is all I could think of. Somehow, they seemed much more important than a mere mortal's life.

The silence was extraordinary after the roar of the engines in my ears for the last four or five hours.

Drifting down was so peaceful. I could see the glow of my plane in the distance against the black sky. There were a few stars out but unluckily no moon to see by but then on the other hand I wouldn't be seen. Looking down I could see a vague outline of what looked like a huge wood. It was too dark to distinguish much. I just hoped I could land without getting tangled up in one of the trees.

There was not a lot I could do so I let the wind take me wherever it felt like. Happily I landed on a large open piece of land. Suddenly terrific pain shot up my leg from my foot, shit, something wrong with my ankle. I felt it gingerly, nothing broken as far as I could tell.

Undoing the parachute from my back and bundling it up as small as possible I looked for somewhere to hide it. If it was found then the Germans would be looking for one very vulnerable RAF pilot. I could hardly distinguish one thing from another but there seemed to be a large branch or tree lying across my path. I hobbled over to it and managed to shove the parachute under part of it. There were some dead leaves lying around so I scooped up what I could and covered the edges of the parachute that stuck out from the trunk. It looked pretty good.

Now I had to make a recce and see where the hell I was. I felt my revolver in one pocket with a bit of ammo. In the other one was my compass, the glass felt intact thank God. Wrapped around it was the locket that Anna had given me before I left. She had pushed into my hand and kissed me. 'Take this Jack for good luck. Think of me and stay safe.'

I remember how awful I felt and told Jack later. I knew he had given it to her for her last birthday. It was beautiful, a tiny antique gold locket with a small ruby in the middle. I know how she cherished it and wore it all the time on a fine gold chain. I tried to give it back to Jack but he laughed.

'It's yours now. You are Jack, treasure it and make sure you bloody well bring it back with you.'

Looking around I could just about make out a mass of trees and bushes. I hadn't the faintest idea where I was. I had a map but couldn't see to read it and didn't want to use my torch not knowing how long the batteries would last. So I had to wait until first light. Hopefully no one had seen me bale out. But the plane exploding would have wakened even the deepest sleeper and someone may well have seen it falling. So I had to get away from it as fast as my wretched ankle would let me. It was pitch black by now so I could do little. I may as well try to rest until it got light, I used my flying gloves and hat as a pillow and laid down.

I must have been a more exhausted than I thought as I fell asleep almost immediately. I woke with terrific pain in my ankle wondering where the hell I was, looking around I appeared to be in the middle of a wood. It was cold and damp, the sky just lightening. I got up stiffly put on my hat and gloves for warmth and walked gingerly towards a gap in the trees. In the distance I could see a river so I decided to follow that. I seemed to walk, or rather hobble for hours.

Then the sun came out and I could see a long way. It looked beautiful, fields of newly sewn corn and wheat were just starting to show their shoots through the dark soil. A pair of buzzards were circling overhead crying with their high pitched call. A herd of chocolate brown cows came ambling up towards me. Great pink tongues licking their wet noses. Staring at me for a few minutes they went back to munching the grass. I could see two or three farmhouses dotted about, where I could smell and see smoke from their chimneys. I kept well away from them though, never knowing if they were occupied by Germans. Not wanting to find out I traipsed on.

The river was wide and five Great Egrets stood like sentinels along the banks, their white wings bright against the dark river. Suddenly in unison they raised their perfect wings and flew high into the sky. Such a sight, for a moment I felt a sense of exhilaration. I would be alright, I had a feeling it would all be okay.

I must have walked for ever, or so I felt. There were no more farmhouses, no civilisation, I never saw a soul. A few more cows and sheep but that was all. The silence was extraordinary.

In the near distance I could still see the silver streak of the river. I decided to keep it in view so I would have some sort of direction. My map was of little help but I would have to stop later and really try and pinpoint where I was. By now I was ravenous. I had a bar of chocolate that one of the ground crew had given me before I left, *'in case of emergency sir!'* I had a small piece only as it may be the only food I would get for a while, so I walked and walked keeping the river in view.

I was getting too tired to think straight. My chocolate had run out. I drunk water from the river which was ice cold and tasted clean. There didn't seem to be any water traffic at all, maybe because of the war. I really didn't know or actually care much. I was starving and exhausted. My feet ached and I was starting to feel sorry for myself. I followed the river while keeping well away from it and hoping that the trees would camouflage me to some extent. I trudged on, my stomach rumbled, I was now more than hungry. I felt light headed and extremely tired, a complete wreck. Could I forage like a gypsy for food, not likely I told myself, I would probably poison myself.

All at once, out of the corner of my eye I saw a flash of red. I crouched down behind a tree and watched as a young girl with a red headscarf cycled by. She had two long loaves of bread in her basket - I almost expected her to have onions hanging around her neck- She stopped and laying her bike down took of her scarf and shook her head. Her hair tumbled down her back, reminding me of Anna with her long dark curls.

Laying back on the river's edge she seemed to sleep she was so still. I stayed crouched down. My ankle was really giving me the gip now and I had cramp in both legs. I wasn't I hoped near enough for her to hear if I moved, but I didn't want to take the chance so I stayed where I was, which seemed forever.

I must have dozed off myself when I heard singing. It was the girl. I watched as she tied her scarf back on and still singing rode off along the river's path. I sat up and stretched myself and waited until she was out of sight then walked warily on.

Suddenly out of the trees came two young boys chasing a boar. Poor thing it was no bigger than a small piglet. They were using sticks as rifles and shouting as they ran but had little hope of ever getting anywhere near the wretched animal. Suddenly they stopped as they saw me, their eyes like saucers. Looking up at me they did the most extraordinary thing. They saluted, so putting my hat on I saluted back. I spoke to them in French which seemed to amaze them.

'You are English but you speak French.'

'Yes, I have a French mother.'

'So do we!' They both said in unison.

'Of course you do,' I said, trying to keep a straight face.

They asked me where I had come from, had I seen any Germans, was I flying a plane, did I parachute out? I answered all their questions very seriously. Then I asked them if they knew where I could get some help.

'Follow the river,' they both chirped 'and you will come to a small village, they will help you.'

I thanked them and saluting me again they ran off in pursuit of their prey. Those two young boys had boosted my morale no end. I seemed to have got back a spring in my step and felt almost happy.

It was starting to get dark, I had a torch in my back pocket but was wary about using it still. There was enough light to see by so on I walked, following the river from a distance. The trees became black silhouettes against the darkening sky. The sun was disappearing behind the fields and a couple of blackbirds were serenading each other in the dying light. Always the first bird to sing and always the last. Nothing changed, life went on as normal.

Then I saw the girl again. She was bending down by her bike. Her back tyre flapped around the wheel, she kicked the bike and shouted something. I tried not to laugh but it was an amusing scene, poor thing, I wonder how far she was from her home. I can't help her I thought, or could I? Maybe this would be my last opportunity. I was starving, tired and the pain in my ankle was getting worse. So putting on my hat and my gloves I walked slowly towards her, I could feel the blood pounding in my ears. I am scared I thought, really scared.

I nearly turned back but I was exhausted and there was no point on wandering around like a lost soul. I came out of the trees and walked hesitatingly towards her. She turned as my feet hit the gravel.

'Oh,' her hand flew to her mouth, 'you startled me. You are an Englishman, yes? Where are you from, are you alone? I heard a plane had crashed in the early hours this morning. Was that your plane?'

'Yes to all questions. The trouble is I haven't the faintest idea where I am.'

She smiled at me, her dark eyes shining. 'You are in Normandy.'

She laughed. 'Don't look so worried I live nearby, you have to come with me. If you are seen it will be bad, the whole area is occupied. Our house is full of German officers, it is horrible. They sleep in our beds, eat our food, while we live in our little Chaumière at the end of the garden.'

'Chaumière, what's that?'

'Ah it is a French word as you must have guessed, it is a small thatched house. Our gardener and his wife lived there but they fled when they heard the Germans were about to move into our house. A shame, they are very old. I just pray they are both safe, my father and mother are very worried about them.' Her eyes filled with tears, 'I grew up with them, it is very sad.'

'Come,' she grabbed my hand, 'walk with me but we must keep well away from the river or we will be seen. We will go through the wood. It isn't far, it will be dark soon so we must hurry as there is a curfew, everyone in by 7.00 pm.'

She shrugged. 'How ridiculous, what do they think we are going to do?!'

I pushed the bike for her, the smell from the warm baguettes was driving me mad. I was starving.

She looked at me. 'You are hungry, yes?'

'Oh yes,' ravenous, 'I can't remember how long ago I ate. A piece of bread would be most welcome, just a little bit'

She gave me a huge piece. 'Sorry there is no cheese to have with it, or even a glass of red wine.' She laughed again, the sweetest of sounds. 'You must come back to my home and we will eat properly tonight. That is a promise, my mother is a very good cook.'

After about twenty minutes we came to a long drive, lined with poplars. They were beautiful, hundreds of these tall elegant trees standing regally along each side. At the end I could see an old black and white timbered house where light blazed from the windows and loud music echoed around us.

'It's the German officers, they have music on all the time, so loud and so horrid.' She winced. 'It is sad to think they are in my home. I really hate them you know, they are very polite and click their heels when they see me but they make me sick. They are too polite, too good looking for their own good as well. Listen, there's someone coming.' She grabbed me by my arm. 'Quick in there.' She pointed to some bushes, 'hide in there I will come and get you when it is dark, hurry.' She pushed me hard. 'Go, go now.'

The bushes hid me well and I sat down leaning against a tree. I was shattered and far too tired to think what I may have got myself into. I must have nodded off for the next thing I knew was the girl shaking my shoulder, 'Monsieur it is safe now, come.' It was too dark to see anything as she led me through the undergrowth. Then we came to a little thatched house, a cottage really, the chaumière. The doorway was low and we had to stoop to go in. Inside there was a wonderful smell of something delicious cooking. The kitchen was lit by oil lamps and a woman stood in the shadows.

'Mama, this is the Monsieur I told you about.'

The woman came out of the shadows, she was tall and attractive. She held out her hand.' Monsieur Beinvenue.'

I answered her in French and both mother and daughter looked at each other. 'You speak perfect French, you never said when I was talking to you in English,' the girl said almost indignantly.

I smiled. 'I liked listening to your accent and your English was as perfect.'

She laughed, it sounded like tinkling bells.' I am an English teacher at the local school,' what's your excuse?'

'My mother is French and she made sure my brother and I always spoke French during the day at home. Then English in the evening, when Father came home.'

She clapped her hands, 'that is wonderful, it will be good for my parents to speak to you as they have little English.'

So it begun, there was to be more deception. But this time it was to be a far more dangerous.

Chapter 11

While George slept that night in the old wooden sleigh bed, with lavender scented linen sheets, Anna sat in the cinema with Jack, Mary and Henry watching a slightly depressing film. *The Stars Look Down'* with Margaret Lockwood and Michael Redgrave.

'I don't think that did much to cheer us,' said Jack.' Bloody miserable film if you ask me.'

'Oh it wasn't that bad,' the others argued.

'Just a typical Cronin film,' said Anna. 'I read the book which was far better and I am sure the heroine looked nothing like Margaret Lockwood with her beauty spot, immaculate make up and coiffured hair!'

They all laughed and with their arms through each other's walked towards the local all-night café. Sometimes if they were lucky there would be sausages on the menu but tonight no such luck. 'Corn beef fritters tonight boys and girls and if you are really nice I might find four eggs to fry!' Mario was the Italian owner; his family had emigrated from Italy 20 years earlier. He was well into his fifties with a large droopy tobacco stained moustache. He, even with rationing, managed to serve up some decent meals. 'Sounds amazing Mario. We are starving!' They squeezed themselves into a small booth with a red lamp above the table and red plush seats, not really all-night café stuff everyone agreed.

'This place always reminds me of a French bordello,' said Henry.

'How many have you acquainted?' said Mary giggling and squeezing his hand.

Half way through the meal, the sirens started, screaming through the night. 'Okay,' Mario shouted, 'everyone down to the basement, quickly. Take your food with you if you can manage but hurry.' There were about twenty people rushing around bumping into each other spilling cups of tea and glasses of wine everywhere while the sirens kept on and on wailing their ominous noise. Then it was as if the very skies had opened spewing out the terrible bombs that rained down outside.

The wooden steps to the basement were narrow causing people to walk down in single file. There was no pushing or shoving. Not a word was spoken. Just the dreadful sounds outside vibrating through the walls shaking the very structure of the building.

Anna was trembling. She was terrified by it all and however many times she heard the sirens and the sickening sound of falling bombs, she could never get used to it. She held George's hand tight wishing it was Jack's instead.

The basement was dark and cold, a small window let a tiny bit of light in. Mario rushed around lighting candles and turning on a gas fire which spluttered into life throwing a red glow across the stone floor.

'It will be warm soon, there are blankets for you all so please take one if you are cold. This is a strong old building you are safe here I can assure you.'

There was a grunt of '*bloody well hope so*' and a few angry words about Hitler. People settled down and wrapped themselves in the blankets, while some finished their meal. The noise outside was stupendous, they could feel the tremors vibrating through the ceiling. No one spoke. Someone was crying softly as the noise went on and on.

The four friends sat huddled together their arms around each other.

'Everyone will be worried about us you know that don't you,' said Mary. 'How I wish we could tell them we were alright, someone needs to invent a phone you can carry with you!'

'Chance would be a fine thing,' laughed Henry and hugged Mary. 'It's rather nice been cuddled up with you all especially this girl.'

Anna smiled at them but her heart ached for Jack, she wanted him next to her with his arm around her instead of George.

She started to think of one wonderful day not long before Jack was called up. It was an early May morning, with dew still sparkling on the grass as they walked through the fields that led off from her house. The river was still pretty full and moving gently. She took off her stockings and Jack tied his shoes together, stuffed with his socks and hung them around his neck. They waded through the water like three year olds. The tall grass was full of ox eye daisies, buttercups and dandelion clocks that spun around as they blew them to tell the time.

Climbing away from the river they clambered over fences where fat sheep scattered in all directions then huddled together like frightened children. Fields full of soft eyed cows lowed at them and turned away to protect their calves that pulled at their swollen udders. The grass was high and still wet with dew. Anna's dress clung and wound itself around her legs. Jack rolled up his trousers and said he ought to have a handkerchief on his head and then he would look just like his father when they were on holiday in Thorpness. Pulling her over he rolled Anna in the grass soaking her. She grabbed at his dark curls and as they moved together they kissed, his green eyes fringed with black lashes turned his girl inside out. Suddenly their kissing became more frenzied more urgent.

'Stop'! Anna pushed him away and stood up her dress clinging to her body, her hair sodden.

'But you look so beautiful,' he said jumping up and pulling her towards him, 'Look at you, my beautiful mermaid.'

'Oh Jack, I am scared, I love you so much but…..'

He smiled. His beautiful smile, his face so serious before now lit up like a child, his green eyes sparkling in the hot sun.

'Oh God don't do that!'

'Do what?' he laughed.

'Smile at me like that and look at me like that.'

'You make me smile. You have turned my world upside down.' He laid his hand on her cheek.

'I love you Anna, you know that, I could never love anyone else, we were meant for each other, and you are all I will ever want.' He caught hold of her shoulders and pulled her tightly against him. She could feel his lips against her face, his hands in her hair. He smelt of summer and wet grass, his lips moved towards her. She opened her mouth and pulled him down towards the soft earth.

At such a terrible time these thoughts made her feel even sadder and she knew she could never love anyone else. George was sweet and did all he could to comfort her but it wasn't the same. It could never be the same as Jack holding her. She could feel tears welling up. Jack smiled at her. 'I told your man I would look after you and that is what I will do.'

Suddenly in the quiet of the room a voice resonated around the walls. Mario was singing, and could he sing. After all the years no one had any idea, his voice was deep, rich and melodious.

'Mario Lanza!' someone shouted then everyone started clapping.

Singing in Italian, his beautiful voice bought tears to their eyes. Then in the middle of it all the sirens sounded, this time for the all clear. Everyone stood up and clapped.

'Bravo, Bravo.'

Mario bowed. 'Now ladies and gentlemen we must all go upstairs and hope some of my poor old café is left standing.'

People drifted slowly up the narrow stairs. Yet again not a word was spoken. Everyone was within their own selves, frightened of what they may find when they left the café.

Upstairs was as before, no damage at all. Obviously the bombing had been on the other side of town. People were hugging Mario and thanking him for keeping them safe and especially for the impromptu concert. He laughed and said it had given him great pleasure to sing to such appreciative people. He watched sadly as he saw everyone leave not knowing what they were to find. He hated this war and hated seeing his adopted city being slowly destroyed by some maniac's orders. He closed the door behind him. Locked up and walked slowly towards his home, praying like everyone else that it would still be standing.

Suddenly Mary started to cry.

Holding her tight Henry whispered, 'shh, it's all over now it's alright.'

'Henry I am scared, what if my house has been hit? The smoke and fire is coming from that direction.'

She was right, the fire seemed very near to where she lived. The friends watched as huge jets of water rose into the night swallowing up great billows of thick black smoke filling the air, stinging their eyes, burning their throats. As the noise of ambulance and fire engines bells rang out across the city they all started to run towards the sound. The terrific heat from the fires hit them before they witnessed the appalling sight that confronted them. A whole row of houses were virtually razed to the ground, half of their walls missing, roofs caved in. Complete carnage.

'Oh my God, it's our house, please let me through,' Mary screamed pushing herself through the rubble. 'I need to find my parents, my sisters, please let me through.'

Someone pulled her roughly back. 'Miss you can't come through, the people from this house were taken away in ambulances, you must go to the hospital. I am sorry but it is far too dangerous to be here, the houses are collapsing as we speak.' Suddenly there was an almighty explosion as one of the houses at the end burst into huge flames.

'Looks like a Gas explosion,' one of the firemen shouted. 'Everyone please get back, get back.'

'Come on,' said Jack I know a short cut to the hospital. Are you okay Mary?'

She shook her head, tears poured down her face. 'Please, please hurry.' Henry grabbed Mary by the hand and the four of them ran as fast as they could towards the hospital.

Inside it was complete mayhem. People crying, shouting, someone was screaming. Nurses were everywhere trying to calm people. It was the start of the Blitz. Well over 2,000 people were killed or wounded that night. It was to go on like that for over eleven weeks. Thousands were killed and seriously injured. It was a living hell that left people devastated. Whole families were wiped out in one go. It was a tragedy too big to comprehend.

Jack rushed up to one of the nurse who obviously knew him as George. She nodded her head and looked towards Mary.

'Come with me please. 'Mary followed with Henry holding her hand. Jack and Anna watched as the ward doors swung closed behind them.

Chapter 12

Jack

I stood with Anna watching Henry and Mary disappear into the ward, the smell of disinfectant and sadness hung around. People were milling about, some with tears raining down their faces, clutching onto each other in their grief. Nurses were trying to calm people, one woman was screaming, it was a dreadful sound to hear and a dreadful sight to see. Someone was trying to calm her but all she did was scream and scream, God help her I thought, what terrible thing has happened to her.

I am used to sickness and death but this was another thing altogether, so many people suffering so much. I took Anna by the arm, 'come over here let's sit down and wait until they come out. I just pray the news isn't too dreadful, poor Mary, God how I hate what this war is doing to us all.'

A nurse came over and asked us to go with her into the ward. I could see Henry standing by the window his back to us. He turned around as we entered. His eyes were full of sorrow. Mary was with her mother who was sitting up in bed with the two children either side of her. Thank God they are okay I thought. Mary lay with her head on her mother's lap while her sisters leant against them both, their little faces pale and frightened.

Her mother looked towards me. 'Oh George, Robert has been killed.' She started to cry.

The children buried their faces deeper into their mother's lap.

'It was all so silly,' she cried, 'we were in the coal cellar where we always go when the sirens sound. Robert said he was sure he could hear the cat meowing in the hall and it would be terrified by the noise and he would go and bring her down. I tried to stop him going upstairs, it is too dangerous I kept saying.'

'I'll be fine back in a tick' were the last words he spoke. He was only gone a few minutes when we heard an explosion then a dreadful silence. It seemed like forever as we all clung onto each other. I was almost too paralysed with fear to move, it was terrible. I managed to reach the cellar door but it was jammed as if something had fallen against it. I kept pushing but to no avail, there was nothing we could do but wait and hope to God someone would come. It seemed hours before we heard shouting, so we all screamed back and the next thing I knew strong arms were pulling us out of the cellar.' She was sobbing now.

Anna and I left the little family circle to their grief and walked slowly through the broken streets. Houses burnt fiercely and smoke lay heavy in the air. It was starting to get light.

After taking Anna back to her house I walked slowly home, Mother and Father were still up.

'Oh thank God George we have been so worried. I went to see Evelyn she has been desperate about worried about Anna as well. What on earth happened?'

I explained how we had been stuck in the café and then the terrible events at the hospital. By now I was completely drained and carrying this 'secret' inside of me was starting to grind me down.

The next morning surgery was chaotic, mainly minor problems, most of them I suspected were just grief and worry. Many patients just seemed to want to talk. The bombings had been too near for comfort and many knew of the houses where Mary's father had been killed. Three other families next door had all died too. It was a dreadful time for everyone and it never seemed to end. Day after day, the bombs rained down on our city.

I went to the hospital in the afternoon to see Mary's mother who was leaving to go home. The children were with her as well as Mary. Everyone was very quiet and the children clung like limpets to their mother.

'We are all going back to the Vicarage. Mother and the girls will stay with us until things are sorted out, it is so difficult to get anything done, no one seems to know what to do with people like us. It is all so awful for Mother. I just wish Father was here.' Mary put her hand across her mouth and shook her head, tears fell down her cheeks. 'I'm sorry. It's just so awful I feel so helpless.'

She rubbed the tears away and gave me a weak smile, 'Henry's coming to pick us up in a minute. He had a service this morning. He said the atmosphere in the church was terrible. The sorrow palpable. He is so lucky that he is able to help people with his words, I think that is why I feel so damned useless.'

Her mother stroked her hair. 'That is something that you are not my darling.' Mary smiled and kissed her cheek.

Henry arrived looking pale and drawn. 'Good to see you George, had a hell of a morning, I took a special service for some of the bereaved, quite terrible.' He ran his fingers through his hair. 'One chap there lost his whole family while he was at work. He sat at the back of the church with his head in his hands and never moved. It was a terrible sight to see, I talked to him afterwards but I am not sure he heard a word I said. Some neighbours are looking after him. I will have to make sure that he is not left alone. We don't want any more tragedies. Last week a young woman hung herself after her children and husband died when their house was hit. Anyway, enough of that. Come on let's go children.' Putting his arms around the girls he looked at Mary and smiled and they all walked out and away from the hospital.

I left them and ambled towards home. The smell of burning still hung in the air. Everywhere there was such devastation. Houses razed to the ground, one street completely obliterated where men were still digging in the rubble for bodies. A young woman stood and watched them, her face drawn and white. She stood like stone and watched as the digging went on and on.

I found myself drawn towards Anna's house. I knocked tentatively on the door. It seemed so quiet here. Away from the horror. Their road of houses was intact, it had missed, like our house any form of bombing. Just the luck of the draw I thought. Nothing more, nothing less, just pure luck. I think if I had believed in any sort of God I would have thanked him for being so kind!

The door opened, it was Evelyn. 'Oh George how lovely, come in, Anna's upstairs. I presume you have come to see her.' She laughed. 'You are the nearest thing she has next to Jack you know that. Without you I am not quite sure how she would be. She has just come back from work, she was out most of last night with the ambulance. You must have seen the devastation not far from here. Anna said it was a terrible night, so many casualties. She has just had breakfast and seems fine now. Ah, and here she is!'

Down the stairs she tripped, her hair hanging lose around her shoulders. How I love it when it is in such disarray instead of tied back with ribbons. My heart turned over. She was so beautiful. My girl I thought, how I want to throw my arms around you, to hold you and tell you I love you. This dreadful pretence is killing me. But I knew the deception would go on and on.

'George, how lovely. 'She ran over and kissed me on the cheek. 'Just who I needed to see. I had a rubbish night last night and feel like been cheered up and you are definitely the one to do it. Let's go down to the river. Mama I promise not to leave the garden, we will just walk a bit and stay near the house.'

'Off you go and enjoy yourself, I will make some tea when you get back.'

The sun shone and the smell of cut grass was all around us.

Skipping backwards Anna shouted. 'Come on lazy bones, hurry up, the sun is shining and all is alright with the world. Well it is, just at this minute in time!'

We sat on the bank of the river. The sun shone like tiny crystals on the water. A few ducks paddled lazily backwards and forwards, stopping now and then to tip their whole bodies into the water. How peaceful it seemed. Great Willows hung lazily, their leaves skimming the river, everywhere seemed so still, so beautiful. It was hard at times like these to believe this land was at war.

I leant against a Willow. Anna sat next to me her sketchbook on her lap. She was drawing the ducks as they played. I knew later she would transfer her drawings to pastel paper ready for the next step. Her talent amazed me. We didn't talk for a while, I sat and watched as the ducks cavorted like children. How I wished I could hold her, tell her everything. It was getting worse, the longer all this went on the more difficult it seemed. Being in such close proximity to her was killing me.

I had to talk to her, all this play acting was crucifying me.

I took a deep breath and looked into those beautiful eyes. 'I know you are worried sick about Jack but listen Anna, I would know if anything happened to him, I am sure of it. We always feel what the other one feels, obviously not all the time but when it is something out of the ordinary it is a form of telepathy. We call it *thought talk*. When Jack was about eight he fell off his bike and broke his arm I h aad dreadfull pain in my elbow at exactly the time he fell. When I had a tooth out it was the same, he was in agony with toothache. I am sure I would have some warning that something is wrong so I am not worried about him and either should you be. It's poor old George you should be worrying about.'

'Oh George' Anna laughed, 'why should I worry about you?'

'Because I feel so guilty with Jack joining up and me being stuck here!'

'That's not your fault and you know it.'

'I understand but it is ridiculous, an innocent heart murmur is nothing,

'Well there is nothing you can do about it. Anyway you are so popular at the surgery and the patients love you. They say you have really changed since Jack left for the war. I heard your Father saying everyone is calling you a saint.'

'That is plain stupid.'

'Okay maybe it is but you are doing a lot of good. You may not be fighting for your country but you are caring for some of its people. So stop feeling sorry for yourself.'

'Oh Anna, you just don't understand.'

'What don't I understand?' she frowned.

'Everything.' He could feel himself getting hot and tripping over his words.

'Well,' smiled Anna, 'go on, what don't I understand George?'

'It's nothing,' I was stammering, 'I just wish I had gone instead of Jack, that's all, nothing else, just that!'

'There is something else. I can tell, what is it? You are starting to scare me George, has something happened to Jack and you daren't tell me?'

'No nothing like that. I am reluctant to tell you because I really don't know what you will think of me when I do.'

'Oh for God's sake, what is it, spit it out, it can't be that bad.'

'Well actually it is, well to me it is. What if I told you I was a conscientious objector and was relieved when I couldn't enlist. What do you think of me now?'

Anna stared at me. 'I find that hard to believe actually, you were so keen to enlist. What changed you?'

'Well it was just the thought that I may have to kill someone and I know I couldn't have done. Maybe I am just a coward after all.'

'Oh George, I can't actually believe you of all people are a coward. Being scared is alright, everyone has a right to be scared. Oh goodness I am relieved I am a girl, I really am. I would be terrified if I had to fight. Anyway you must have known you wouldn't be accepted, surely?' Did Jack know how you felt. I bet you never told him?'

'I did actually and he was okay about it, he promised to keep it under his hat as they say. He did mention that I would probably be put in the tower or shot. I can't imagine what Father would say had he known, probably disown me or something.'

'I doubt it,' said Anna, her voice sounding so sad that it made me feel dreadful. Christ why on earth didn't I tell her the truth. What is wrong with me, stupid, stupid, stupid.

'You will promise not to say anything won't you, I couldn't bear my parents knowing.'

'Of course, and for goodness sake stop looking so miserable. You look just like Jack when he's in one of his black moods, and anyway listen to me.' She put her hand up to my face and turned it towards her, her beautiful grey eyes soft with compassion.

'George. Thank you for being here for me so much while Jack is away, you have kept me sane, I am so grateful, I really, really am. I don't think you have any idea how it has helped me being with you while he is God knows where.'

'You don't need to thank me Anna. Jack would have done the same if I had gone to war. I said I would look after you and I will. I love your company and I miss Jack dreadfully too so it is doing us both good.'

She turned around and looked at me her eyes now filled with tears, she leant over and kissed me on the cheek. How I didn't grab her I don't know. What a nightmare I kept thinking. This is sheer hell.

We sat there for about an hour just talking of nothing much. It was so hard not to stroke her beautiful hair not to kiss her soft cheek, not to kiss her beautiful mouth. How long can I keep this up? I just needed to share this agony with someone but who?

Chapter 13

Mary's family stood at the graveside. The sun shone on them. It should be raining thought Mary. Raining in sympathy it's far too beautiful on such a sad day. The thought of never seeing her beloved father again seemed too dreadful to contemplate. She found it very hard to understand the finality of it all and holding tightly onto her mother's hand, while her little sisters hid their faces behind her skirt she wept silently for them all.

Around them were freshly dug mounds of black earth with flowers wilting in the hot sun. Henry looked quite exhausted. There had been four funerals that day already. Mary noticed how he had aged in the last week. It was like being on a roller coaster the way things had changed from the happiness of their wedding only five weeks ago to this day of sorrow. She wondered what was going to happen next. It was a like bad dream; unreal yet so real.

Walking away from the graveyard people spoke quietly to each other, some had lost their own loved ones during the bombing so their terrible memories came rushing back. A few of the women found it hard to control their emotions but most did, they had to. This was the time to mourn atfor their own when this day was over. So it was a very subdued little company that made its way back to the Vicarage, while tears were softly shed and hands held tight.

Family and close friends stood talking quietly to each other in the garden where flowers and apple blossom filled the air with their perfume. A soft breeze stirred the leaves of the aspen. It was a perfect spring day. Anna watched as Mary talked with her mother and Henry. She thought of the wedding such a short time ago, It had been such a wonderful day; the sun had shone briefly. Robert had been such a proud father when he walked Mary down the aisle and now here they were mourning him. It was all too sad to contemplate.

She ached for Jack. For his arm around her, for him just being here. Where was he? I just wish I had some contact with him she thought and sighing she turned away and walked towards her parents who were talking to George .

'You okay Anna?' George said putting his arm around her.

'Yes I'm okay, I was just thinking how sad it all is today and remembering the beautiful wedding such a short time ago. It all seems too horrid somehow.'

Henry's dog Clarence, a massive black Newfoundland lay panting under a tree while Mary's little sisters stroked him kissed him, then cuddled up against him like two little puppies. It was a beautiful sight that somehow made things feel less tragic for a second or two.

Mary smiled at her mother and squeezed her hand. 'It's going to be okay Mum, I promise, we have each other. Henry and I will look after you all, Dad would have wanted that.'

After the funeral, Anna and George walked slowly back with their parents to their homes. There had been no siren to disrupt the little gathering at the Vicarage which helped dispel some of the gloom people were feeling. The roads around them were almost clear of traffic. A few cyclists were out but otherwise it was very quiet, too quiet somehow. They walked past the road where Robert had died. The houses open to the skies, some with no roofs, some with no walls but the majority of them just great mounds of rubble. Everywhere they turned there seemed to be some sort of devastation.

'Don't you find this so unbelievable that we are living in times like this?' Anna stood looking at the dreadful sight, 'What's it all for? I know war is war, but it is so wretched, so cruel. Mary's family destroyed for what?' Jack put his arm around her, 'Every war the same questions are asked and there are, and never will be answers. Things will never change, that is the tragedy. There will always be wars where there are human beings. A sad fact but oh such a true one, we will never learn to live together. Go back as far as history is recorded, nothing really has changed, just the ways of killing are more sophisticated and more deadly.'

Later that evening George and Anna sat together by the river, it was getting dark but somehow they needed to be outside, the day had been a bad day and being with nature seemed the right thing to be doing. Watching his girl deal with the pain thinking that it was him at war was so hard it was killing him. It was much the same at home the sorrow made it a sad place to be at the moment. So many times he had wanted to blurt out to his parents the truth and so many times he never did. His mind was a jumble of confusion. If George died, God forbid, what was he to do, be George for ever? Say goodbye to Jack? The whole thing was a huge nightmare that had no intention of going away. He felt completely and utterly out of control and very, very alone.

Anna turned to him. 'Oh George please hold me tight.' Her face crumpled. 'I am so frightened that Jack will be killed and there is nothing anyone can do.'

Tears fell heavily down Anna's face as he held her and a familiar smell of peppermint and after shave seemed oddly comforting to her. 'You smell just like Jack did,' she whispered.

'Do I?' George shrugged, 'It's probably because I've been wearing his aftershave and nicking his peppermints, I'm sorry if it upsets you.'

She smiled up at him, 'No it's rather nice being reminded of him somehow.'

Looking at these two you would presume them to be young lovers clutched in each other's arms. The girls unkempt hair hanging lose and dark against the white of the boy's shirt, but looking closely you would see something else in the boy's eyes, not just sadness but sheer confusion.

Chapter 14

One Month Later: Jack

I have been working most nights at the lab. Trying to put the penicillin culture through a *Recovery Process* so it could reach its crystallised form. I then needed to dissolve it in a saline solution so it would be ready to be used on a patient through injection. It was one hard long tedious job and I was exhausted.

It was around eleven at night, I had left the surgery at eight that evening and cycled to the lab. It was difficult to see where I was going with the blackout. My light was covered except for a pinprick which did little good, so I was always rather relieved when I reached my destination without causing damage to myself or anyone else on the road. The lab was all closed up, no one around, thank goodness. I had no desire to talk to anyone at the moment. I just felt so damned tired.

Turning on the lights I looked around the room, there were cultures and microscopes waiting to be used but somehow I had no energy to do any work and felt quite drained with it all. I really thought George would return and we would laugh together at the deception we had caused, but now it was not to be. I sat down my head in my hands and cried, the first time real tears had come and it was a relief to shed them. I had felt choked with the agony of it all.

I don't know how long I sat there, how long I cried, but I felt shattered and ready to go home, everything could wait until tomorrow. I was just too tired to think. Suddenly, I thought I saw a movement over on the other side of the room. Just one lamp was on, the blackout curtains making the lab darker than normal. I looked again, peering into the gloom, but there was nothing there. Then suddenly where there had been a movement a veil-like curtain seemed to appear. It was almost like a waterfall but somehow more like the trembling of leaves through sunlight, but nothing really substantial. I thought I could hear a sound coming from the veil but the sound was in my head at the same time. I couldn't seem to decipher it. I pressed my fingers hard into my forehead the voice was there again. I looked at the veil it was shimmering with a strange light. A black shape in the centre of it, it looked like a figure. I couldn't be sure, but I concentrated harder and the voice came again and the shape moved. It *was* a figure. A man. The voice was saying something I couldn't understand.

'George?' I whispered, ' it is you isn't it, speak to me again, I can't hear you. Where are you, are you alright? Please answer me, please.'

'Again I heard a faint voice, it sounded like 'alright, alright.' Again the words, alright, it sounded like I am alright. I shouted now. 'What, I can't hear you George, are you alright, you said alright. Oh God you are okay say it again, say it again. Then a faint sound.

'Yes I am okay Jack, I am okay!'

Suddenly there was a blast of cold air then nothing. Everything had disappeared. But it was going to be fine it was going to be just fine I knew it

I remembered how many years ago when we were both young boys George had fallen into the river on his bike, breaking his arm in the process. It was then that he had contacted me in just the same way. I had cycled like a crazy thing to find him, there he was grabbing tightly to some rushes with the bike on top of him. Neither of us had ever forgotten it and only once had mentioned it.

'Guess that was telepathy' I said, 'Guess so,' George replied.

I had to see Anna, tell Mother and Father. I started to laugh, he's alive. The bloody man is alive, thank God, thank God. I cycled like a maniac all the way home, not caring how dark it was. I felt as though a ton had been removed from my head. My brother was alive, alive!

Chapter 15

George

I was given hot soup and bread when I first arrived at Isabelle's, it was like nectar after so long without food, then I must have fallen asleep in front of the fire; for the next thing I knew Isobel was asking if I would like a bath. She said she had put out some of her brother's clothes for me and I was about his height so they should fit.

The room I was in belonged to Regis. It was full of football memorabilia, he played for the local club and was destined for greater things but the war had got in the way, so at the age of 19 he was fighting for his country instead of kicking a ball around. I sat on his bed and realised how lucky I had been to land up here instead of lying in the wreckage of a plane. I felt Anna's locket in my pocket and took it out and looked at this little golden jewel and thanked the Lord for it. Who knows if it saved me, but something did.

I thought of how I had been sweet on Anna when we were younger; how I rather hoped she would fall in love with me but somehow, which I never could understand, it was Jack that stole her heart. I gave in willingly, they were so right together and there were always other girls to conquer. Even so Anna would always hold a special place in my heart.

Going down stairs I could smell that wonderful aroma of something splendid cooking. In front of the huge inglenook a man lay sleeping in a large leather arm chair, a newspaper open on his lap. I guessed it to be Isobel's father. In the kitchen I could hear her talking to her mother, so I crept quietly in and found them both sitting around a table.

They looked up when I walked in and smiled. 'You look just like Regis,' said Isabelle. Both of them looked sad and there were tears in her mother's eyes.

Sitting around the fire before supper Isobel's father, Lucien, asked me what had happened. Why had I crashed? There wasn't a lot I could tell him without giving away too much information but I gave him a vague outline of how I had been shot at and where the plane had gone down.

Isabelle and her mother were appalled that I had to bail out. We talked of how lucky I had been to escape. Lucien talked of his son Regis who had been called up and was now in the army.

'But we have no idea where he is, we worry everyday about him.'

I said how I understood as my parents would now have probably received a telegram saying I was missing so all I wanted to do was contact them somehow.

'We have no phone lines here and there is no communication at all, it is frightful. No one knows what is going on from one day to the next. There are dreadful stories circulating about Jews in Paris and other cities being rounded up, taken off in lorries and never seen again. It is a bad time for France.'

I did feel a bit like the prodigal son and was certainly treated like one. The family couldn't have been kinder. That night we feasted on a delicious rabbit casserole and we talked and talked while an old black range chuntered away in the background, next to where lay a rather old black labrador snoring gently An oil lamp gave some light to the room. Occasionally someone would put a large log on the already roaring fire that glowed behind its black iron bars, with candlelight glinting on the brass handles.

'Electricity,' said Lucien, 'is virtually non-existent and as scarce as the food on most people's tables.'

Lying in the beautiful old wooden sleigh bed that night was heaven, even if the bed was a little short for a tall man. Made for a Napoleonic Frenchman I thought.

It was so quiet, not a sound to be heard. I looked at my watch by the light of a huge yellow moon that hung like a great golden orb outside the window. It was only 11.00 pm but it had been one hell of a day. I still found it so extraordinary that I was lying here enjoying the sheer joy of being safe. How damned lucky I had been.

Chapter 16

That night when Jack cycled home to wake his parents and tell them the news of his *'thought talk'* with George, was the beginning of a calming time for the family. Nell and Ernest knew of their children's telepathy, neither of the boys had ever gone into intricate detail about the visions, that was their private world to be shared with no one but themselves. Yet they had seen how each boy could feel the same sensations as the other especially when danger was around the corner, so there was no question of them disbelieving. That night the three O'Brien's slept the sleep of the just and when waking, life seemed kinder to them all.

'Tomorrow I will tell Anna the good news,' were Jack's last thoughts as he slipped gently into oblivion.

When he told her the next day, she was wide eyed and frowning. She doesn't believe me were his first thoughts. Why should she, it all sounds so bizarre and unlikely.

'Well?' He said looking at her. 'Say something.'

'That's amazing,' she gasped, 'unbelievably amazing. Oh I wish I had been there to witness it all, you are so lucky,' and she threw her arms around me.

'Thank God, so you do believe me, I was so sure you wouldn't. Why do you believe me, how do you know I am not making it up to comfort you?'

She looked at me, her eyes were shining. 'I believe you because the same thing has happened to me. Well sort of, not so dramatic but even so pretty weird too. Listen, and I'll tell you?'

'When I was a little girl I was sitting on my bedroom window sill, watching the snow falling in the garden. Suddenly a woman appeared from nowhere screaming and running around in circles, with blood pouring from her hair. For some bizarre reason there was a red stiletto heel embedded in her head. I was about six years old and have little memory of it really, but I can still see the blood staining the snow to scarlet.. I don't think I knew what was happening to be quite honest. I remember screaming and my mother came up. I pointed out the window, still screaming. Apparently I was hysterical and wouldn't stop crying. So I was picked up and taken down stairs wrapped in a blanket, given some hot milk where I sat by the fire with Mama. I remember little but I was told the story when I was about twelve if I remember rightly. That is when Mama told me that both her and her mother were 'fey' and could see things others couldn't. I did like the word fey, it sounded like fairy. So I was rather pleased about that. After that I had several other experiences, but nothing as dramatic.

Mama also told me that a week later in the local paper there was a headline. '*Husband kills wife with one of her red stiletto shoes.*' It had happened miles away over the other side of town; there was the date and the time of the murder and it was the exactly when that I had seen her in the garden. So you see George, I do believe you, so very much.'

She leant over and kissed me on the cheek. It was all too much for a young man, in love with a girl he couldn't tell. I just wanted this farce to be over but I was not sure it would ever be resolved.

Chapter 17

George

It has been a whole month since I've been 'rescued' by Isabelle. One whole month of happiness yet the worry and indecision of not really knowing what I was going to do seemed unfathomable. I had no contact with the world outside; no communication to let my family know I was safe. It was killing me knowing that the dreaded telegram would 1 have arrived already, saying *'missing in action.'*

I had to contact them somehow. I had to. There must be a way I thought. I closed my eyes and tried to think. Maybe I could find someone with a shortwave radio but then I knew no one at home who had one, so that was a pointless exercise. Jesus there must be a way, some way. Then suddenly it struck me, of course. *'thought talk'!* We had done it when we were young, why not now.

I sat on the edge of the bed, it was late. After midnight, there was no moon that night just a heavy mist that hung over the land like a great cloud. How to start. I'd had no sense of Jack trying to contact me so it was all new. Could it be done out of the blue. He must think of me a lot so if I could get through to him when I am in his thoughts, it would be just luck but I had to try.

I concentrated as hard as I could pressing my hands hard against my temples. Thinking his name, trying to imagine where he would be. Nothing happened, I tried again and again. This went on for a good half an hour. I was just about to give up, when suddenly there was something.

I squeezed my eyes shut, nothing, what had been there had gone. I felt exhausted. I stared out into the fog of the night then suddenly I saw a shimmer behind the window like a transparent curtain. It moved backwards and forwards and there were shapes in it and around it. I pressed my hands harder against my head, then I saw it, a dark shape, with a lamp and a figure. I stared harder, it was Jack, in his lab. He was hunched over with his head in his hands. He was crying. I could hear the muffled sound of a man in pain.

Willing him to see me I *'thought talked'* him. Suddenly he looked up, his image was very vague, but I concentrated as hard as I was capable, then I heard his voice. The image started to fade then became stronger.

I could hear his voice in my head, 'George?' It was Jack's voice like a whisper. 'Are you safe, tell me for God's sake!'

I shouted as loud as I could. 'Yes Jack I am okay, I am okay.'

I had to hope he heard me, the vision was getting weaker and weaker. Then a cold wind seemed to whirl around the room and it all disappeared. I was sweating like a pig and my head throbbed, but we had *'thought talked*. We were in contact. It was going to be alright. I felt as though I could sleep forever as an overwhelming sense of relief washed over me. Now everyone at home will know I am safe I thought. Thank the Lord. I climbed into bed and was asleep almost immediately, the first time I had slept easily. Let Jack sleep well too were my last thoughts as beautiful sleep rocked me in its arms.

Chapter 18

One sizzling Sunday Anna sat in her studio, her atelier. It was actually just an old converted gazebo in a pretty ropey state. Nothing much had been done other than having the sides glazed in, it was now waterproof but freezing cold in winter and boiling hot in summer. Even so it was her private space and she loved it. Nestling in the corner of the garden near the willows, looking over the river that lay still and silent in the hot sun, she was away from the city of London and the devastation that lay all around. The Blitz was over but the bombing still went on and on. Each day there was this overpowering fear of what might happen next. It seemed, she thought, like the sword of Damocles hanging over everyone's head.

Thank goodness I have my painting she mused as she stood looking at the beauty that lay around her. Four white swans sailed regally up and down the river some with cygnets nestling in their feathers; it was all too quiet she thought, the calm before the storm. Please not she prayed, let us have a little peace for a while.

Earlier that day she had been painting her little sisters who refused to sit still, with blue ribbons tied in their hair and in their 'party' dresses they looked like little angels which they certainly were not. They insisted on fidgeting and giggling all the time and the gazebo was tremendously hot even with the blinds pulled down.

When it was cold there was a brazier in the corner with a chimney poking out of the roof, not brilliant but it took the ice of the windows, she would explain to those who came to sit for her. The inside was painted the palest of yellows. Like sitting in the sunshine she would say, even when it is gloomy outside. On the wooden floor there were a couple of old Persian rugs she had picked up in a jumble sale, a bit ragged but just perfect for what she needed. There were always flowers from the garden everywhere, normally in old paint jars. I have to have flowers she would say, they make me smile.

The sisters sat on the old blue velvet couch which sagged dreadfully in the middle. Fat cushions hiding the worst of the lumps and bumps from the broken springs.

They had their gas masks slung around their necks; they wore them continuously. Evelyn had tried to explain that it wasn't necessary when they were at home but they insisted so she left them alone.

'You can your gas mask boxes off while I draw you,' Anna suggested.

'Oh no, Mama said we have to have them with us just in case.' Frowning, their little faces appeared really worried about the whole thing. Hugging the boxes closely they looked at Anna for reassurance. Poor little things she thought, what a rotten time for them.

She had tried to position the girls in a way as near as possible to her favourite painting by Renoir. Where two young girls, around their age, sit with a book open on their lap. In his painting they are wearing little brown lace up boots. These were impossible to find so Anna had put them in thick men's socks to give the impression of boots. This caused trouble!

'They're so itchy and scratchy,' cried Victoria. She was a year older than Elizabeth at twelve and a real little madam.

'I'm taking them off!'

'No you are not,' shouted Anna. She was fed up with the girls. They kept on talking and moving constantly while Elizabeth sucked her thumb wrapped in an old piece of blanket. 'My losh-losh,' she called it, therefore her face was hidden most of the time.

'Stop it, both of you!' She was exasperated. She had been painting them for about an hour and they were driving her mad.

'Go away both of you, scat, and tomorrow we will do another hour and if you promise not to fidget I will bring the new kittens so you can hold them. Now go away and annoy someone else.'

A cat, named Jazzman by the girls, had arrived out of the blue one day and was still with them a year later. Jazzman had turned out to be a Jasmine after all and had just delivered her third litter much to the girls delight.

Anna watched her sisters as they ran towards the river. The hot sun shining on their long auburn hair turning the ends to scarlet. Dangling their bare feet amongst the swans, who swam off indignantly with their heads in the air. Then as they ran up the garden she could hear them singing.

She watched them with love and affection and prayed. 'Keep them safe. Whoever you are up there. Just keep them safe that's all I ask.'

Turning away from the window she collapsed onto the couch. That had been one long hard hours work. The painting was taking shape and would be finished with a couple more sittings.

Swinging her feet up she laid down as she waited for George who was due later. She was to paint his portrait, a surprise for his parents.

There had been a lucky break for her. Her father, who working in parliament had got her a couple of commissions and after that the work just kept coming in.

'It is all in the eyes,' people would say. 'She captures the very essence of their persona in her portraits, you can almost see them thinking.' So now she was to have her very first real exhibition, which she was working towards. Maybe one day I will paint our prime minister she dreamed, maybe one day.

She had drawn all her life from when she was old enough to hold a crayon. It's part of me she mused, like a musician has his music. Like a singer has his song. A writer his pen. It was part of her very being, her psyche. Everywhere she went she took a sketch book, if she had drawn something special she would transfer it to thick pastel card sometimes making a watercolour sketch first to gauge the colour. She was never happier when she was at work. It keeps me sane she thought in this crazy mixed up world, especially now.

She sighed and closed her eyes feeling herself dropping off. That lovely time between wakefulness and sleep. Jack was running towards her, his arms outstretched; calling her name over and over again but the faster he ran the further away he seemed. Trying to run after him her feet were rooted to the ground, however hard she fought she could not move. It was terrible, she knew if she didn't reach him he would disappear. She screamed out his name but no sound came from her mouth, and she watched in horror as he vanished into nothingness.

Suddenly she felt a kiss on her mouth and waking with a start she saw George standing over her.

'George did you just kiss me?'

'Good Lord, hardly! No, of course not, as if I would. You were shouting out Jack's name it was he who kissed you not me!'

Anna rubbed her eyes, 'Of course. He was running towards me but couldn't reach me and I tried to run but couldn't, it was horrible. Could it mean something sinister?'

'No, just a dream. Not surprising, he's on your mind all the time. Look are sure you're not too tired to paint, I can come back another time?'

'No it's fine, I had the girls here earlier they were such monkeys. I was exhausted by the time they left I must have fallen asleep but I am perfectly fine now.'

'Where do you want me to sit?' Jack looked around the gazebo. He loved coming here, to him it was a little bit of paradise away from the problems of the world.

When he was the 'real' Jack they would sit here in the evenings listening to music. Anna would lay on the couch with his arms around her. His beautiful girl, his princess, now he had to pretend yet again. Oh let it be over, he thought, let all this pretence be over soon.

'Can you sit in that armchair by the window? I only need to do the top part of you so if you want to read or something that's fine or I can put some music on.' 'Music would be good, any Glen Miller? Rather keen on him somehow makes the most amazing sound with his clarinet. Very big in The States. Hopefully he'll be coming over to entertain the troops, not sure if we will ever get to see him though, but rather hoping we can.'

So the artist and the sitter were as one while the music floated around them and the sunlight slanted through the white blinds.

'You know George I find it uncanny that you have that little dip below your nose just above your top lip. When I painted Jack last year he had exactly the same tiny dent, quite bizarre. How your parents differentiate between you boys is a mystery to me. It is like painting the same face.'

She smiled, 'It is rather nice, I feel as though I am painting you both at the same time! By the way I don't suppose you have had any more 'talks' with Jack have you?'

'Nope, 'fraid not, but I am not worried I just know he is okay, and you must think the same; that is the only way we will get through this you know that.'

'Yes, I know. Anyway that's it for the day. An hour and a half is long enough for you and my back is aching.'

She stretched up and arched herself backwards her hair hanging lose down her back. She was so beautiful Jack thought, he could hardly bear it, my girl. If only I could talk to you Anna. Somehow I have to get the strength up, to face you and tell you everything.

Chapter 19

Jack

After telling Anna about George I felt a lot lighter and more positive than I had for a long time. Hopefully now we had got through to each other, George would find some normal way of contacting us.

I was to sit for Anna later so after surgery I wandered up to her house, I walked around the back where the gazebo stood white and shining in the sunlight. The river beyond lay still and silent. It was all so peaceful. Denying the chaos we were in it was a little bit of paradise in a time of darkness. A few swans glided elegantly up and down ruffling the water slightly. Willows dipped their leaves in the water and the sun shone hot on my back, everything was alright in the world, just for that minute in time.

I could see through an open window Anna lying on the old velvet couch. Her hair hung loose over one arm, she seemed to be asleep. I crept quietly up the few wooden steps and tiptoed into the gazebo. Her mouth was slightly apart, her lashes dark against her pale cheeks. My Sleeping Beauty, time for the Prince to wake her. I leant over and kissed her lightly on the mouth She jumped up and glared at me 'George did you just kiss me?' I laughed. 'Of course not, you were calling out Jack's name, so it was him, not me. As if I would.'

She smiled, her eyes glistening. 'I was dreaming of him, so I guess it must have been!'

Sitting in the old armchair she started to draw me, Some Glen Miller was playing on the turntable record player, it was almost like the old days, just the two of us. Blinds drawn, music on, and a lot of canoodling! Not now sadly, no more of that. I was George and George had to behave himself. More's the pity I thought.

How extraordinary, she said it was that I had the same little dip below my nose that Jack had and it was rather like painting him again. I laughed it off feeling extremely uncomfortable about it all and wishing things were different. How could I get out of this dilemma, how the hell could I?

There had to be a way out of all this mess. I have to do what I have been thinking of over the last couple of days. I will do it tonight I thought and tried to relax and let Glen Miller's clarinet wash over me.

The light started to fade so I helped Anna clear up. There were pastels all over the table and on the floor. Her face was streaked with black and red.

'Have a look at yourself you look like a Red Indian,' I laughed.

She looked at herself in the old silver mirror. 'Oh God, what a state, I always get in such a mess, every time. I think I need a bath or a dip in the river. The river is very tempting. I am so hot I think I will jump in, are you coming?'

'What, not like this?'

'Why not? Great fun, I will take my skirt off, you take off your trousers then we are halfway decent in case anyone sees us.'

She spun around whipping off her cotton skirt and running towards the river, her long brown legs flashing in the sunlight. Taking off my trousers, I followed her. The river was still cold as it was early in the year and also extremely muddy and squelchy underfoot but swimming out to the middle was better. Not deep enough to do any amazing feat but enough to vaguely dive. I watched as she turned upside down and came up with her hair hanging around her face.

'Wow, you look just like a mermaid, a beautiful mermaid!'

'Shut up George, you sound just like Jack.' She giggled and disappeared again. This was driving me mad, time to leave.

'I'm off Anna, need to get back and prepare for evening surgery. Don't drown will you.' And picking up my trousers, I walked up towards the house, feeling rather self-conscious of my white legs.

That night after supper and surgery I cycled over to the vicarage, Henry and I were to meet up for a drink later. I pushed my bike up the path, it was pitch black. How I hated the blackout, it was so depressing, no lovely warm light to welcome you anymore.

Mary told me that her mother and sisters were to go to stay with her aunt in Devon, she was her mother's older sister who was married with three children much the same age as her girls.

'They are to go down tomorrow, they catch the afternoon train. There are so few running at the moment they were lucky to get a seat. I think Mum will be happier away from the bombing with the girls. She hasn't been sleeping and is very jumpy when the siren goes off. I will miss them all but it is much better for them.' I agreed and hugging her shouted for Henry to get a move on.

That evening sitting in the local pub I was trying to pluck up the courage to tell Henry all about George and me. I needed some 'Dutch courage' and knocked back an extremely large scotch before my pint.

'You okay old chap? You look a bit twitchy and that was one hell of a snifter. Is something worrying you, hope everything is okay at home?'

'Yes all good, just something I need to get off my chest and I am not sure how to go about it. If I tell you can you keep it to yourself? It is rather a delicate matter and I thought you may have some advice to give me, being a Vicar and all that.'

Henry laughed, 'a confession?'

'Well sort of, not sure how to start?'

'At the beginning as they say. Don't worry I won't bite. Look George I have known you and Jack since we all went to school together. I am sure there is nothing that would surprise me about you two!!'

'Well it isn't anything to do with girls for a change. It's just. Oh God, I don't know how to tell you. This is crazy, I feel such a fool, maybe I shouldn't burden you with all this.'

'Well you certainly can't stop now. Spit it out old man, it can't be that bad.'

'Oh but that is the trouble, it is. The worst thing I have ever done and that is a fact.'

'Good grief, you haven't killed someone and hidden the body?'

'Good heavens no of course not, nothing like that. I almost wish that was all it was actually.'

I took a deep breath and started to talk, I talked for nearly half an hour. Afterwards I felt completely drained.

I looked at Henry. 'Well, there it is the whole wretched story of deception and it is all my doing. If I had been any sort of man this would never have happened.'

'Stop beating yourself up man.' He leant over and looked at me. 'It is a pretty radical situation I must say. But what is done is done and I can see no way of turning back. So you will just have to play along and hope it all works out, which,' he paused, 'I am sure it will.'

So it was done. Someone else knew the sordid story that was tearing me apart. We both sat for an hour or two, drinking, smoking and trying to think of a way out of the mess I was in. There seemed to be no answer. As Henry said. I had to grit my teeth and get on with it and pray to God that George returned safely and life could return to normal. But nagging in the back of my mind was should I tell Anna, should I tell Anna?

Chapter 20

George

Today I have been here in Normandy with the Henots for over two months.

There is vague talk from Lucien about getting me out of France, through Spain and then Gibraltar. It is an ongoing subject but nothing definite has happened, I will just have to wait but it is hard. Missing the family is bad enough but knowing they don't know where I am or if I am alive still preys on my mind incessantly, even after the ''*thought talk*'' with Jack. I just need to give them something solid to hold on to, a bit of telepathy is all well and good but not substantial and definite. Nothing written down in black and white; no phone call, nothing at all really when I think of it.

Last night after we had finished supper I told the family the story of me Jack and the switch. They sat in silence, not a word was said. The old stove muttered gently to itself while the dog joined in snuffling like an old man. The grandfather clock ticked slowly as I spoke. I'd had a glass or two of Lucien's calvados after supper and I guess it had loosened my tongue a bit. But I knew that I had to explain what had happened. They were risking their lives sheltering me, so the least I could do was tell them that I had been living a lie. And they needed to know this.

So I told them the whole complicated scenario, right from the beginning, not mentioning the '*thought talk*.' Now that really would be pushing it a bit, really asking too much from them.

After I had finished they all stared at me. Not quite open mouthed and wide eyed, but slightly bemused by the whole thing.

Isabelle looked at me, tears welling up in her eyes. She took hold of my hand. 'Oh George, how hard it must have been holding such a secret to yourself and I am so pleased you wanted us to know.' She smiled and looked down at our hands held together. My great rough paw and her small soft hand with delicate shell pink nails. I squeezed it and my heart lurched. She tilted her head to the side questioningly and looked at me with her dark eyes. They were navy blue with green lights, cats eyes I called them, they were irresistible.

Then something happened. It felt like a jolt of electricity running between us. She smiled and lowered her eyes. That is when I realised I had fallen in love for the very first time, not lust but love, friendship had come first and now this. I felt slightly overwhelmed by it all. Me George O'Brien being in love. Extraordinary. I had realised it earlier on in the day when shopping for Isabelle's birthday present when it hit me that this was the 'real thing,' as they say in the movies.

That morning I had been in town trying to find a present for her. When walking along the back streets I discovered a little *Brocante* almost hidden by the lilac wisteria that covered its frontage. The scent lingering in the senses long after passing through the door; a door so low I had to stoop to get through it, a bit like the sleigh bed, obviously made in Napoleonic times!

An extremely large Madam sat in an old armchair by the window with an extremely fat cat on her lap. She jumped up as I walked in, the fat cat rolled on to the floor and landed in a furry heap at her feet where it shook itself and waddled into the back of the shop.

Did I want any help? Yes probably. Picking up a cloisonné box lined with white silk she handed it to me. It was tiny, the enamelled turquoise and blue was stunning, it is eighteenth century she informed me. Who was I to argue with her. Then she showed me a pair of pearl drop earrings. Not quite as old, but last century monsieur. Your friend will like it all I think. If I liked she could make me a *petit paquet*. I would like very much I replied. She disappeared into the back of the shop where a great deal of activity went on. Paper rustling, scissors snipping and the fat cat told in no uncertain words, to get off the table at once or…. I missed the last bit! At last Madame appeared, holding aloft a masterpiece in her hands. A *petit paquet* wrapped in gold and silver tissue paper; pale blue silk ribbons flowed down the sides and tiny pink paper roses were sprinkled over the top. 'It is beautiful, thank you so much,' I said.

'It is for someone special I am thinking, no?' She asked.

'Yes I suppose it is.' Isabelle was definitely special.

'You love this friend no?'

'Yes I said, 'I think I probably do.' Of course I did. I had been falling in love with this beautiful French girl from the first time I saw her.

After paying Madame, which it seemed, an astronomical amount of francs, I kissed her on both cheeks, making her blush alarmingly and give a strange little throaty laugh.

I almost skipped out of the shop. I was ten foot high. I wanted to shout, to tell the world. 'I am in love, I am in love. Do you hear me?!'

Two young girls glanced at me and dissolved into a fit of giggles, running off then turning around to blow kisses at me. I laughed and an old man washing the pavement outside his shop laughed too and shook my hand. Life was pretty good right now; definitely pretty good.

That night we were to celebrate Isabelle's twenty first birthday. Three of her friends, two

142

who taught at the school with her were coming over, staying the night as the curfew was 7.30 pm.

Isabelle's mother, Marie-Claude had told him how hard it was to get hold of decent food at the moment. She said the Germans, who seemed to have huge financial resources scooped most of it up and although there was no rationing yet, times were getting to be very hard. She was lucky though; her sister and husband had a farm across the way where they managed to get their cheese butter and cream from them. Also a goose they were to eat that night and the occasional chicken and eggs, which was a godsend.

I sat with Lucien by the fire and drunk a small whisky with him.

'Gives one an appetite' he insisted.

I didn't think I needed to '*get an appetite.*' I was starving again.

I watched while Isabelle and her mother laid the table in the sitting room. Not in the kitchen I was told, as this was a special occasion and so it was to be.

In the middle of room stood an old round table, it's beautiful patina catching the light from the huge log fire. The fireplace itself took up most off one wall, with room enough to sit inside with ease. A white damask tablecloth was laid down with great care over the table, then crystal glasses and blue patterned plates were added. It was like a ritual, quite fascinating to watch.

Afterwards the girls joined us. Isabelle along with Laura and Emily from school and Sologne, the little waitress from the Café du Sport, where we had our lunch most days.

Marie Claude bustled around in the kitchen. My 'laboratory' she called it where I make magic. Meanwhile the three girls giggling like schoolgirls, were all dressed up to the nines. Isabelle looking amazing in a black shift dress with her hair lose around her shoulders. She had lipstick on and what I think was mascara.. The first time I had ever seen her wear make-up. Her mouth looked invitingly luscious; it was hard to keep my eyes off her.

She glanced over at me and held a small glass of Madeira up. 'Here's to you George, thank you for dropping by!' She laughed and her small white teeth glistened against her red mouth. 'Santé' everyone said and raised their glasses. 'Here's to George.'

I bowed my head, 'Here's to the Henot family for saving my life.'

The girls laughed. Isabelle had filled them in earlier and explained everything. They too had brothers fighting in the war and were eager to hear what I had to say, so there was a lot of talk and laughter.

I watched with joy this beautiful girl with her dark hair hanging down her back and her eyes shining. I will give her the present when everyone else does I thought, if I do it quietly away from everyone she may be embarrassed. I was going to have to play this very carefully I thought. This could be the most important time of my life.

'*A table!*' Isabelle said and we all sat down. Candles were lit in bronze candlesticks. Heads were lowered and grace was said. Then the food arrived. First Isabelle bought in pâté de fois gras with hot buttered toast and fig jam. The first time I have eaten anything quite so exotic. It was heavenly, a delicious sweet white wine accompanied it. There was a lot of talk and laughter about how their house was requisitioned as a German headquarters and surprisingly how well-mannered and respectful the men were. Which seemed to surprise them all, and me too. They had managed to get most of their personal belongings out before they arrived. A lot of the linen, glasses, crockery, cutlery and cooking stuff. Wine from the cellars, (most important Lucien informed me). Their books and framed photos of the family, they even managed to get their piece de resistance out with great difficulty, which stood now in the corner of the room. A rather lovely walnut piano which shone as the table had done in the firelight.

In between all the banter more food was bought in. Slices of a golden goose covered with a glazed orange sauce, surrounded by tiny new buttered potatoes, on a huge blue and white plate. It looked and tasted sublime. Then Lucien poured out some rich red wine into the beautiful glasses.

'Here's to the chef.' I said clinking glasses with the others.

So we ate and ate. Then came white soft cheeses. 'From my sister's farm.' Marie Claude told me. A wooden bowl of green salad was dressed by Lucien. He tossed and turned the leaves for what to me seemed far too long; he informed me he was '*fatiguing the salad.*' That is exactly what Mother would say at home! It was a meal I never forgot.

Then Isabelle bought in a tarte aux pommes that she had made. Thinly sliced apples, cooked in butter and covered with an apricot glaze served with thick cream. 'It is all too much for a mere mortal,' I said to my host, which caused much laughter.

After we sat around a roaring fire and drunk dark sweet coffee out of tiny porcelain cups, and Lucien's calvados, made from his cider apples. He said he was allowed by law to make a certain amount after making his cider. He smiled and said that he always made a little extra in case anyone dropped in.

Then the presents were opened, it was almost midnight, we had been eating and talking for nearly four hours.

Laura, Emily and Sologne gave Isabelle a beautiful navy blue silk shawl embroidered with green flowers. 'To match your eyes!' They giggled. Putting it around her bare arms she got up and walked up and down, making the girls laugh even more.

Her parents gave her a pearl necklace that had been her grandmother's. To be given to her now she had turned twenty one. Her father fastened them around her neck, where they seemed to glow pink against her golden skin. She was so lovely.

Then my turn came and I passed the 'petit paquet' to her. She opened it slowly, making sure no paper was torn. She undid the silk ribbons and unwrapped the silver and gold tissue paper.

'Oh,' she looked over at me, 'Why George, it is beautiful. How did you know?'

'Know what?' I looked at her.

'That I collect cloisonné, and this is the most beautiful of all my pieces. And the earrings, they are divine. I will wear them now, they match my pearls, look.' Fastening them on she tossed her head making the pearls dance in the light. She leant over and kissed me on the cheek and whispered, 'thank you I love it all.'

Then we all sung Happy Birthday. It sounded pretty much like the English version but in French. What an evening. Goodnights were said and as I climbed the stairs I heard the girls laughing and talking as they washed up the chaos that was left.

That night as I got into my little sleigh bed I thanked whoever was watching over me for such an evening. How I wish I could believe in God, it would be so nice to have something to cling on to. I thought vaguely of maybe talking to Henry when I got home but somehow I was too tired to think much about anything. The moon hung golden in the sky as I got into bed. The sheets felt warm. I could feel the heat on my toes and pulling back the covers I found a large stone water bottle. I smiled, such good people I thought. Wait until I tell Jack when I get back.

Chapter 21

Jack

It had been a long day, surgery was busy in the morning. Then again in the evening. It seemed to go on forever. Father had to go out to an emergency house call so I had all his patients to see too. It was almost 8.00 pm by the time the last one left. I started to pack up ready to go home when there was a tentative knock on the door. It was Rachel the nurse, she poked her head around the door and whispered. 'There is a Mrs Barrett here with her child, the woman is really very agitated. Can you see her?'

'Of course,' I sighed. 'Show her in.'

The woman was young and seemed to be in a panic.

'It's Rose.' She said. 'She scratched herself two days ago on some barbed wire, when we were out for a walk. I washed her arm and put some disinfectant on the cut but it seems worse this morning. Can you have a look at it please?' Rose was about four, a pretty little thing with blonde curly hair and blue eyes. She had a slight fever, her arm was inflamed and a little swollen, nothing too drastic. But I was a bit concerned that there appeared to be a red streak running upwards from the wound. I cleaned it again and poured some strong solution over it. Bandaged it and gave Rose some aspirin for her temperature and told the mother to come back tomorrow if it hadn't improved.

When they left, I thought how red the wound had seemed and hoped to God it wasn't what I thought.

There had been a young man in the hospital last month with a streptococci infection, after falling and cutting his knee badly on some broken glass, causing septicaemia. He was dangerously ill and would die unless his leg was amputated. It was a drastic measure. It saved his life but he would never be the same again. The surgeon said there had been four cases over the last year in two other hospitals, with the same infection resulting in amputation. Two of them had sadly died.

'So needless.' He'd said angrily. 'If only the government could manufacture this damned Penicillin. They really need to pull their finger out. They know full well the troops on the front are desperate for it, as we are here in the hospitals.'

He had heard it was been used on troops in America and wondered when on earth it would reach Britain. I so wanted to talk to him of Florey and my lab but was not sure if I should. Probably what I am doing would be illegal, against government policy. Damn that I thought.

Lives are more important than political correctness!

That night I went to the lab. I had managed to get the penicillin to the *'recovery process'* and obtain its crystallised form. Now it needed to be dissolved in a saline solution before it could be ready for injection. Could I get it to that state in time, if young Rose worsened?

I worked long into the night and managed to dissolve enough in the saline to use, in case Rose deteriorated. But I had to take make sure I had enough. I didn't want to run out. That would be catastrophic. I was quite sure that it could do no damage and if there was even the slimmest chance she would recover it had to be worth the risk. But first I would need to talk to the doctor in charge, to see if he would be willing to use the child as a guinea pig and of course explain it all to the mother. That night I slept fitfully worrying about tomorrow.

The next morning surgery was busy again. Most chairs were occupied. Rose was there with her mother when I arrived. I called her straight away into the surgery. Her mother had been crying, her eyes were red and she looked as though she hadn't slept. The child was pale and when she showed me her arm I saw that the wound had started to fester, that her arm was red and swollen. Her fever was way too high and she seemed slightly delirious.

Her mother looked at me while tears ran down her face. She sobbed. What's wrong with her doctor? She's getting worse, she is so hot and sleepy. I'm scared doctor; really frightened.'

I tried to reassure her and suggested as casually as I could, that maybe Rose should go into hospital for a few tests to see what the problem was. Luckily a bed was found for her after phoning around. Father took over my patients and I drove Rose and her mother to the hospital. I stopped by the lab and picked up the penicillin. Hoping to God there would be enough, And that by some miracle it would work.

The hospital was overflowing with casualties from the bombings, but a bed was found for Rose and she was squeezed into a children's ward, where a lot of shell shocked and injured children lay.

Luckily George was a colleague of the surgeon on duty. They had worked together many times before and I had met him when researching childhood diseases. He obviously presumed me to be George like everyone else did. But all this deceit was nerve wracking. I tried to be as casual as possible, hoping he wasn't going to ask me any pertinent questions about their social relationship!

He examined the child and seemed concerned. 'It looks like a streptococci infection, not a lot we can do George. Just a matter of waiting for the fever to subside hopefully and to keep the wound as clean as possible. I just pray we don't have to amputate.'

We were away from the bed and talking as quietly as possible, while Rose's mother sat by her child kissing her face and holding her hand. She was white with worry. It was then I mentioned the penicillin. His eyebrows shot up and he looked across at the child then back at me.

'Good heavens I had no idea you were working with Jack. I remember you mentioned that you were concerned with him being called up and that it would put an end to it all his research. How wonderful that you have carried on and managed to get the penicillin to this stage. Well done. But I have to ask you is there a risk?'

'No, unless she has a bad reaction but we can't find that out without using it. We have to take the chance. But I don't want you to be involved if you are worried it is above the law. I will take full responsibility. I have enough penicillin hopefully for quite a lot of doses. Well?'

'We have to put it to the mother of course. Do you want me to talk to her, or shall I leave it up to you? Being her doctor she may feel more at ease with you.'

'Mrs Barrett.' I said taking her hand. 'Rose has what is called a streptococci infection which causes blood poisoning.'

She gasped and looked at me in horror.

'But there is a good chance that we can halt the progress of the infection by using a new drug, something called Penicillin.'

Looking up at me, her eyes full of anguish she grabbed my arm and in a broken voice whispered. 'Rose is dying, isn't she doctor?'

'No, but she may if we don't do something fast. There is a slight risk she may have a bad reaction to the drug but there have been no problems so far with clinical trials. Are you happy with that?'

'If you think it is the best thing to do doctor. I just want her to get better. Please do what you think. But she can't die. She can't.' Clasping my hand in hers she looked imploringly at me.

'Dear God' I thought let this work. 'It has to.'

No way did I mention any chance of amputation. The poor woman was going through hell as it was. There was no point of making things worse. I remember George telling me that it was one thing a doctor or surgeon dreaded. 'To talk of amputation to a patient.' He said. 'Is almost as bad as telling them they have a terminal illness.'

Rose was treated with regular doses of the penicillin over four days, while her mother sat with the child for the whole time, sleeping in a chair. Then on a mattress next to her, after a nurse said it was ridiculous to expect the poor woman to function with no sleep. So she made up a bed on the floor.

In the first twenty four hours Rose started to recover. Her fever subsided and the swelling improved. By the fourth day she was sitting up in bed eating and giggling. I still had enough of the drug so she was given it for three extra days. By this time she was up and running around the ward. It felt like a miracle. Seeing the light return to her mother's frightened desperate eyes made all those long nights in the lab worth every second.

That night I rang Florey who was back in England.

I told him the whole story. He laughed. 'You do know Jack that this drug is supposed to be a military secret kept from the Germans!' He was delighted about Rose. He said '*The Lancet*' had published the fact that, four or five patients had survived their illnesses and now at last scientists had encouraged the government to allow doctors to use the drug. On and off the battlefield.

'So Jack, let's just hope the government will listen this time. I am in discussion with the medical board at the moment so I will keep you posted with any progress. It is so good to hear such positive news. Well done old chap!'

It was then I wanted to tell him I held a secret, not a military one but a pretty serious one. But it seemed a pointless exercise. It would be just to appease myself. He never questioned why I hadn't been called up, so I didn't mention it. I did feel very guilty and I knew would have to live with that guilt until George returned.

Going into the ward to say goodbye to Rose and her mother, I saw the child standing there, her teddy clasped tightly in her arms. She looked up at me and smiled. Her blue eyes sparkling. 'Mummy said you made me better and I must say thank you.' She put out a chubby little hand. I took it and bent down to kiss her. 'The magic drug made you better Rose, not me. Now make sure you don't go sticking nasty things into yourself, promise.'

She giggled, 'I promise.'

Her mother shook my hand and tears of happiness welled up in her eyes. 'Thank you doctor. I will never ever forget what you have done for us.' Then holding Rose by the hand she walked out through the swing doors.

Chapter 22

George

Next day being a Sunday was a lazy one, I must admit I did have a bit of a sore head after such an evening, but it was of little consequence. I was in love and everything was as it should be, quite perfect. Whether Isabelle felt the same was another matter entirely. I would have to play my cards right and not make a mess of it all, as I do seem to have done quite a bit when it comes to the female of the species.

It was nice to be away from work and have time to relax. I had been working with Lucien who owns the only pharmacy in town. His assistant, a young boy had been called up so I fitted in perfectly. The story we had concocted together seemed entirely plausible. I was Lucien's sister's child who came from the south of France where I was an apprentice working with the local pharmacist. I had a heart murmur preventing me from being enlisted. How ironic I laughed when we were planning it all.

I spoke fluent French so I passed easily for a Frenchman. No one questioned me and the locals were very friendly. Knowing I had a heart problem they were most considerate and treated me like cut glass.

Every lunchtime, exactly at midday Lucien and I would eat in the Café du Sport by the river. There we had the 'menu de jour,' which was always a mountain of food. Three courses, with cider, wine and water on the table. I was convinced that the French had an alarm clock in their stomach, as exactly at midi they were always starving hungry. All the shops would shut and the town would be virtually deserted, while every café and restaurant overflowed with ravenous Frenchmen and women.

The only drawback being the amount of German officers eating in the café. Sitting there in their jackboots talking and laughing loudly as though they owned the place made for uncomfortable feelings.

A lot of them had got a taste for pastis, the pale green liquid that turned opaque when water was added. Absinthe having been the far stronger but banned due to a spurt of alcoholics and suicides. So pastis was the next best thing and far weaker, but enough to make the officers talk voraciously. None of them even bothering to try to speak French. They would just speak louder which made me feel like belting them. Some could be incredibly rude, except for one young officer who at least tried out his dreadful French and always acknowledged us when we walked in. I had a feeling he was sweet on Solonge the way he looked at her, that would not bode well I thought.

Some of the Germans were billeted in Lucien's house and they would nod when they saw him. Maybe utter a few words but other than that they kept themselves to themselves.

Lucien told me that he was rather hoping they would be leaving soon. He had heard rumours that a lot of the Germans were moving out, but there had been no official confirmation.

'So it is probably just hearsay,' he grunted. He was very sanguine about it all and said it was just a matter of time. He had heard there had been talk of Hitler having sent over three million soldiers and tanks into Russia, taking the Russians by surprise. And now the USA were supplying to the USSR, so maybe this was the beginning of the end.

I hoped he was right. But somehow doubted it.

Lucien knew the proprietors of the café and told me that Sologne, who had been at the birthday party, came from the next village, her fiancée had been killed at the front. She waited at table and became very subdued when the Germans got loud and teased her. I could see her trying not to cry. Poor child I thought, if I was any sort of man I would do something but I had to keep a low profile. Oh how hard it was not to get up and hit them. Lucien said she had been a bubbly girl and always would wear her long blonde hair lose around her shoulders. With her pale pink lipstick and pretty clothes a young man was bound to fall in love with her. And he did. His name was Jean and they got engaged just before he was called up. He promised to return so they could be married. He was killed at the front in the first week. Just another statistic in this dreadful war.

Now she wore her hair in a bun, no lipstick and always black clothes. Like a widow in mourning I thought. It was hard to compare her to the young happy girl at the party. How hard it must be for her to serve these men when her lover had been killed by the likes of them. I pitied her and I would make a point of talking to her which seemed to brighten her a little. Lucien laughed and said she was falling in love with me. Oh if only he knew that I was about to tell his daughter of my love for her. What would he make of that I thought? I was soon to find out.

One afternoon after lunch I left Lucien and wandered into town. I. had never been in the great church that stood in a square surrounded by shops and houses. It was a beautiful piece of architecture built in the sixteenth century. I walked up the old stone steps to a massive wooden door, tightly bolted.

'Damn!' I said out loud, then I saw just next to it a smaller door. Trying that it swung open to reveal a wood panelled lobby. There were two doors either side of the panelling. I pushed one open and immediately the smell of incense filled my senses, taking me straight back to our church at home. I was a catholic, not a practicing one by any means. Of course my parents were. Both Jack I had been dragged to communion every Sunday as young boys, but the older we got the more we grew away from our faith. And now it was very seldom either of us went anywhere near a church, much to our parents dismay

The church was quite impressive. It felt more like a cathedral with its huge stone pillars holding up the roof. Great hammer beams stretched across the roof from one side to another. The altar was exquisite. Maybe a little bit over the top with all its gold leaf and cherubs flying everywhere, but quite magnificent. The stained glass windows were a sight to see. Mostly brilliant blues and greens had been used with great flashes of crimson. At the opposite end just by the entrance was an amazing rose window, way up near the roof. An intricate design of different coloured pinks, reds and golds which, with the bright sun streaming it through flooded the white stone floor with a haze of an unearthly pale rose and silver light.

I stood there looking up at the breath-taking beauty of the window for a long time.

On each side of the church stood stone alcoves with statues of the Virgin Mary and Saint Theresa, and many other saints; who they were, I had no idea. Lighted candles stood next to them. Little pieces of paper with prayers for loved ones were slotted into a wooden lattice. Some of the prayers were heart-breaking and I had that old feeling of wanting to kneel down and cross myself, but I felt it would be wrong, like playing a part.

There were a few people praying in the pews. One person with a red scarf around her head was bent over her hands. Crossing herself she got up to leave. It was Isabelle, she smiled when she saw me. 'I thought it was you,' she whispered, 'I saw you wandering around but wasn't sure if it was. How lovely to see you, I had the afternoon off so decided to cycle down here before going home. I love this old church I have been coming here since I was a child, are you a catholic?'

'A relapsed one, unfortunately.' I smiled rather weakly.

'No such thing, once a catholic always a catholic. I love this church, I feel at peace here. I can forget about the wretched war and what it is doing to France. It is my solace and keeps me sane.'

We walked down the steps into the street. People were starting to gather around. Lunch was over and the afternoon had begun.

'Come and have a coffee with me; do you have the time?'

'I would love that.' She smiled, that sweet smile which made my heart beat faster.

There was a little café just opposite the church, with tables and chairs on the pavement and a green awning keeping out the sun. An elderly couple sat at the next table but otherwise it was empty.

'The whole town is on tenterhooks.' Isabelle sighed. 'It has changed from a happy community to one of suspicion and fear. Everyone is wondering what is going to happen next. A young girl at my school thinks we will all be put against a wall and shot. She really believes it. She is terrified because she is Jewish. She has been hearing and reading about Hitler and the deportation of Jews and how families have been taken from their homes and sent to camps. She says she can't sleep at night. Her parents are talking of leaving but where would they go. It is terrible what this war has done to good innocent people.' Her eyes were full of tears. I leant over and wiped one that had got away, her face softened.

'You are so kind to me George, thank you.' Again my heart turned over.

We sat in the warm sunshine and drunk our *petit cafés* and talked. I told her of Anna and Jack being in love. How when I had gone on leave he had said it was so hard keeping up the pretence. I told her how dreadfully guilty I felt leaving him in such a predicament, that it was preying on my mind night and day. I was on the point of telling her of our *'thought talk'*. Then I had a feeling, being such a devout catholic that she would probably poo-poo the idea. I would wait and tell her once I had told her of my love for her. But when will that be I asked myself. Pull your finger out man. Life is too precarious at the moment for hesitation.

I looked at my watch. I was late for work. 'I will see you tonight, I have something to tell you.' Now I had done it.

She looked puzzled. 'Something nice I hope? Laughing, she ran off to untie her bike from one of the plane trees that surrounded the square.

Chapter 23

There was uneasiness in this little town of St Samson Sur Seine. An air of quietness, where before there would have been the sound of laughter, gossip and arguments.

Most young men were at war, so it was mainly, women, the elderly and the very young that walked the quiet streets.

Around the square stood Norman houses crammed together. Interspersed with shops. Amongst them the inevitable boulangeries. Three hairdressers, a poissonerie, a couple of epiceries, a chocolatier, two greengrocers, a dress shop, a shoe shop and a hat shop and Lucien's pharmacy of course. An ironmongers and at least four butchers plus two charcuteries and several cafés and restaurants.

It had been a bustling town, but no longer. There seemed to be a huge lethargy hanging over it. The two hotels which had been so popular were now the home of German officers, as many of the larger houses like Isabelle's were. Not many people ate out now, mainly office workers and labourers at midi. Gone were the days of the four hour dinners at grand restaurants. Most people ate at in the privacy of their homes, away from danger.

Even though food was starting to get scarce they ate well. That would never end they promised each other.

Down by the Seine stood a solitary flag pole where the French flag had proudly hung. Now in its place hung the Swastika, the Tricouleur having been torn down and burnt in front of the mayor and the inhabitants of the town. They had been ordered to be at the quay side at exactly 8.00am one morning. The women had wept and held each other. While their men were fighting for their country they could do little except hope and pray it would all be over soon. It was a dire time for this little town. It seemed to be holding its breath in sheer fear of what was in store for them all. It was a bad time for these poor people.

If you stood outside the shops in the main street you could almost reach out and dip your toes into the River Seine. The huge expanse of water separated the village of Le Plessis La Rue, - where Isabelle's family lived -from the town. The only way being to reach St. Samson was by a little *bac* – a small flat bottomed ferry - which took the inhabitants from both sides of The Seine to their homes and work.

Every day Lucien and George would cycle from their village to catch the *bac*. It would ferry them over the water, along with tractors and a few cars, but mainly it was pedestrians and bicycles and sometimes a few farm animals that needed moving from one farm to another.

The ferryman with his black beret, a yellow Gitane cigarette hanging from his lips, was as old as the hills. His face a network of lines, with his smiling eyes as blue as the sky he somehow made everyone's day a little brighter. No one knew how old he was but there was talk of him having lived in St Samson for over 90 years, along with his wife of the same age. Occasionally she would join him on the *bac*.

Dressed in a faded black shawl covering her long white plait of hair, wearing a well darned patterned skirt and tiny wooden clogs she would smile her toothless smile while smoking her white clay pipe. These two were the very epitome of so many of the local Normans. Many illiterate, but they were what made St. Sampson Sur Seine what it was. Simple people, living simple lives. Then of course there were the aristocracy with their big houses and servants and ordinary people like Lucien and his family. Each one's world being turned upside down, by one lunatic. Adolf Hitler.

George enjoyed the journey morning and evening. Somehow being on the move made everyone seemed more cheerful. Even though the length of the crossing was only ten minutes there was always a great deal of shaking hands and kissing going on. A sense of camaraderie which seemed to be lacking on the mainland.

Chapter 24

Across the channel in an English garden, in a newly painted white gazebo lay Anna Cooper on her sofa, with a book in her hand. It was late afternoon and she was asleep.

All day, along with Mary and a lot of other helpers she had been hanging her paintings in the Town Hall. It was to be her very own exhibition. She had exhibited with other artists but this was to be her work alone. Most of the paintings were commissioned portraits that weren't for sale but she hoped it would get her some more work even so. There were paintings of the streets of London, the people of London. The river with the swans and ducks and a variety of work she had done over the years. She had been so nervous saying to Mary that she was sure she wouldn't sell anything, and people would think she was showing off.

Mary looked at her, rolling her eyes and told her 'to shut up and stop being ridiculous. 'Look at, all the eminent people you have painted. Not the Prime Minister yet but don't forget you painted Chamberlain before he became Prime Minister and Churchill is bound to come and sit for you in your little house by the river.' She laughed and kissed Anna and told her to stop looking so miserable.

Lying on the couch Anna dreamt again of Jack. He was still running towards her and she was still rooted to the ground but now in this dream it was George running away from her and she was still unable to move. She woke with a start and sat up. She was crying. Wiping the tears from her eyes she thought of Jack and how much she missed him, and the tears flowed again. She brushed them away and walked wearily up to the house. It was getting late and George was due round to pick her up to go the cinema. Dear George, she thought, what would I do without you?

While she was sleeping Jack had been on the phone to Howard Florey. Now that the production of penicillin had got the go ahead and was being manufactured in large quantities, Florey had asked if he would think of coming up to work with him and join his team. They needed more researches, as most young men had been called up. How tempted he was. It would be a dream come true. Dare he? He would have to explain to his Father that as George he had been primed by Jack. That he was pretty adept now at the processes penicillin had to go through, but that would mean a locum and they were thin on the ground due to the war. And what about Anna, he would feel like he was deserting her. He told Florey to leave it with him for a couple of days and he would think about it seriously.

He had everyone driving him mad lately asking why he never went out with girls anymore. What's happened to the George we know they would all say. Even Anna was nagging him. 'I have a friend called Amy. Really pretty, she is coming to the dinner dance on Saturday. I bet you'll like her, definitely your type.'

The night of the dinner dance arrived. Dressed in his white tie and tails Jack duly arrived on Anna's arm, along with Henry, Mary and Amy. Amy was petite, with baby blue eyes and a rosebud mouth, wearing a meringue of a pink dress, definitely George's type. But as for Jack having to dance with her and be polite was anathema to him; while sitting next to him was Anna, whom he wanted to scoop up and whirl around the dance floor. To kiss her hair and mouth and tell her how he loved her.

There were eight of them at a round table with twenty other tables situated around a dance floor. A Big Band playing 'Swing' kept everyone entertained. Young girls in their evening dresses stood in little groups together. There were very few men for them to dance with so they kept themselves to themselves. Then a crowd of American GI's strolled in. The girls giggled and nudged each other and threw back their hair and lowered their eyelashes. Meanwhile, the men who had arrived with their girls looked with distaste at this intrusion. The master of ceremonies went onto the stage. He whispered to the band leader who signalled to the band to stop playing.

'Ladies and Gentlemen, I would like to introduce these young men from The United States of America, who are here to fight alongside our own soldiers. Please welcome them, they are a long way from their homes and families, thank you. Now please start dancing and enjoy the rest of the evening.'

There was a huge round of applause as the band struck up once more. The GI's introduced themselves to some of the guests. The young men looked suspiciously at these well uniformed alien men chatting up their girls.

Jack went up to one of the men and shook him by the hand. 'I say Harry you never mentioned you would be coming tonight.'

'Hi George. We didn't know we would be until the last minute. We were in your local pub when this guy came in and invited us to join the dance. So here we are. Not sure if we will be that popular with everyone, but that is what it is like everywhere, so I guess it is bound to be the same this evening. People seem to think we are from another planet!'

Jack laughed. Come and meet my friends they will treat you like human beings. That's a promise.'

'Harry this is Anna, Mary, Henry and Amy.' Amy pouted and wriggled around on her chair.

Jack and Harry had met in the library when Jack was researching some medical stuff. Harry was at the same table. Glancing at what he was reading, Jack saw it was the virtually the same as his research. Their eyes met and that was the beginning of a new friendship. Harry was training to be a neurologist, in his final year at university. Jack talked to him of the penicillin road he'd been on and of the child Rose. All this intrigued Harry, as he was researching diseases of the brain in young children and babies. Jack talked to him and became fascinated in the work he was doing. He took him to his local and introduced him to English ale.

It's warm *and* it's flat.' He exclaimed in horror.'

Jack hooted with laughter. 'You'll get used to it old man!'

He was George to him of course, not Jack. Again the pretence. He started to feel as though he was on a roller coaster to disaster. He had to sort this mess out, but how. Alone he would sigh and put his head in his hands and groan.

Chapter 25

Sitting in the lounge room late one evening, with a large scotch in his hand Teddy sat with his feet up on the leather pouffe. His bare feet enjoying the heat from the coal fire. It had been a long day at Westminster and he was glad to be home. Being one of the many Press Secretaries in the government he was kept on his toes night and day and now the war was at its height it was mayhem. Most of the time he was quite exhausted.

In the other armchair sitting with her feet curled up under her, sat Evelyn reading, her long dark hair obscuring her face. She looks as young as she was when I met her he thought, remembering the gawky girl he had asked to dance so many years ago.

For the last couple of days his lost twin boys had been preying on his mind. He knew it was because of all the death around him. The newspapers were full of the war and casualties. Every meeting seemed to involve it. Every official paper he had to read was full of it. There was no getting away from it. Death was in every nook and cranny of his thoughts, and night and day he lived it like so many others did.

Evelyn never mentioned her twin boys; it was as if they had never been born. After their deaths both of them had gone through the motions of being parents to Bertie.He had felt them drift apart like paper boats on a pond, each going in its own direction. He had thought of nothing but what was happening to them both. It had torn him apart. Every time he started to talk of the babies she would turn away and walk from the room. It was the hardest time of their lives.

'Evelyn.' Teddy got up, and sat on the pouffe, he leant over and took her hand.

She looked up and smiled, her beautiful smile. 'What? Don't look so serious, what's the matter, no more problems at work surely? I thought you had sorted all that out.'

'No, that's all dealt with. I was just thinking of the twins.'

'I know. I spoke to Nell the other day, she said there has been no news from George for well over three months. She is convinced he is dead. She looked so worn out, not like the vibrant Nell we all know.'

'I meant our twins. The babies.'

'Oh.' She uncurled her feet and got to get up. He held her hand tightly as if would lose her, again.

'Please stay Evie, let's talk. It has been years now and we never talk of the twins. Life is so precarious at the moment. Maybe this is the right time. I know I was useless when it happened. I didn't know what the hell to do. I was too young. Too full of myself. Being involved with the government went to my head and I am sorry, so sorry.'

She didn't pull away this time. She looked at him, her eyes full of tears. 'I hated you, you know. I blamed you for their deaths.'

'I know.' He said. 'And I didn't know what to do when you turned away from me all the time, as though it was my fault. I thought you would leave me.'

She looked at him her eyes full of hurt. 'I didn't know what to do either and it was all so terrible. Like a nightmare that I couldn't wake up from.' She was really crying now.

He put his arms around her and she sat their upright her hands clasped tightly on her knees. 'I used to dream of them all the time you know.' She smiled. 'They were my little blonde angels, running towards me, their kisses like butterfly wings. Sometimes I still have the dream, but it is not the same. I can hardly see them now; they seem to be fading away from me.' She was sobbing.

'Shh, shh.' He said and held her as if she was a child herself until the fire turned to ashes and the room grew cold.

Just down the road Nell and Ernest were having a late supper in front of the fire. Surgery had gone on way over time. Jack had gone to see Anna so it was just the two of them. They were talking of him and how they were missing him and worrying.

'Surely we will hear something soon' Nell sighed. 'It's been three months now, and nothing.'

'I know I have tried to find out anything that would tell us of his whereabouts. All I know he was flying Spitfires as a reconnaissance pilot. It is obviously all hush hush.

'I am scared he is dead.' She lowered her knife and fork and tears fell onto her plate. She sighed and felt for her handkerchief. 'I know the twins were supposed to have had their ' *'thought talk''* but it is so fragile. So little to cling on to. All I want is to hear is Jack's voice, or at least know he is still alive.'

Ernest leant over and took her hand. 'Nell, we have to just hope and pray he is okay. I am sure we will hear something soon. Please try not to upset yourself. I will speak to Teddy tomorrow, okay?' He smiled. 'Now eat up this delicious omelette and you will feel better. How you make eggs taste so beautiful is beyond me!' She smiled at him. 'Maybe being a French woman, bought up in a French household has a lot to do with it.'

'Nell, you know something, I am really almost more worried about George. He has changed so much. He seems so quiet and reserved. Don't you notice it? Not the George we are used to. Where are all the girlfriends for a start? There was always some young lady on his arm. He spends so much time with Anna. You don't think he is starting fall in love with her? Now that would be an interesting situation!'

'Oh I hope not. I do know what you mean though, he is different with me too. He was always so loving and always had something to talk about, but now he seems to have withdrawn into his shell. Maybe it is the worry of Jack. He probably feels guilty because he couldn't fight like him and all his other friends who were called up. It could well be that of course.'

'It is probably just that. But one positive thing is, the patients adore him. They call him a saint. I must admit he is very good with them, even more so than before. Maybe the war has changed him. I know it has me. Live for the day. 'Carpe Diem' as one says.' Life is so fragile, who knows what tomorrow will bring.' He leant over and took Nell's hand, come on let's stop worrying and enjoy the rest of the meal. Tomorrow is another day.'

Chapter 26

Anna

My exhibition went well. Such a relief it is over. I was so nervous. For three days I had people coming to see my work. I was amazed there were so many, a lot of Father's colleagues from Westminster, my friends of course and strangers who had heard or read about me. I was lucky and sold an awful lot, so now I can afford to buy some decent stuff for the studio. A new couch for starters and a proper heater and a new rug. All very exciting. The only thing that was missing was Jack. It is so weird without him.

George bought Harry along. He is really nice, considering he is American! Not brash like a lot of the others seem to be. Very polite and considerate and he does have the most amazing smile. I don't think I have ever seen such white teeth. He arrived with a large box of chocolates and best of all some nylons. Real ones. No more staining my legs with gravy browning and drawing a line with an eyebrow pencil for the seam! It is by far the best present ever. He bought one of my little sketches of the swans on the river. He said it was for his sister, who also paints, so I was very flattered.

But there is a problem of sorts. He wants to take me to the cinema. No strings, he promised. But am not sure if I should go. I asked George who was a bit sarcastic to be honest.

'It's up to you Anna, Jack isn't here so I can't see it will matter. What the eye can't see the heart can't grieve over.'

That made me feel very uncomfortable. He was a bit iffy after that for a couple of days. Obviously he thinks I shouldn't go. So unlike George to be like that, so I suggested he came with Amy and we went as a foursome. He said that would be a good idea. Maybe he felt I would be safer with him there.

So to the cinema we went. '*The Great Dictator*' with Charlie Chaplin was playing. It was packed. We got seats in the circle which weren't too bad. I sat next to Amy and the boys either side of us. Harry had bought popcorn from his PX, also great bars of American chocolate. The film was good and so was Harry! He didn't try anything. On the other hand Amy never left George alone. Snuggling up to him and trying to hold his hand. It was really rather amusing. George wanted nothing to do with her. He is a strange boy at the moment. I can't make him out.

Chapter 27

Jack

Being George is a disaster. Harry asked Anna out to the cinema. She wanted to know what I thought. Well I felt a bit like knocking his teeth out actually but I said that Jack wouldn't know, so it was up to her. I was fed up to be truthful. He's a good looking guy with more to offer than I could at the moment. At the exhibition he arrived with chocolates and he actually bought her some nylons. I mean, nylons of all things! Flowers would have been more appropriate. She suggested that maybe I could take Amy to the cinema, make up a foursome. So that's what we did. We saw '*The Great Dictator.*' It was hilarious, with Charlie Chaplin playing two parts. One as a Jewish Barber in the Ghetto and the other as a mad general, called *Adenoid Hynkel,* obviously supposed to be Hitler. Very near the knuckle but extremely clever. The only thing that spoilt it was Harry sitting next to Anna. I sat next to Amy, who spent the whole time cuddling up to me and even putting her head on my shoulder. It was a nightmare. Something has to give or else I will.

Chapter 28

George

When I left Isabelle I ran back to work. Apologised to Lucien for being late but it wasn't a problem apparently as it had been very quiet.

'Tonight.' He said, 'I have some good news for you.' So, I had good news to tell Isabelle and he had good news to tell me. I couldn't wait to get home. Hopefully the good news was about getting out, but then on the other hand it wouldn't be good news leaving Isabelle. Maybe I shouldn't say anything. That afternoon my thoughts were everywhere except on the job. All I could think about was how to go about confessing my undying love to Isabelle. And what Lucien was going to tell me.

That evening as we cycled home, with the sun just starting to set, it was the end of Spring with the smell of Summer all around, the trees still full of blossom, the air fragrant with their scent, it all seemed so idyllic. Then a great line of German cars roared past us with swastikas billowing out on their bonnets. Reminding us all of the underlying misery that occupation brought with it.

Sitting around the table in the kitchen Lucien suggested a glass of pastis. He made his own, completely potent, completely illegally. He said the Mayor always asked for it when he visited as did the local gendarmes, so therefore that was alright in their eyes and in his!

'Santé. ' He said, raising his glass.

We were alone. Both the women were out. The old black Labrador lay under the table snoring gently. The range grumbled a bit and we both sat and enjoyed the quiet moment. The war seemed a long way away. I wondered what Lucien was thinking, was he thinking of those Nazi jackboots walking up and down his stairs in his house and sleeping in his bed? How hard I realised it must be for them all. To be occupied must be the ultimate degradation. The very idea of an army moving into your country and the population being run by a regime that was slowly destroying Europe and having to kowtow to these people was beyond imagination. When the war started I remember how scared Mother was, that we too would be occupied, to be ruled by a Germanic government instead of the monarchy. It didn't bear thinking about.

'Well young George I have found a way of you contacting your family.'

I looked at him in amazement. 'Oh my God Lucien, how, why, what when?' I was laughing it was too good to be true. At last there was light at the end of the tunnel.

'Well I have friends who have contacts with England using a shortwave radio. They are part of an Escape Route out of France. It is only feasible to send at night when the signal is strong enough, usually from 10-10.30. Then the messages are picked up by military intelligence in London. Due to problems, they have had to keep their heads down for a while that is why there has been such a delay, but now things are up and working, so if you write a message I will get it sent tonight. If you are up for it.'

'Up for it?' I shouted. 'I'll say!' Grabbing hold of Lucien's hand I shook it as hard as I could. 'Oh I can't tell you how excited I am, it is the best news ever. Thank you so much.'

'Also there is a good chance that we can get you out through the Escape Route. It won't be immediately but hopefully within the next month or so. It's a dangerous mission but hundreds upon hundreds have reached Neutral Spain safely. There is of course a risk but I think you will be happy to take it somehow.' He smiled and raised his glass. 'Here's to freedom and home!'

I should have been more excited, but all I could think of was leaving Isabelle. It couldn't have come at a worst time. Even so the news that I can get a message sent home was a huge relief. The thought of my family receiving the news made me want to whoop with joy.

Soon after my conversation with Lucien, both the women came back from visiting Isabelle's friend and her family. It was the young Jewish girl Isabelle had talked of. Her parents and sister were living in fear of their lives. Rumours had been circulating that an elderly Jewish man in the next village had been taken away the night before. But both women were very sceptical and thought it was just gossip and nothing more.

At supper that night Lucien told the women the news. They were both delighted and hugged me. I said I was excited about getting a message to my family and of course being able to get home soon. Maybe I was imagining it, but I am sure and really rather hoping that Isabelle's face dropped a bit when she heard I would be leaving soon.

That night I wrote my message home.

When Lucien went out on his bike to deliver it I made an excuse to go into the garden, hoping Isabelle would follow me. It was a balmy evening and the smell of blossom filled the air. The sky was full of stars and it was so quiet. No lights shone from the main house, meaning the Germans were absent for the time being. It was always slightly uncomfortable, knowing that there were Nazis living at such close proximity. .

That morning I had decided I would go back to the little Brocante and see if I could find a ring that wouldn't break the bank. Lucien had paid me that morning so I felt decidedly rich. I always gave some back for my rent which they without fail refused to take but I insisted. It made me feel better somehow. The Brocante was actually busy for a change. Three or four young German officers were browsing. They clicked their heels and nodded when I walked in. Somehow I never could get used to them, with their polished jackboots and beautifully pressed uniform. To me they seemed more like robots than people and I always felt dreadfully uncomfortable in their presence; as if suddenly I would feel a heavy hand on my shoulder, then the words. 'Ah ha we know who you really are come with us!'

Madame was delighted to see me, especially when I mentioned I was looking for an engagement ring for my fiancée.

'Ah the lady with the cloisonné box? You do love her after all'!

I laughed. 'Yes Madame you were so right. Indeed I really do love her.'

I found a tiny amethyst ring set in white gold. Madame estimated it to be about 100 years old. I loved the idea maybe it had once belonged to someone else who was crazily in love. She placed the ring inside a little ivory heart shaped box lined with red velvet and again it was wrapped in a *petit paquet* with ribbons and flowers.It was perfect. I couldn't wait to give it to Isabelle that night.

Sitting down on the bench by the old oak tree and lighting a cigarette, I tried to think what I was going to say to my girl. I felt like a youngster again with my very first girlfriend. She had been fourteen and lived next door. She wore white socks with little black patent shoes, done up with a button and ribbons in her hair. We were sitting outside in her garden on a night much like this, while our parents were playing Canasta inside. I kissed her, a child's kiss, and she kissed me back. We held hands and said nothing. We kissed again and held hands again. I asked her to come to the cinema on Saturday morning and that was it really. My first love. Now here was my real and last love, walking towards me with a coffee pot and cups on a tray.

'I thought you may like a coffee and a calvados to celebrate.' She laughed.

I moved up and she sat next to me. Dipping a lump of sugar into my calvados she sucked it. 'This is very French; you men drink it and we women are allowed just a taste. A bit mean really don't you think?' She looked at me her eyes were sparkling. She was speaking in English. 'So you go back soon to your family, you must be so excited.' She looked at me and put her head on one side. 'You don't look very excited.'

I grabbed her hand, nearly making her coffee go everywhere. 'Isabelle I am in love with you. Really, truly deeply in love. I have never felt this way before, of course I have had girlfriends.

Too many really but you are the first girl that has made me feel this way.' I could hear myself gabbling on so stopped and held her hands tightly.

She leant over and kissed me, her lips so soft and tender. I kissed her back. I felt her hands in my hair, then she was holding me and crying, kissing my eyes my cheeks, my mouth, her hair swinging against my face smelt of Rosemary. I was trembling now and could feel tears welling up in my eyes too.

Isabelle leant against me, her head on my shoulder. 'George, I love you so much, so much it hurts.'

I looked at this beautiful girl. My girl, soon please God to be my wife. 'I love you too, so that is just perfect and to make it even more perfect here's something to make it really special.'

She took the present and looked at me. 'Oh George, I think I am going to cry again.'

'Please don't. You can once you've opened it.'

Again, as before with the cloisonné box and the earrings she unwrapped the ribbons and the tissue paper with great care, then when seeing the tiny heart shaped box she gasped as she opened it.

'Oh George you must put it on my finger, will you?'

So feeling very gallant I got down on one knee. 'Isabelle Henot will you marry me?'

'George O'Brien, I will.' She flung her arms around me kissing me furiously. 'The ring is beautiful and it fits perfectly, you are so clever. Oh how I love you, love you, love you.'

'Well.' I said with huge relief. What do we do now? Should we marry before I go and get killed, then you will be a widow. There is a chance you know that, or would it be better to wait until this damned war is over?'

She sat back and her eyes were shining. She looked so beautiful it made my heart ache.

'Dear George.' She was still talking to me in English, her accent was adorable. 'I want to marry you now. I loved you the minute I saw you in your RAF uniform, looking like a very lost and hungry little boy. You have made these last three months the happiest I have ever known, but now you are to leave us.' Her eyes were full of sadness. 'What will happen to us? You will go away and forget me and we French will become prisoners of the Nazi regime and have to learn to speak their language. I can't bear it.' Bursting into tears she threw her arms around me.

'I don't believe any of that.' I exclaimed. 'Along with the Americans we will get rid of the bastards. That is without doubt, so you must not worry and as for me forgetting you, that is not going to happen. I want to marry you, to give you babies. We will have at least four!'

We both laughed and held each other. I couldn't let her go. I felt if I did she would disappear into thin air.

'Thank goodness for that, and now.' I said. 'Maybe I should speak to Lucien.'

I explained that is what one did in England. I wasn't sure what the protocol was in France.

She shrugged. 'Pretty much the same I suppose. Never having been in this position before I am not a hundred percent sure, but Papa would like it if you did. He may so no of course!'

We sat and talked until the cold drew us inside. I kissed her again by the back door and we went into the kitchen holding hands.

Her mother was there sewing by the range, she looked up and smiled. 'Hallo you lovebirds!'

Isabelle looked surprised. 'What do you mean?'

'Look at you both, you are shining like the stars in the sky!' Putting down her sewing she came and put her arms around us.. Lucien and I have been wondering when you two would realise your feelings towards each other. To us it was so obvious!'

We looked at each other. .Isabelle giggled and put her head on my shoulder, I squeezed her hand.

'Were we that obvious?' I asked.

'Oh yes.' She laughed. 'Very! You know, it is so very lovely to see such happiness in these dark times. Listen that's Lucien, fingers crossed your message got through.'

My message had gone and been received. A huge wave of relief washed over me. Thank God now everyone will know I am safe. Now I can enjoy the short time I will have here with Isabelle.

Lucien was delighted with our news. The four of us sat in the kitchen that night and spoke of our plans and whether we should get married before I left or wait.

'It is up to you both.' Lucien looked at us. 'You are adults and things are so different now. What you both decide we will go along with. Who knows what will happen to us all. We are occupied by a Nazi regime, so to me anything is possible.' Sighing he rubbed his hands wearily across his eyes.

Chapter 29

Jack

At long last we have had a message from George. Three long months with nothing; it was very short, but oh so very welcome.

It was brief and to the point. *'All okay. I am safe in France. Living with nice family. Hope to be home soon. Jack.'*

Mother and Father were beside themselves with joy. Mother couldn't stop crying. Father laughed with relief. It was a good moment for us all.

I went around to tell Anna, she was in her Gazebo drawing. It was getting late and the sky was darkening, golden light from the lamps in the window glowed faintly. She would draw the blinds once it was dark, but for now the little studio looked rather splendid with the shadows throwing dark shapes across the lawn.

I walked up the rickety old steps and tapped on the door.

'Anna, it's me!'

'Hallo me.' She smiled and came over and gave me a kiss on the cheek.

'I have wonderful news of Jack, Anna, a message got through to our parents. He is safe, with a family in France and there is talk of him getting out soon.'

She sat down on the sofa her dark eyes full of tears. 'Oh that is so wonderful George. Wonderful, wonderful. My Jack is safe and he is coming home. Oh George, I can't tell you how happy I am. Quickly I must tell Mama.'

Grabbing my hand she pulled me out of the Gazebo and ran up the garden shouting. 'Hurray, Jack is coming home.' She was like a child, twisting and turning her hair flying out from her face her dress swirling around her legs. My Anna, my beautiful Anna.

That night there was a celebratory dinner at our house, with Anna and the family as well as Mary and Henry. Somehow Nell had concocted an amazing dish with eggs, not sure where she got them from! They tasted incredible, quite delicious. We toasted Jack and the whole evening was a one of happiness. But I could feel the hand of deceit on my shoulder the whole time. I had to, whatever else I did, talk to Anna.

Henry and I went outside. I made an excuse that I wanted to have a look at his car as I was thinking of buying it, once I had saved up enough petrol coupons.

'Phew.' I feel exhausted. 'Tell me what to do Henry what would you do if you were in my place. God forbid!?'

'Tell Anna. You have to now. She knows George is alive and well so I am sure she will be understanding about it all.'

'Bloody hell, Henry, I just don't know. I have a feeling she will hate me and that will be the end of us as a couple. Oh how I wish this had never happened.'

I lit a cigarette and Henry pointed out that I already had one alight in my mouth.

'Oh God, I am in such a fucking mess. I don't know which way to turn, but you're right I will tell her, tomorrow. Though right now I need another drink, come on.'

We went inside and both got slightly drunk.

Chapter 30

George

That night I sat in bed, reading Flaubert's Madam Bovary, Isabelle had lent it to me telling me it would be good to read it in its original language. I had read it in English and loved it but reading it in French was an eye opener. It was so beautiful and I realise now how much the words had been lost in translation. It was unbelievable how much better it was in the original language. It is known that a translated book loses its soul. How true, it was like reading the story for the first time. But to be perfectly truthful I was actually finding it hard to concentrate. All I could think of was my beautiful girl lying in her bed just across the hall. It was hard not to knock on her door but her parents were too close for comfort. So I gritted my teeth and kept reading.

Suddenly there was a tentative tapping on my door. My heart lurched. 'Come in,' I whispered.

She did. Standing there in a white satin dressing gown with her bare toes peeking out stood Isabelle. Her hair hung lose around her shoulders, she was so desirable that something else lurched as well. She walked over and sat on the edge of the bed.' I just wondered how you were and thought maybe you would be a bit lonely, so if you like I can keep you company. Is that okay?' She looked up at me under her lashes and smiled.

I held out my arms and taking off her gown she slipped naked into them.

'I'm not a virgin you know.' She whispered in my ear.

'Thank God for that, I wouldn't have known what to do if you had been.'

She giggled and pressed her warm body closer. She smelt of lemon soap and toothpaste. Her hair lay soft against my chest as she kissed my neck and my face then our lips met. I had been with a few or probably more than a few girls, but this was different. This was what it must feel like to be in love, really in love, not just lust. It was overwhelming. We lay together not moving, our bodies tight against each other. Then she moved away from me and smiling she laid her hand on my cheek, her dark eyes full of desire. 'Make love to me George.' She reached up and pulled me down and again our lips met, her mouth slightly open. She sighed and we moved together as if we were one. Her body so soft beneath me. I could feel her hands in my hair and then her sweet cry as she buried her face in my shoulder. We lay like that until again she smiled at me and kissed my face, her hands running through my hair. Her mouth was soft and I felt her tiny teeth bite my bottom lip. She whispered. 'I love you George, love me again.'

This time I felt I knew her body so well and we moved together with a passion I had never known or felt before.

After she looked at me her eyes shining. 'Do you think it can get any better? If it does I may well fly to the moon and play among the stars!' She laughed and I held her tight, never ever wanting to let her go.

So it was decided. We were to marry as soon as possible. Somehow, and I never found out how, Lucien managed to get me a false passport under the name of George Lacour and was able to rush the wedding through; the Mayor being a great friend of the family. I am not quite sure what excuse Lucien gave him for having to do everything in such a rush. But I had an idea!

A week later we had a civil ceremony in the Mairie. Afterwards there was a blessing in the church, with just close family and a few friends and surprisingly Madame from the Brocante was there. It turned out she was an aunt of Lucien's. Also Sologne from the Café du Sport. Who Isabelle told me later was seeing the young German officer who frequented the café, so she was being teased mercilessly by the other officers. It sounded a dangerous game to me and I hoped it wouldn't be harmful to either of them. But I wasn't so sure. Most of all I wished more than anything that my family could have been there too, but we had promised each other that once the war was over we would have a special ceremony, for absent friends and families.

Isabelle took my breath away when I saw her. She had changed from a white shift dress and jacket for the civil ceremony. She walked down the aisle towards me, wearing a long white satin gown with lace at her throat and wrists and a cream ribbon wrapped around her tiny waist falling to the floor. Her hair entwined with tiny white flowers was piled on top of her head with a full length veil covering her face. She lifted it when she saw me. Clutching my hand tightly she smiled. I couldn't take my eyes of her. This was my wife. This beautiful creature standing next to me was Mrs. George O'Brien. I felt as though I would explode with the sheer joy of it all.

Chapter 31

Anna

Sitting by the river one late afternoon my bare feet dangling in the water, I was watching with delight a mother moorhen and her babies swimming up and down in front of me. First they all went up river then turned around and swum back. This went on for a good half an hour, it was so lovely to see. I managed to get a good sketch of them which I will transfer to a canvas and do an oil of it. The colours will be rich and I will enjoy working with something other than watercolour or pastel, even though I do find it the most difficult of the mediums but the smell of the paint is like an aphrodisiac to me. I often feel I would like to eat the paint straight from the tube, it looks so inviting! I was missing Jack more than usual which was making me feel a bit downcast. We hadn't heard any more news from him and I was trying hard not to get in a state about it and so I was trying to involve myself in work.

I had gone out with Harry again. George looked a bit disapproving about the whole thing. I can never really understand why, it's not as though he is Jack, but maybe he thinks I will fall in love with this American and disappear into the wilds of Texas with him. Not likely. Harry is nice but he isn't Jack. Even so it is a treat when he spends money on me. I know that sounds so materialistic but a girl can't have enough nice things, especially when the world is in such a mess. We always go to really nice restaurants and dance halls and I must admit he does dance extremely well. He tried to kiss me the other night but I managed to wriggle out of it somehow and he hasn't tried again. Another thing. He wants me to wear his ring. He says it's an American custom when you like a girl, it's just to say we are going out together, apparently. I said I would think about it. He is probably angling for a bit more than a kiss. Well he can keep on angling for all I care, I have no intention of that happening.

Mary thinks he is nice and says it will do me good to enjoy myself while Jack is away. ',You don't have to have a mad affair with him', she said. 'Just a bit of fun.' But I wasn't sure about it. I would feel I was cheating somehow.

Last night was a bad for air raids. The sirens were sounding all evening and well into the early hours, stopping around dawn. It was ferocious and terrifying. Luckily we were all at home so we went down into the cellar as usual. Mother and I had made it as cosy as possible. There were makeshift beds and rugs covering the old stone floor and a couple of camping stoves for cooking and making tea as well as food, drinks and books, playing cards and of course board games, oil lamps and boxes of candles, a couple of paraffin heaters and the inevitable first aid kit. Actually, it was really rather nice if it hadn't been for the air raids! The cellar was pretty sound as it was quite a long way under the main house, but even so the dreadful noise seemed to vibrate through the walls. Father decided we should all play charades to keep the girls happy, which they thoroughly enjoyed. Then I got them into to bed where they cuddled up with their gas masks and were asleep straight away. I envied them so. I never slept, just lay awake terrified every time a bomb exploded. It was so awful and the noise was tremendous even down in the cellar. God knows what it was like outside.

I thought of my WVS friends who were on duty that night and prayed they would be safe. Last week two of the ambulances girls had been badly hurt by debris falling from a bombed house. Why more of us hadn't died was a miracle. Everywhere was fraught with danger, it was a terrible time to be alive.

As blessed dawn broke the all clear sounded. We could breathe easily again for the time being. So bundling the girls up and putting them in their own beds we three sat down in the kitchen, thanking God the house was still intact. It was too dark to see anything outside. We had lost all the electricity so candles were lit, tea was made and we relished the quietness. No one spoke for a while, we were all exhausted but happy to be alive. I wondered how much damage we would witness once it got light.

As the new day arrived we realised the next street had been hit really badly. The sound of both ambulance and fire engine bells echoed around the houses. The smell of smoke was evident and we all sent up silent prayers that once again we had been spared. The gods had been on our side.

I went back to work and again witnessed the horror and destruction all around us. The street next to us had lost a whole terrace of houses and the fires were raging out of control. I drove with another WVS girl who I had got to know very well. She was older than me and seemed immensely sensible so I always felt better when she was a passenger!

That day will be forever imprinted on my mind. We must have taken God knows how many wounded to the hospital. Some were walking wounded but some were beyond help. It was a living hell. I will never forget the smell of burning flesh and the smoke stinging our eyes and throats. It was all a confusion of sheer and utter carnage. Stretchers were loaded into ambulances, someone would bang on the roof when they were all inside and we would drive off through the streets, trying to be as careful as possible with our precious cargo.

I have one big, big problem. I think maybe I am starting to fall in love with George. I am wondering if it is because he is so like Jack but I never ever felt a thing for him before. I am trying to analyse it all, there is something about him that I have never noticed before. I can't put my finger on it but I am really scared that I am actually falling for him.

Also, I feel somehow that he feels the same way. There's nothing concrete to put my finger on but it is the way he looks at me when he doesn't think I can see him. And I am sure he kissed me that afternoon when I was asleep. I am almost convinced of it but really still unsure -it seemed so *'Un George Like!* - Now I have a dilemma. Do I tell him or do I keep it a secret? I will look such a fool if he doesn't have any real feelings for me. God I wish I knew what to do. I also have this huge guilt that I am betraying Jack and what on earth would he think. It would split the boys up and I can't be responsible for that. I probably will just have to keep it to myself. Hey ho, I really don't need this, I really don't. I realise that I am behaving badly but we are at war and that to me is a good enough reason to be reckless.

Coming out of my daydreaming I saw George coming down the garden. 'Can I intrude or are you too busy?'

I laughed. 'Never too busy to see you!'

He did look a bit serious and didn't say a lot after giving me a perfunctory kiss on the cheek. I carried on drawing and could feel him watching me, I turned around and he looked at me. 'What?'

'Nothing, just thinking.'

'About what, about you.'

'Me why?'

I looked at him his eyes as green as Jacks, his lashes as dark, his black hair far too long and curly. He was beautiful, no doubt about it. If I hadn't known any different it could have been Jack sitting next to me.

'George?'

'Yes.'

Then a shout from the top of the garden. It was Henry and Mary, both laughing and running down the lawn towards us.

George looked at me. I smiled. 'It can wait, nothing important.'

'Hallo you two. Hope we're not interrupting anything but we have some news we thought you might like to hear.' Henry nudged Mary. 'Go on you tell them!'

'I'm pregnant!'

I jumped up and threw my arms around her. 'Oh, what marvellous news. When. How far gone are you? Oh this is so exciting!'

'I know.' Mary smiled at me. 'I wanted to tell you before but I had a bit of a scare so wanted to make sure the little thing was well and truly ensconced within.' She laughed patting her stomach, which I noticed was very round.

'The baby is due in four months and I want you to be its godmother Anna. Will you?'

'Will I. You bet I will, thank you so much. I am very honoured.' And I did a silly curtsy while the men looked at me as if I was crazy.

'Anyone for tea. I have a kettle in the gazebo, come and help Mary?'

Mary got the cups and saucers and teapot out of my lovely old pine cupboard, I had requisitioned from the kitchen. Mama gave it to me so she could buy something more modern, to me it was just what I wanted.

'Well.' I said. 'You must be so excited; do you mind what you have?'

'Not really, as long as it has ten toes and ten fingers. Wouldn't it be wonderful if we could find out before it was born, then I could paint the nursery blue or pink. But don't think that will happen somehow. But I would love it if you could paint a mural on one wall. Of course if you have time, now that you famous. I heard that Churchill is sitting for you, how do you feel about that?'

'Terrified to be quite honest. I am to go to Downing Street next week for the first sitting. I couldn't believe it when Papa told me, I thought he was joking. I feel so privileged but even so it's all a bit daunting.'

Putting the tea things on a tray we went down and sat by the river with the men. It was a glorious day; the moorhens were still there entertaining us. It was getting cooler and the sky was turning pink and turquoise as the sun started to set. Everywhere seemed so peaceful. It was hard to realise that the war was raging all around us. To be quiet was all we wanted.

'Any news of Jack?' asked Henry.

'Not a dicky bird.' Said George. 'But we should hear something, he's supposed to be on his way back soon.'

'What about Bertie, Anna. Anything?'

'Only that his ship is safe. No more news, all top secret!' I sighed, worrying about Bertie and Jack was so ghastly. Oh how I wish everything was back to normal.

Chapter 32

Jack

Well that was a bit tricky. I was so ready to tell Anna everything and she was about to tell me something when Mary and Henry arrived. They are to be parents, such good news to know life goes on normally with all this mayhem around us.

Had even better news this morning, we received another message from George. It was short and to the point, all we needed to know in a few words.

'Am leaving tonight, will be out of contact en route will phone when arrive safely! Jack'

Mother was delighted and burst into tears again. Poor Mother, she has been so stressed since he left which makes me feel dreadful. I must try and be a bit more like George, they have such a good relationship. We do too but somehow she is more relaxed with him, so I will make a concerted effort from now on.

I have come to the conclusion that I had better bite my lip and keep stum about the switch after nearly blurting it all out the other day. I am so glad I didn't. I need more time to think how the hell I can resolve it all, which was actually doing my head in.. Not sure how long I can hold out to be quite honest. The close proximity to Anna is frightful. I know she is going dancing with Harry this week, I heard her telling Mary and she was deciding what to wear. Oh God it is all too much, what the hell have I got myself into?

Now that penicillin is being used in hospitals and for treating the troops it is hard to remember how dreadful it was without it. So many limbs amputated. So many lives snuffed out. It really is a miracle drug and I am so glad I was involved in it all, even in such a small way. Little Rose is doing really well and I see her mother now and again and she keeps me up to date with her progress. I received a hand drawn Christmas card from the child that touched me greatly.

I am, in between, surgery, researching into traumatic brain injury and post traumatic amnesia. Quite fascinating. I have managed to get some help from the medical board, so I can set up my laboratory with the necessary equipment. At the same time having to keep it all quiet as this is Jack's domain not mine as George, is all very stressful somehow. Oh to have my life back.

Knowing George is on the way back thrills me and at the same scares the shit out of me. How on earth are we to explain what we did when he returns? I have to sort something out before that happens. It is up to me to do the decent thing.

He is the one in danger, while I sit here on my backside.

Anna is definitely going dancing with Harry she informed me this morning, over coffee in Mario's café. She even asked me what she should wear.

'I don't want to look too overdressed.'

I felt like saying don't go. Stay here with me. I will dance with you if you promise to wear your silver sheath dress that makes you look exquisite. But of course I didn't. I just grunted a bit and said. 'It's up to you.'

She is very excited too, as our Prime Minister, Churchill has asked her to draw his portrait. It is such an honour for one so young. Now she will really be sought after! I am thrilled for her of course but how I wish it was me, Jack she talked to all about it. Not George.

The bombing has seemed to have worsened. Even though the dreadful Blitz is over, it is still terrible. As a family we listen avidly to the BBC every minute of the day, and the news is as depressing as ever and there seems no end to it all.

One good thing that has come out of the BBC is a new programme called 'Desert Island Discs' with a chap called Roy Plomley. I listened to it with Anna the other morning in the Gazebo. Such a clever idea. The guest has to choose ten of his favourite pieces of music. Then pick only one to take to the island, also a favourite book. Already there is the Oxford dictionary and the works of Shakespeare. They have to chose also an inanimate luxury. Anna and I had great fun choosing our own music, books and a luxury. But I had to think like George as our taste in music is very different. I love jazz and big band stuff he is more classical and loves musicals so it was all a bit dodgy. Anna loved the programme and we have promised to listen to the second guest next Sunday. Do hope it lasts. Nice to have a bit of frivolity on the radio for a change.

The poor girl had a bit of a shock the other day. She was helping some injured into her ambulance when there was an almighty gas explosion from a bombed out house and she just missed being hit by falling debris. I hate the thought of her being in danger, but she loves her job and says she is happiest when she's driving the ambulance and being of some use.

The other day she sat with some poor old chap whose wife was buried under the rubble of their house. She held his hand while the firemen carried out their gruesome job of looking for other survivors. There were none. His wife had been killed and he was in a dreadful state. He kept telling Anna that it was their sixtieth wedding anniversary next week. Poor kid, not much fun for her but she never complains. I think I am falling more in love with her every day!

Chapter 33

Anna

Goodness that was definitely good timing on Mary and Henry's part. To think I may have blurted out my love for George. It doesn't bear thinking about. I have to keep it to myself, it is a pointless exercise and it will hurt too many people. So to cheer myself up I have decided to go dancing with Harry after all. I didn't really want to but it will be nice to dress up for a change. Even so I rather wish it was Geeorge I was dressing up for as Jack is not here but I will wear my silver bead dress, it is his favourite so I can imagine I am dancing with one of the O'Brien boys. Maybe I am being a bit fickle. There's no maybe about it of course I am. It is most unlike me. I have always been so loyal to Jack. I must pull myself together and think of Jack not George from now on. This war does funny things to one's way of thinking!!

My silver dress is fabulous, it is covered in beads which sparkle and move when I walk. It is very figure hugging, with tiny crystals sewn around the edge of the scooped neckline. Long tight sleeves to my wrists, with deep purple velvet buttons from the elbows downwards. Over it I will wear my little mink stole Mama gave me. With a silver clasp in my hair and my drop silver earrings. What to do with my hair I haven't decided yet. I have a little silver clutch bag which will set it all off. I actually feel quite excited about it all. It is rather nice to have a bit of fun for a change after the last awful couple of days.

I was driving my ambulance, all alone this time, as I was just returning to the hospital and had dropped the other WVS girl off on the way back. As I reached the street leading to the hospital there was a fire raging with firemen frantically trying to put it out. Three or four houses were burning furiously. A couple of people were pulled out alive as I arrived but I saw three or four shrouded shapes lying on the ground.

There was an old man sitting on an upturned bucket. His head in his hands. No one seemed to be taking much notice of him. I stopped the ambulance and got out to see if I could help. He was pretty old with white wispy hair covered in flakes of black ash. His blue veined hands covered his eyes. I crouched down next to him, 'Hallo my name is Anna, I am one of those WVS girls who make cups of tea for people and drive around in ambulances. Shall I see if I can rustle up a cup?'

He looked at me, his pale eyes flooded with tears which began to roll down his face. 'It's Mavis, she was in there.' He pointed to the remains of his house. 'I went to buy a paper not far away when the siren went. I tried to run back but I had these old slippers on and I fell over.' He pointed to his feet. 'I couldn't get up for a bit, and by the time I got here she was gone. Blown away. She's lying under that sheet just there.' He nodded towards a small shape lying near his feet. 'So, I thought I would stay next to her until they take her away. I want to go with her.' He looked at me. 'It was going to be our sixtieth wedding anniversary tomorrow you know. What I will do now without her?' His hands were shaking and he started to sob, great wracking dry sounds. It was a terrible thing to see.

Then an old woman scuttled over and put her arm on his shoulder and looked at me. 'I knew his wife we were very good friends.' She brushed her tears away. There did seem to be an awful lot of crying going on these days. 'He wants to wait and go to the hospital with her. I see you are a WVS lass. Can you take him? Then he can go through all the rigmarole with you and could you bring him back here after? Or is that asking too much. I expect you are very busy.'

'Of course Mrs?'

'Oh call me Molly, Molly Riley. I'm a widow myself, have been for a couple of years before this awful war started, so I know how he's feeling. Poor old Percy. They had planned a party for tomorrow, sixty years of marriage.' She shook her head.' It's all so pointless. All this.' She swept her arm around. 'All this bombing. What good is it doing? You tell me.'

'I know it is a bad time for everyone. Now don't worry, I will take Percy with me and bring him back. Where do you live?'

'Number eight, just over there.' She pointed to a row of untouched terraced houses. 'That last bomb just missed us. Terrible racket there was goodness me, I can still hear me ears ringing.' She touched my arm and smiled. 'Thank you miss. I'll see you later.' She hobbled off. Her white hair in curlers. Her flowered dressing gown flapping around her feet.

The next day I called in to see Molly Riley and Percy at number eight. They were having breakfast in her tiny kitchen and she insisted I join them for a cup of tea. Percy was very quiet and grunted a sort of hallo, then went on eating his toast.

'How's he been?'

'Not too bad, considering. He has been a bit weepy and keeps talking about the cake Mavis had made for the party. He seems a wee bit disorientated still.'

'Tell you what my good friend is a local doctor. I'll see if I can get him to call in after surgery this morning, if he isn't too busy.'

So later I went with George to see how things were. The little kitchen was warm and cosy with an old fashioned cooker in one corner and a smell of something baking. Molly was sitting at the table with Percy when we walked in. Her hands covering his. She looked very serious. 'Oh miss, thank you so much for coming and you doctor. Percy's not doing too well at all. He seems very confused and keeps calling me Mavis.'

After George had examined him, he gave Mavis some tablets and told her to make sure Percy had one three times a day. 'It's a tranquillizer, it will make him sleepy which is a good thing. I will come and see him tomorrow. Mrs Riley aren't you Rose's grandmother? I met you when she was recovering in hospital'

'Oh of course you are that wonderful doctor that saved my granddaughter's life. How can I ever thank you? Poor little mite, seeing her so ill was terrible for my daughter. Her only child suffering like that. It was that magic drug that did it she told me.'

George smiled. 'It is a magic drug you're right and now it is saving the lives of our boys at the front, you have to thank two men for that not me. Alexandra Fleming and Howard Florey, between them they have changed the world of medicine for ever.'

Molly looked at George. 'My husband died of septicaemia after cutting his arm at work. It took him three weeks to die. I will never forget it. They had to amputate his arm but he was still terribly ill and suffered so much it was awful to see. So when little Rose seemed to be going in the same direction it was like a nightmare to me and her mother. So I really do have something to thank you for young man.'

When we left George suggested we went for a coffee. Pushing our bikes through the rubble, the smell of smoke still hanging in the air, we arrived at Mario's. It always felt a bit like home somehow, it was full of people finishing their lunch. Rationing had really hit now so poor Mario was scrabbling around for decent food but somehow he managed it. He had got hold of a load of pasta, which really was a luxury, and with his beautiful sauces made of simple ingredients that tasted so exotic the place was always overflowing. He threw his arms around us and said how glad he was we were still alive!! It was said with tongue in cheek but we knew what he meant. Everyone seemed to know someone who had either been bombed or even killed. It was a bad time to be living.

Sitting at one of the tables with its red checked tablecloths, drinking cups of Italian coffee - no one ever could work out how he managed to get hold of such things, no one asked either - we talked of Jack and the last message and of Mary and Henry. Then the subject of Harry came up and George started to interrogate me, or it felt like it! When was I going out with him? Why was I going out with him? Had I decided what to wear yet? So weird, I couldn't imagine why he was so interested all of a sudden.

If it had been Jack asking I would have understood but not George. Maybe he is sweet on me after all, perhaps I was right. So I answered all his questions and when I said what I was wearing he said he hoped it wouldn't be a bit over the top. Such a strange thing to say. Anyway I just laughed it off but it was a bit uncomfortable after that, so we drunk up our coffee and left.

Chapter 34

George

Well the time has come for me to say goodbye to Isabelle and her family. The escape committee has been in contact with Lucien and I have, what they call, a *'local helper'* meeting me. He will be my guide and hopefully lead me to safety across the Basque Pyrenees. I am to leave once it is dark, I must say I feel very ambivalent and apprehensive about the whole thing, as I am quite happy and content with my new wife by my side and in my bed. I don't think I have ever known happiness like this to be honest and leaving Isabelle is going to be one hell of a wrench.

Last night we had a 'farewell' supper just the four of us. It was a sad yet happy time. Marie Claude again excelled herself and the food was beautiful. How she manages with such scarcity amazes me. I guess having a sister who owns a farm helps. We had a delicious roast pintade, well two actually. Never heard of them so it was a real treat. It tasted a bit like a pheasant but not so gamey. Before we had fois gras which was amazing. In fact it was, yet again, a veritable feast.

That night lying in bed together, Isabelle cried softly, so I could hardly hear her. I felt her tears against my face. We made love slowly as though we wanted to make it last forever, then again and again. Falling asleep in each other's arms I could hear the nightingale singing, I had heard him almost every night since I arrived. I realised then, how I would miss everything. How can I bear to go and leave my girl? I may never see her again. God only knows what will happen to her. I just have to pray she will be safe, there is nothing else I can do.

The next morning Lucien went to work in the morning, *'leaving me to rest as I had a long journey ahead of me,'* he said as he left. But I was like a cat on hot bricks and couldn't sit still for long. Isabelle and her mother fussed over me like mother hens plying me with coffee and beautiful pastries they'd made. Then as dusk started to fall I gathered my small possessions together and kissing Marie Claude goodbye I gathered Isabelle in my arms and held her as if I could never let go, I could feel her shaking sobs against my chest and my tears fell too. I kissed her tearstained face and lips and whispering *'adieu'* I walked out the door with Lucien.

Walking away from the little chaumière -with its daffodils on the roof holding the thatch together which always tickled me -was hard. I looked back, Isabelle, stood silhouetted in the doorway. She waved and then turning around, she went inside, gently shutting the door behind her.

The main house was in darkness so no Germans to worry about. We seemed to walk for a long way in silence, following the river at a distance so as not to be seen. Suddenly out of the darkness a torch flashed twice, then twice again. Lucien returned the signal and after a few seconds a figure emerged and walked towards us. It was a youngish man, wearing a black beret and carrying a revolver. He embraced Lucien by kissing him on both cheeks and shook my hand. Lucien turned to me. 'Bon chance, mon brave,' and put his arms around me. 'I will miss you.' He smiled, turned around and walked away.

'Come.' The young man beckoned. 'My name is Remi. 'Follow me, it is a long walk but there will be a bed and food when we arrive. This will be your first step to freedom.' He smiled, showing a lot of rather discoloured uneven teeth and offered me a cigarette. It was one of the yellow Gitanes a lot of the locals smoked, very potent. Also explaining his brown teeth. I accepted. It may help the nerves I thought.

About three hours into our journey we stopped and rested against some rocks. It was a balmy night and star filled with a yellow moon to guide us while we kept well away from any sign of habitation. Remi passed me one of his cigarettes which were starting to become quite addictive. He told me to have a swig from his flask. It was calvados! Rough and strong but very welcome.

We trudged on for another three hours or so then Remi flashed his torch, twice. In the distance two flashes came back. Remi signalled for me to lay low until he let me know it was safe. Dropping to the ground, revolver in hand, he squirmed his way long the ground, then came the flash of his torch, so crouching as low as I could, I crawled until I reached the house. Inside was dark with a couple of candles on a table where five people sat. A youngish woman and a man with two young girls and what appeared to be their grandfather. Also an elderly couple who seemed far too old to me to be venturing on such a journey. They smiled and signalled me to sit down, while the old woman got up and bought me over a bowl of soup. It turned out they were the owners of the farmhouse. Remi told me that hundreds of escapees had passed through their hands. 'Once everyone had slept,' he said. 'We will be travelling to the next 'safe house.' These elderly couple gave one the feeling of a kind of peace. I felt more relaxed than I ever thought I would and drinking the hot soup I sent a message upwards to whoever, for getting me this far safely.

Next morning before it was barely light we were given bowls of strong black coffee and amazingly freshly baked bread, with great slabs of butter and white cheeses. Madame smiled, showing surprisingly white teeth interspersed with a gold one right in front, then signalled us all to eat. The bread was delicious and I watched while everyone dunked chunks of it into their coffee. I tried but decided it was better without. Then after a lot of kissing and shaking of hands the seven of us left on the next stage of our journey.

Fortunately it was quite warm, although the sun was veiled by clouds. No one spoke for a while, then Remi explained that we would be walking for most of the day but he had provisions so we wouldn't starve.

Everyone relaxed a bit and I looked around at the scenery, it was late summer nearly autumn and the fields were full of corn and wheat. There were goats and cows wearing bells around their necks and the sound echoed around the hills. It all looked so bucolic and peaceful. It would have been a pleasure to stroll through this beautiful land if it hadn't been for the dangerous mission we were all on.

The family with the grandfather kept much to themselves, so I fell back a bit to walk with them. The woman was very shy as were her two daughters, but after a while they started to talk to me. Her name was Miriam, her husband Joseph and the old man was called Reuben. The daughters Camille and Aimee, they were about the same age as Victoria and Elizabeth I guessed, both very pale with black rings under their eyes, they looked exhausted . It turned out they were all fleeing France as they had been threatened by some German soldiers that were billeted near to their farm. They were insulted and threatened, called filthy Jews with lewd comments about the mother and her daughters. The men had laughed and promised to be back the next day to take them away. That night they had left their home and walked into St Sampson where they knew there was a contact. That contact was Lucien.

They had been at the safe house for three days waiting for Remi. The girls cried as the story was told. The grandfather too looked exhausted by the whole thing and I wondered if he would actual manage the journey, he seemed so frail. Then I realised, this was the same family Isabelle and her mother had visited. When I told them that I was married to Isabelle they were delighted and exclaimed how wonderful it was to be with someone who belonged to such a lovely family.

What a terrible thing this war is I thought. Lucien had told me that it was mandatory in all French occupied towns and cities for Jews to wear the Star of David pinned to their clothes. It was a yellow star with the word Jew inscribed on it. Even the youngest of children were forced to wear one. It made me despair that so much hatred lay within the human mind.

We stopped twice en route for bread and cheese washed down with cheap red wine or water. The wine was coarse but with the food it did the trick somehow and cheered everyone up.

That night there was another safe house, this one was on high ground hidden amongst a forest. Remi went through the same procedure with his torch and once again we were welcomed. This time by a young woman with a small child at her side. Remi explained that her husband was also a guide and had been gone for over a month now. He said the girl was worried, but used to it all even so. There was soup again to eat with bread and cheese and wine of course. Mattresses were placed on the floor with a blanket and pillow on each. Tomorrow is another day were my last thoughts as my head hit the pillow.

Chapter 35

Jack

I have been thinking such a lot about George at the moment, wondering how he is getting on, has he left yet? where is he? And how good it would be to meet him en route wherever that may be!

I have been considering doing some *'thought talk'* but not sure if I could reach him this time, but will give it a try.

I have been having a hard time with Anna. She is definitely going dancing with Harry and to make things worse she is actually wearing the silver beaded dress that makes her look a million dollars. It is crucifying me.

We went to Mario's for coffee and I think I was giving her the Spanish Inquisition as she got a bit huffy when I kept asking her lots of pertinent questions. I rather wish I'd kept my mouth shut.

I do worry about her, especially when she is driving her ambulance. She said she had a near miss the other day when there was a gas explosion as she was helping people into the ambulance.

Also I met Rose's grandmother which was quite unexpected. She was caring for some old chap whose house had been hit while he was out getting a newspaper. When he got back his house had been blown apart, along with his wife. He was obviously in a bit of a state so Anna asked me to have a look at him. He must be well into his eighties, I thought as I sat with him at the kitchen table. I remembered Molly Riley and we were both rather pleased to see each other. She's a kind old soul. I vaguely remember Father and George talking a few years ago of her husband and how he had suffered for so long from septicaemia. Thank the Lord for the beautiful penicillin. Too late for him but it saved his granddaughter's life, maybe there is some justice after all.

I have decided finally that I have to talk to Anna and *'own up'* to this mess I am in. I will wait until she goes out with Harry otherwise she will think that is the reason for telling her my guilty secret. So I have been keeping busy with my research. The grant I got has helped a lot with equipment I need. I haven't told anyone as that would more than likely give the game away - why on earth would George be spending so much time in Jack's lab, and all that nonsense-.

So after surgery I creep away to my lair, I have been reading up on the GOAT (The Galveston Orientation and Amnesia Test) It's absolutely fascinating, what it does is determine how orientated a patient is after being in a coma and how to assess different elements of the amnesia. A lot of shell shocked soldiers are been monitored and have been found to be in such a bad state that they know neither who they are, or where they are. The fascination with comatosed patients is urging me on. When they come out of the coma a person will sometimes take days or weeks until they regain some memory. The symptoms of post traumatic amnesia in a lot of soldiers is being researched into. The findings are so interesting that the more I learn the more I need to know.

One of the most intriguing situations is the 'psuedocoma.' Where patients appear to be awake but cannot speak and are completely paralyzed. To me this must be the ultimate hell on earth. Trapped inside a body which is completely shut down, while one's brain works as normal. Often the cause can be from some form of lesion on the brainstem. The patient is in a vegetative state yet their brain is working. The worst of all situations it seems to me.

I remember when reading '*The Count of Monte Cristo*' and how Dumas described a Monsieur Noirtier de Villefort '*as a corpse with living eyes.*' He had been in this state for six years and the only way he could communicate was when his 'helper' pointed at words in the dictionary, then he would blink when the word was indicated. That was written in the 1880's as was Zola's '*Therese Raquin.*' He talked of a paralyzed woman '*who was buried alive in a dead body with only language in her eyes.*' How strange that these men would be talking of this terrible condition long before it was medically proven. I longed to discover more.

At least all this kept me slightly distracted from the presence of Anna everywhere; but right now I needed to see her, just to be near her.

Unfortunately for me. I turned up at her house at exactly the wrong time. It was about 7.00 pm on a beautiful evening. I thought maybe I would catch her in her gazebo. I get withdrawal symptoms when I was away from her.

I walked down to her atelier but it was all shut up and Anna was nowhere to be seen, so I knocked on the back door and went into the kitchen.

Evelyn was in the middle of cooking and turned around with her lovely smile. 'Oh George, how lovely, Anna I am afraid to say is on her way out. Hang on let me see if I can catch her before she leaves.' Wiping her hands on her apron she went into the hall and shouted up the stairs. 'Someone to see you Anna.'

'Okay I'm coming,' and down the stairs she came. A vision of loveliness in her silver dress. Her hair hanging lose around her shoulders. With diamonds in her ears and her hair and a small mink stole over her shoulders, she looked ravishing.

'Why George it's you. I thought it was Harry.' There was a knock at the door. 'Wait that sounds like him.'

Oh and yes it was. There he stood in his dress uniform looking as handsome as ever. In his hand a long box and in the other a huge bunch of roses and under his arm an enormous box of chocolates. How I hated him just then.

Elizabeth and Victoria came tearing down the stairs their pigtails flying. 'It's Harry, it's Harry.'

'Hi kids, here, and don't eat them all at once!' So the chocolates were for the little ones and I guess the flowers would be for Evelyn, which they were. She came out of the kitchen flushed from cooking, looking almost as beautiful as her daughter. Harry was charm personified. He kissed her on one cheek and handed her the enormous bouquet of white roses.

'Why Harry, they are exquisite.' She buried her face in the flowers and smiled. 'Oh the perfume is lovely, thank you so much. I will go and put them in water straight away.'

Handing the small box to Anna he almost bowed. 'And for you beautiful lady to wear tonight.'

'Oh Harry it's so lovely.' It was a cream flower, which looked like wax. I had no idea what it was, he tied it around her wrist with cream ribbons.

'It's a camellia, how amazing. I love it.' She stood on tiptoe and kissed him on the cheek.

I thought I might hit him or be sick, not sure which first. There was too much *'loveliness'* going on for my liking, I could feel my hands clenched by my side. Time to go.

'Well I'm off, lots to do. Have fun and be good Anna.' I gave a half-hearted laugh and waving goodbye went out the front door, tempting to slam it, but I shut it as quietly as I could.

I felt like screaming, so decided to go for a long walk. Hoping that no sirens would interrupt me.

Walking along the street I passed the church where Robert was buried. I found his grave and paid my respects, then decided the church would be a good place to be for a while away from the stress of Anna and her new found love.

Sitting in a pew I sat quietly and enjoyed the peace. A distant memory flooded back of George and Father discussing the case of a man in a pseudo coma at the nearby clinic. He had been locked in his body for six months or more. Completely paralyzed and voiceless, needing artificial respiration. The only communication he had was eye movement. His wife would hold up the alphabet and painstakingly he would blink for each word she pointed to. It was exhausting work for both patient and helper. It made me even more eager to find out how patients dealt with such an alien world.

As I sat there I suddenly felt and saw that strange movement that I had experienced all those months ago, again it was in a corner, this time near the altar, again a shimmering veiled curtain, I sat there mesmorised, it had to be George trying to contact me again. The apparition started to change and there was an indistinct form wavering like a black mark against the light, then I saw him, he seemed to be surrounded by trees and water somewhere. I felt his voice in my head. I shut my eyes and pressed my fingers into my temples. The voice came again, unclear. I could hardly hear it.

Then suddenly the words, 'I am on my way Jack, a lot of walking but I am on my way.' Squeezing my eyes tight, I could almost see him. It was so vague but he was there. I could hear the sound of water falling and the scent of grass was intense.

I concentrated as hard as possible. Then *'thought talked'* him back. 'I hear you George, stay safe old chap.' I could feel his presence near me, then like last time there was a cold draught of air. The curtain seemed to swing away and then there was nothing. A huge feeling of relief overcame me. He was alright. He was coming home. Thank the Lord, my brother was safe. That's all that matters I thought. There would be time to tell Anna the secret but not now. Not yet.

Chapter 36

So now we have George on the Escape Route to Spain…

What else is going on?

Well Jack is deep into research of Pseudo-Coma patients and Amnesia in Comatosed patients and doing his pieces over Anna and trying to decide when to tell her his secret

George is thinking of Isabelle and how much he misses her. Whilst wondering when the hell this dreadful journey would end. In between caring for an old Jewish grandfather and hopefully keeping up the spirits of the rest of his family.

Anna had her first sitting with Churchill in Downing Street. Who turned out to be much kinder than she imagined, making the portrait painting a joy instead of just hard work. In the meantime she is constantly worrying about Jack and if she will ever see him again.

Isabelle is thinking of George and wishing she could tell him he was to be a Papa in seven months' time!

Lucien is in the process of helping another four airmen, who crash landed last week and have been staying in a 'safe house.' Hopefully they will leave tomorrow for Spain.

Regis is back after being shipped home with bad shell shock and is in the local hospital recovering.

Sologne is still going out with her German officer but it is all done under cover. She thinks she is falling in love with him.

The bombing in the meantime had been pretty horrendous but still leaving our heroes and heroine's homes intact.

Mario's café had a near miss blowing part of the roof off but he managed to keep the place open even so. He has discovered a new recipe for a beautiful sauce for his home-made tagliatelle so he is a happy man and still entertains the clients with his magnificent voice.

Mary and Henry's baby is due soon.

Bertie is home on leave for a week or so before he joins his ship, so Evelyn and Teddy are enjoying his company for a brief moment.

Victoria and Elizabeth are still making mischief. They are being home schooled as Evelyn is terrified of them leaving home while the bombing is going on.

Nell and Ernest are trying not to worry about Jack. While their suspicion of George and Anna's relationship deepens.

Percy is staying with Molly Riley and feeling more stable after the death of Mavis. In fact he has made a small vegetable garden which is flourishing much to Molly's delight and he bought two fat hens which are supplying them with two eggs a day. So between them their lives aren't as bleak as they could be.

Rose is doing well and goes with her mother most Sundays for lunch at her grandmothers. Percy is teaching her how to whistle.

Chapter 37

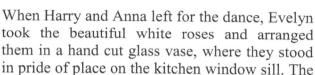

When Harry and Anna left for the dance, Evelyn took the beautiful white roses and arranged them in a hand cut glass vase, where they stood in pride of place on the kitchen window sill. The little girls gobbled up most of the chocolates and promptly felt very sick and had to lie down, much to their mother's dismay.

Walking into the dance hall with Harry Anna felt beautiful and it showed. Her silver dress sparkled in the lamplight. Her dark wavy hair hanging down her back shone and her smoky grey eyes were filled with wonder. The hall was beautiful. It had been draped everywhere in white silk, -actually disused parachutes- great candlesticks flamed along the walls where the American flag hung over the stage. A big band played Swing. There were long tables groaning with the weight of huge amounts of food; lobsters, crayfish, great sides of beef, other dishes of every sort imaginable and enough alcohol to drown in. It was an eye opener to Anna when there was such rationing at home. She revelled in it all and drunk far too much champagne, letting Harry put his arm around her and lead her out to dance. Her head spun with it all. He taught her to dance the *Lindy Hop and West Coast Swing*. She loved it all and for the first time since Jack had left she felt good to be alive.

The food was delicious, and sitting around a table with Harry and his friends she thought that she could stay like this for ever. Amy was there, pouting and throwing her blonde curls around and dancing with gay abandon. One very handsome black officer monopolised her for most of the evening, much to her delight. While dancing with him Amy imagined her parents faces if she bought him home for tea. She had never seen, let alone danced with anyone who wasn't white and English. It was all very intriguing. She found him beautiful with his great smile of flashing white teeth and his impeccable manners towards her. And when he called her Honey she could feel her toes curl.

It started to get late and Anna said she should be getting back. 'One more dance.' Harry insisted.

'Just one!' She laughed. 'It's after midnight, Mama will be having kittens if I'm not home soon.'

Walking out into the cold night air Anna drew her mink stole around her shoulders. Harry put his arm around her and turned her towards him.

'You are so beautiful Anna, I was so proud to have you as my partner. All the men were so jealous of me.'

She laughed and he kissed her, long and hard. It made her head spin. Pushing him gently away she looked up at him her eyes shining. 'Oh Harry we mustn't.'

'Why not?' he frowned. 'You enjoyed it didn't you?'

She blushed and lowered her eyes. 'I want to go home please Harry.'

He looked at her. 'Okay Honey whatever you want,' and taking her elbow they walked towards a sleek white car. They had gone with another couple in their car to the dance, but now they were to go back alone.

He smiled at her. 'Don't look so worried Anna, I won't take advantage of you if that is what is worrying you.'

Opening the car door for her he walked around and got into the driving seat. He offered her a cigarette, lighting it for her. Just like Jack she thought guiltily. They sat there smoking together. He put his arm around her and she laid her head on his shoulder. Kissing the top of her head he started the car up and drove her slowly home through the deserted streets. The smell of burning lingered in the air. It was eerily quiet. Then suddenly, ripping through the air came the screech of a siren. Putting his foot on the accelerator Harry drove like a madman arriving at Anna's just as the heavy, ugly sound of German bombers could be heard in the night-black sky.

'Come inside. 'She pulled him in and ran down into the cellar where her parents and the girls already were.

'Oh thank God.' Evelyn turned as they came in. 'I was so worried about you.' Hugging her eldest daughter close she thanked Harry for looking after her. Ernest was busy trying to get some news from the radio but all he got was a lot of interference. He grunted and turned it off.

'Cup of tea anyone?' He said putting the kettle on the little camping stove.

So there they were, the Cooper family and one rather alarmed young American officer in the cellar with candles lit and the smell of the paraffin lamp taking off the chill of the room. Almost at once there was an almighty explosion, which sounded too near for comfort. The little girls started to cry and were immediately comforted by Harry, who gave them some chewing gum which seemed to do the trick. Neither of them knowing quite what they were supposed to do with it just that on no account must they swallow it!

The bombing went on most of the night and as dawn broke the all clear sounded.

Ernest, feeling extremely apprehensive about seeing what damage that first explosion may have caused to the house, opened the cellar door carefully and peered into the darkness of the stairs. They were still standing. He walked cautiously towards the kitchen. No damage there. He walked through into the hallway and into the sitting room. All intact. With a huge sigh of relief he shouted down to the others. 'All clear and okay everyone.'

The girls scrambled up the cellar stairs like the children they were and holding hands whooped around the kitchen together.

Evelyn sat down heavily on a chair. 'I was convinced we'd been hit, it sounded so near. I had better have a look outside.'

Slowly unlocking the front door she peered up into the greyness of dawn.. It was almost light. A thin rain was falling and the smell of burning was all around. She walked down the path and looked up the road. All the houses seemed okay then turning around she looked down towards the town, where huge flames were shooting up from what was left of several houses. Walking back towards her house, she closed the door gently behind her.

Everyone looked up as she walked back into the kitchen.

'Well.' Said Ernest. 'Much damage?''

She burst into tears and walked towards her husband. 'The houses at the end have been hit, I don't know how many, I just know that there were huge fires burning. Oh God Ernest that is where the Bishops and the Mitchells live. All those children. Dear God in heaven I can't stand it. Will it never end?'

Ernest took his wife in his arms and laying her head against his chest she wept.

Harry got up. 'Anna.' I have to go, or I will be shot at dawn for being AWOL!' He bent down and kissed her on her cheek. Going over to Evelyn and Ernest he thanked them for everything and offering his deep felt sympathies he walked out into the rain.

Chapter 38

George

It has been nearly three weeks since I left Isabelle and she is on my mind constantly. How I wish I could hold her in my arms. Being out of contact is dreadful. I feel as though part of my life has gone forever, it is so difficult not to think like that, to be positive. Being so exhausted most of the time doesn't help one's mood much somehow.

We are getting to more hilly terrain. Not quite mountain country yet but it won't be long as the Pyrenees can't be that far away. I am very worried about old man Reubedn. He informed me proudly that he would be ninety next week. He is very frail and he let me listen to his heart once I had explained that I was a doctor. Having no instruments I pressed my ear hard against his chest. The beat was weak and irregular, his pulse too and he seemed very breathless, I knew at this rate that no way could he last the journey.

Stopping at yet another 'safe house' I suggested to his daughter and family that he should stay here and rest. I knew he was dying but it seemed unnecessarily cruel to burden them with such sad facts. Turning to her father the daughter sat down next to him, where he lay on a mattress and holding his hand spoke to him. Tears filled the old man's eyes and dripped down his pale tired face. He shook his head from side to side. 'No, no don't leave me, please don't leave me here to die.'

'You're not going to die Papa. You need to stay here until you are stronger, and once you are well you will be able to join us.'

He shook his head even more wildly and trying to sit up he whispered. 'Take me with you, please.' And clutching her hand he lay back wearily on his pillow.

The family looked at me. I felt like God making decisions for them. I asked them to let me talk to the owners who were busy eating at the table. Explaining the situation to them I made a suggestion, they both agreed, so it was decided.

'We are going to make a stretcher to move your father. We will take turns to carry him. It is the only solution but it should be alright.'

I knew that he would never make the whole journey but it would be kinder to let them think he would.

So a stretcher was made. Wooden poles were found in the barn and cut down to size. A large piece of canvas that covered the haycocks in the rain was found and sewn around the poles. It was perfect.

Next morning just as day broke it was time to leave. Laying the old man on the stretcher and covering him with a blanket, we bade *au revoir* to our hosts and set off on the long journey home.

Luckily the day was clear and sunny and the old man slept most of the way, his granddaughters holding his hands while we all took it turns to carry him. He was very light so it was not a drama.

We reached our next 'safe house,' which was set quite high up in the hills, away from anywhere. There were goats grazing all around us, much to the young children's delight, who fed them with buttercups and grass. The house was bigger than normal and Miriam and the children had actual beds, while us men made do with mattresses on the floor. After eating, we Remi, Joseph and I sat and talked. Remi had an endless supply of cigarettes that he kept in his haversack. We all took one and relaxed for a while. He said we were making good time and were over a quarter of the way there.

I went to check on the old man who was sleeping alongside his family. His daughter said he had been coughing and sneezing a lot. That to me sounded bad, more likely to be pneumonia. Known in medical circles' *as the old man's friend.*' He had a fever and he seemed slightly delirious. The most frustrating thing to me was having nothing to ease his symptoms.

That night sleep evaded me so I crept out the back door and looked up at the night sky. There were a myriad of stars, millions of them. You could see for miles and it was as if the whole universe was in front of me. It was mind blowing. Of course I had seen stars before but nothing to compare to this. It made me feel infinitely small and unimportant. I could remember when Jack and I were about seven or eight and Father gave us a chart of the night sky. He showed us where everything was. To us at that age it probably meant little. It was just there and we accepted it. We would find Orion and The Milky Way and always Venus and Jupiter and the North Star. Then we would rush back to tell our Father what we had seen.

It made me think of Jack and I wondered how he was coping being me. Poor chap. Knowing him he probably wasn't coping frightfully well, so again I felt guilty for landing him in such a mess. Sitting down on the back step I could hear the noise of the small cascade that flowed down from the rocks behind the house, into a small stream that ran through the garden while the smell of the wet grass filled my senses with a kind of peace. Maybe I could try and contact Jack. I looked up at the lacework in the sky and concentrated as hard as I could, this time it was far quicker and I could feel Jack near me. I ''*thought talked*' him saying I was doing alright, I could vaguely see something, and he seemed to be in some kind building, it looked a bit like a church, but knowing Jack I doubted it! There was a shimmering movement like a curtain in a breeze, I heard his voice around me, the sound in my head, then a great gust of wind and he was gone. I walked back into the house and lay down on my mattress and fell asleep almost immediately.

Next morning Madame was already up making coffee for everyone and slicing up great hunks of hard cheese. She had baked bread for us like most of the others had done, which always amazed me. The trouble these people took to make us so welcome. Showing a kindness that was well beyond the call of duty. Their bravery astounded me. They knew full well if they were caught they would be shot. It made me feel very humble. Such ordinary people in such extraordinary circumstances.

The old man seemed slightly better and even managed some coffee. So yet again the strange little group gathered together and carrying the stretcher we started our walk towards freedom.

Chapter 39

Anna

Well I am in a quandary. I seem to be in love with three different men! Am I behaving atrociously? Probably. Am I being fickle? Definitely.

Last night with Harry was wonderful, he makes me feel beautiful, and treats me like a princess. I know Jack tells me I am lovely and how much he loves me but there is something about Harry, maybe that is because he is American and calls me *'Honey,'* but quite honestly I don't know anything about him, he could be a serial murderer for all I know!

George has been a bit off with me lately. Anyone would think he was jealous of Harry, which makes me think he is falling in love with me after all. I do sound terribly vain and spoilt and I'm not really. I don't like myself that much. My nose is too big and I am too tall and my hair is too curly. The only thing I like about myself are my eyes which are like Mama's. Now she is really beautiful, I will never be like that.

I am on duty tonight and I just hope and pray there are no more bombings. Houses in our road were bombed to oblivion. Both families didn't stand a chance. I had known the Bishops and the Mitchells since I was small. Their children were younger than me so I didn't have a lot to do with them. Luckily the Bishops girls were in the country with their grandparents but the three Mitchell children were killed along with their parents, it was horrendous. We seemed always to be going to funerals. It is hateful.

Arriving at the hospital this morning to start work I saw Amy there in a WVS uniform. I could hardly believe it. She is such a flippertigibbet, who would have thought she would join up.

She waved and came over to me. 'I've joined the ranks as you can see.' She laughed.' The uniform is a bit itchy and my hat's too big but I want to do something to help.' Tears filled her eyes. 'I just need to do anything, anything to help at this terrible time. My aunt and uncle were killed a couple of nights ago. Their house was bombed, luckily their two girls were in the country with their grandparents. Oh it's too awful, she was Mother's only sister.'

I stared at her. 'Was their name Mitchell?'

'Yes, did you know them?'

'Very well, they lived in our road. The house next door was bombed too, everyone was killed, including three children. I put my arm around her. 'I am so sorry Amy that is terrible to hear.

Got time for a cuppa, I am on duty in half an hour. What about you?'

'I've just finished been doing paperwork and am off home but I would love a cup of tea please.'

We sat in the little canteen and I got to know this girl. She wasn't what she seemed. With her hair drawn back in a bun and no make-up she looked completely different. How we judge people by their looks and I admit to being the worst culprit. It turned out she was an only child of academic parents and had fought against academia and gone to drama school, much to her parent's dismay. She was spoilt. Her words. She said they would do anything to make her happy.

Before the outbreak of war she had been in a few shows, mainly in the chorus line but now all theatres were closed due to the bombing and blackouts, there was no proper work for her. She admitted being at a loose end so decided to do something constructive.

'I'm out of my comfort zone Anna and flailing about a bit, but hopefully I can learn to drive and be more useful.'

We discussed the dance with the American boys. Amy said Shane, the black American, was lovely. She was so tempted to take him home to meet her parents, just to see the look on their faces! He was a musician and played the saxophone. After I had left the dance he had got up on stage and joined in with the band, she said he was quite amazing. Then we discussed Harry. Amy was a bit doubtful about him. She didn't know why, maybe just a bit too nice she suggested. I knew what she meant and we laughed and said. What were nice girls like us fraternising with American soldiers anyway.

We sat and talked until I was ready to go on duty and arranged to meet tomorrow.

I kissed her goodbye and she put her arms around me, her eyes full of tears. 'Thank you Anna, I feel a bit better now.'

As she left I thought again of how I was behaving in such a cavalier way and needed to grow up. Oh God this is crazy. Last week I thought I was falling in love with George what can I do. I need to talk to Mary. She is so rational and sensible, unlike me.

That night after work I went and saw Mary. Henry was out so it was just the two of us which was nice. We sat by the fire and drank hot chocolate. She talked of how the baby had kicked so hard last night it had woken her up. As I looked at her, she seemed to glow as if she had an inner light hidden somewhere. I thought how you would have to love someone a terrific amount to want their baby. Did I love Jack enough, or maybe Harry? I told Mary all this and she laughed and said, Harry was just a diversion and I was being ridiculous. I felt better after that crazy conversation and decided I would just let Harry spoil me. No more, no less.

Harry phoned me the next day and asked me out to the cinema. Why not? It is all innocent, so I told him I would love to go. We went with Amy and her new man. Everywhere we went people looked at us. I think it was the fact there was this beautiful black Adonis on Amy's arm, and a beautiful white one on mine!

The cinema was packed but we managed to find pretty good seats in the stalls. Everyone was there, ostensibly to see the film, but what they really wanted to see was The Pathé News. There was a deathly hush as the music started and the news began. Of course it was dire as always. Hitler had sent over 3 million soldiers and thousands of tanks into Russia. Surely things could get no worse, but of course it did.

The film cheered everyone up a bit. It was the romance between Nelson and Emma Hamilton, with the beautiful Laurence Olivier and the exquisite Vivien Leigh. I wallowed in it with glee. Not sure what the others thought but I had a feeling neither Amy or her man gave a damn. She was cuddled up next to him with her blonde curls nestling under his shoulder. The boys had supplied us with great bars of American chocolate, which, to be honest, I was never quite sure if I actually liked. Somehow it wasn't like our lovely milk chocolate, but beggars can't be choosers so I ate it greedily.

Harry put his arm around my shoulder and held my hand in his. I thought of Jack and felt miserably guilty so ate another square of chocolate. I sat up stiffly not wanting to encourage him. After he kissed me last time I felt dreadful, as if I was betraying Jack, so I made sure I didn't succumb. But I so wanted to. He smelt delicious, some sort of after shave I guessed. That, along with the smell of the cigarette he was smoking, made me feel slightly heady. I could feel his arm heavy on my shoulder, with his hand hanging loosely. Out of the corner of my eye I saw his wrist, heavy with a gold watch wrapped around. He was really rather divine I realised. There was something about him, so I shifted a bit and sunk lower into my seat and turned and smiled at him. He grinned back and kissed me gently on my forehead.

Going out into the cold night air with blackness all around us, we walked with torches to a bar the boys knew. It was down very steep steps into a basement where the sound of music blared out. There were young American soldiers hanging around outside, smoking and drinking. Some with English girls on their arms. Inside lit by red lights was a small dance floor, where a girl was singing soulfully while a jazz pianist accompanied her. I had never heard music like it before. Harry informed me it was *West Coast Swing*. I had no reason not to believe him! Whatever it was I loved it.

There was a bar in one corner of the room. The boys bought Amy and me Manhattans. I had heard of them but never had one. They were quite delicious. The place was a fug of cigarette smoke. It was wonderful. It was a different world. I could get used to this I thought. Watching Amy and her man with her head on his shoulder, why not, I thought. I am enjoying myself. Life is too short, I may get blown up tomorrow. I laughed, he pulled away from me. 'What's the joke honey?'

'Nothing, I am just having such a good time, that's all,'

'Good.' And he kissed me. I had never been kissed on a dance floor before and I had never drunk two cocktails so quickly either. It was all rather splendid I thought, and closing my eyes I sighed and moved gently to the music.

Chapter 40

George

That morning the sun was warm on our backs. Summer was turning to Autumn and the terrain had changed, becoming far more mountainous.

The old man, Reuben, slept on his stretcher while his grandchildren took it in turn to hold his hand. It was a very evocative picture and I wished I had my old Brownie Box camera with me. But I had a feeling the picture would stay in my memory, for a long time to come!

We stopped and ate our bread and cheese, with the gentle sound of the cascades around us, while a herd of golden Limousin cows, with bells around their necks looked at us curiously then wandered off to munch at the lush green grass. The almost mystical sound of their bells echoed around the hills as they swayed slowly from side to side. Strange black butterflies drank nectar from the wild flowers that grew in such profusion. If we hadn't been in such a dangerous situation it would have been idyllic. I watched as the children skipped their way up the mountains, and hoped and prayed we would all arrive safely at the next safe house. We were leaving the centre of France, travelling towards

Agen and Toulouse. Then onto Ariège, and God willing, into Spain.

I watched the old man, as Joseph and Remi carried the stretcher. The sun was hot on my back. Everyone was shedding their clothes. It was going to be one long hot day.

We had been walking for nearly six hours with a couple of breaks. It was still ferociously hot.

'Not a lot further.' Remi said, passing me a flask of rather warm water. 'We are making good time.'

We walked along together in a pleasant silence, broken suddenly by one of Reuben's granddaughters tugging at my sleeve. 'Doctor, Grandpère is very cold. Please come at once.' Her frightened eyes darted from Remi to me. 'Mama says he is dying.' She looked up at me in bewilderment, biting her lip, trying not to cry.

I grabbed her hand and walked back to the little group huddled around the old man. His hands were ice cold, his breathing shallow. I felt for a pulse it was very faint. Everyone was staring at me. Miriam crouched down at her father's side. She looked at me, her eyes begging me to say something.

'Your father is dying. It won't be long now, I am so sorry.' This was always the bit I hated. It made one feel like God. 'He's in no pain. He is peaceful, I want you to know that. He is ready to die, he isn't fighting. It will be a gentle end for him. I promise.'

She smiled. 'Thank you doctor. You are very kind, it is good to know.'

Joseph leant over his wife and taking her arm lifted her up from the grass. Putting his arms around her she buried her face in his shirt.

The last hours were hard ones. There was little talk as the sun started to slip behind the horizon. The air was sweet with the scent of wild rosemary and thyme. Songbirds filled the air with their final song of the day. We carried the old man on his final journey, with his granddaughters still holding his hands.

Suddenly, Reuben opened his eyes and tried vainly to sit up. I put my arm under his frail body and helped him. He looked around at us all and smiling he whispered. 'Listen, the most beautiful sound you will ever hear, the farewell song of the birds.' Then a tear, like a stone rolled down his cheek. And he closed his eyes.

I like to think that the joyous sound of the birds helped him in his last seconds. I have a feeling, seeing the light in his eyes that it did.

We trudged up the steep hills towards our destination. The two grandchildren clutching their mother's hands, while Joseph and I carried the covered body to the next stopover.

It was dark when we reached the safe house, but a huge yellow moon hung in the sky to guide us. We were all exhausted.

I explained to madam and monsieur what had occurred. That the burial had to take place as soon as possible.

Joseph had explained to me that the body must be washed and buried almost immediately. Sounding almost apologetic he looked at me and shrugged.' It is the Jewish way.'

So that night we buried old man Reuben. The night was soft with stars and the sound of cicadas could be heard all around us. Remi, I and Joseph constructed, rather badly, I must say, a makeshift coffin. Madam kindly gave Miriam an old velvet curtain with which to line it. After washing her father he was placed gently down onto his soft bed, for his last and final sleep.

We found the perfect spot for the old man's resting place at the end of a meadow, a little way from the house, next to a small mountain lake, where the earth was soft and pliable.

Joseph stood by the grave and spoke kindly of his father in law and then he spoke the memorial prayer *'El maleh Rachamin'* I had never heard such a beautiful prayer. Of course I understood nothing, but the words washed over me like falling crystal water. When we lowered the coffin slowly into the ground, I watched as the family said *'Kaddish.'* Another Jewish prayer, which Joseph had informed me *'was reserved especially for the mourners and would be recited by his daughter every day, for the next eleven months, then each year on the anniversary of her father's death'.* It was again beautiful to hear. But the words that I thought were Hebrew turned out to be Aramaic. '*The language of Jesus'* Joseph told me. The 23rd psalm was spoken by us all, and Miriam, her face pale and drawn threw three spades of earth onto the coffin. I watched as she washed her hands in the small lake -I learnt from her later that this was a ritual of the disassociation from death and impurity- then kneeling down as the coffin was buried beneath the sweet green grass, she let her tears fall. It all seemed rather lovely somehow. I thought if I had been an old man of ninety, fleeing my oppressors, I would have been happy to be laid to rest in such beautiful surroundings, in such a beautiful way.

Chapter 41

Jack

Thinking of George, knowing he was alive and well did take the edge of worrying about my love life. Or lack of, with Anna. Surely it would be best to tell her everything and just hope and pray she would understand. But I had a feeling it wouldn't be as easy as that.

When I told Mother and Father about George and our *'talk,'* I could see mother visually relax. She always seems so clenched these days. I wonder if she would worry about me as much as she does George. I was getting paranoid. Of course she would I told myself. It was then that I realised that all this secretiveness had to come into the open. It had gone on too long. I knew and I am sure that George was safe, so maybe now was the time. It always did seem to be the time. But I, being pathetic, did nothing about it.

I found Anna in the Gazebo. She was painting but this time painting the walls. She had redone them again in pale yellow, so the room was full of sun even on a grey day like today. She looked lovely. Her face streaked with paint. Her hair piled on top of her head, half of it falling down and an old shirt covering her dress. My girl, I thought, my girl.

'Hi George.'

Oh God, she's even starting to talk like bloody Harry. I smiled rather weakly and kissed her in a brotherly way on the cheek. She smelt of Pears soap and paint. I could have grabbed her there and then, thrown her onto the couch and….. Oh God this is driving me mad!

'How was the dance by the way?' Hoping it had been a disaster.

She smiled. I thought rather dreamily. As if she was remembering it all. 'Super actually. Amy is in love with a rather dishy black soldier. I have a feeling it may turn into something serious, if the cinema episode has anything to do with it!'

Oh hell. She had gone to the cinema with the wretched man as well, what on earth else has she done? I felt like punching the walls. Making great holes in the new paintwork. I think I hated everyone at that moment.

'Oh I see. So we may be seeing a GI bride in our midst then?'

She laughed. 'Who knows? Apparently he is very wealthy. Well his family are, his father is a diplomat in Washington so she would have a good life. But not sure what her parent's reaction will be. They are a bit funny about anyone who isn't British, let alone American and black!'

'What about Harry then?' I was torturing myself, but it was almost pleasurable, a feeling of self-destruction. 'Is he going to steal you away too?'

'Of course not.' She looked indignantly at me, 'I'm in love with Jack, you know that.'

'You have a funny way of showing it, wouldn't you say?'

'George, stop being so horrid. It's only a bit of fun. I get bored and Harry spoils me as Shane does Amy. We enjoy the dancing and all the goodies we get.' She giggled like a schoolgirl.

I felt like slapping her.

'Well I'll let you get on then.' I moved away to the door.

She reached out and grabbed my hand. 'George, what's the matter? You sound so cross. You're not Jack you know, telling me who I can and who I can't see.' Tears filled her eyes, she looked so vulnerable so young.

I felt like kissing her.

'Oh ignore me. I've just had a bad day at the office as they say. Surgery was a nightmare. Anyway as I said, I will let you get on.'

She squeezed my hand. 'Don't go, stay and have some tea with me. I'm tired, I 've been painting all morning and need a break.' She smiled wistfully at me making my heart lurch. This girl what she did to me.

'Okay, I'll put the kettle on.' I lit the little camping stove and found two cups and saucers and her little cache of rich tea biscuits. One a day only, due to rationing she would always say.

Rationing was hard at the moment. I know it was driving Mother mad. She loved to cook and it was a struggle for her to dish up anything decent, so she said, but it tasted as good as ever to me. Everyone had food coupons and tried to eke the food out for that week. My patients moaned about the lack of food, worrying their children wouldn't grow as there was so little to eat. So I spent a lot of wasted time dishing out tonics, which were really of little benefit but it reassured worried mothers. A lot of them grass widows, with their men at the front.

Mother had a list on the larder door of what she was allowed. It is imprinted on my mind!

Per Person Per Week

4 oz. butter

12 oz. sugar

4 oz. bacon

2 eggs.

We took our tea and our one biscuit outside and sat down by the river, which was in full flood and fast flowing. Some ducks were enjoying themselves and swans were there begging for crumbs.

'Anna, I want to let you know that I was in contact with Jack again and he assured me all was okay. I could see little, but strangely I could smell fresh grass and hear what sounded like a waterfall. He sounded okay. I thought it would make you feel a bit better, knowing he was doing alright.'

She flung her arms around me and kissed my cheek. 'Oh such news George, thank you, thank you. I do feel better, much better.'

We sat in friendly silence and drank our hot sweet tea, savouring the biscuits.

'George, do you think this war is going to go on much longer? I thought the bombing had calmed down but last night was dreadful. I was on duty and there were so many people killed and injured, so many houses reduced to rubble. It was terrible to see. I sat with a woman who had been blown out of her front door when the bombs fell. She was alone in the house and was lucky to be alive. I waited with her until an ambulance turned up. I was on 'tea duty' keeping the firemen and wardens fed and watered. You know, even after the Blitz we are still running mobile canteens everywhere. What would these brave men do without us amazing women to look after them'? She laughed and threw back her hair. Her long slender throat the colour of cream. How I wanted to kiss, it to feel her hair touching my face, her hands through my hair. I think maybe I was going slightly mad.

'I do worry about you Anna, look how many of you girls have been killed. You are so near all the bombing; do you realise how dreadfully dangerous it is? I tended to another young WVS girl last night. She died in hospital. She was 19 years old.'

'Yes I know, she shared the driving with me sometimes. Both her brothers are fighting at the front. Can you imagine how terrible it must be for her parents? I pray every night that Jack and Bertie will come back to us soon. I wonder at times like this how I can stand it all, that's why I let Harry spoil me. It is a release from all this horror. Please understand, I mean nothing by it. I still love Jack and always will you know that.' She leant her head on my shoulder. 'Dear George, you are my solace you know that. You are the nearest thing to Jack I have, so when you are angry with me it is as though it is Jack having one of his black dog days. Be kind to me please.' She looked up at me her grey eyes glistening with unshed tears, I felt like a first class shit. I kissed her on her forehead and put my arm around her. We sat like that for a while, watching the gentle movement of the river.

Suddenly, the silence was broken by Elizabeth and Victoria hurtling down the garden, Elizabeth clutching something in her arms.

'Look Anna, look Uncle George. Daddy bought us a puppy, we're going to call her Mischief. Isn't she super?'

We smiled at each other. A little bit of joy at such a dismal time was the best distraction ever. There would be time enough for me to talk to Anna. It was rather a relief to be quite honest, so I joined the girls as they tumbled in the grass with the little black puppy, laughing as they dipped its paws in the river.

'Uncle George.' (Jack and I were honorary uncles.)

'Yes Victoria?'

'Why do you pretend to be Uncle George, when you're really Uncle Jack?'

Good God. I felt cold all over, what was this. What on earth was she saying?

'Good heavens.' I laughed. 'What on earth can you mean? Why would I pretend? I am George, George O'Brien GP and twin brother of Jack,. Son of Ernest and Nell.'

'But you are Uncle Jack really. I know you are.' She giggled and rolled on the grass with the puppy.

What the hell I thought, what on earth has bought this on? I felt slightly sick, hoping the conversation would go no further. Oh but it did.

Anna frowned at her. 'What are you going on about Victoria, that's a silly thing to say isn't it? What made you say something so stupid?'

Poor little Victoria. She blushed terribly and looked down at her feet. 'Well he is different from my Uncle George. He's just like Uncle Jack, that's all.'

'Explain then.' I said wondering what the fuck she was going to say.

'Well, you look at Anna like Uncle Jack does when she's not looking. Sort of soppily and all lovey-dovey.' She giggled and pressed her hand against her mouth. 'And most of all when you smoke, you hold your cigarette just like he does.' She picked up a twig on the grass and pretended to smoke. She held it between her thumb and index finger. Then lifted her chin up and blew hard. 'When the real Uncle George smokes, he smokes like this.' Putting the twig between her middle and index finger, she blew imaginary smoke into the air and turned her head to blow the smoke away from her face.

Dear God, she's right. How on earth did she pick that up? I have to laugh this off, right now.

'Well now, that is amazing, aren't you a clever girl then. Maybe Jack smokes like me over in France. What do you think Anna, do I look at you all soppily?' I shifted on my feet, trying to look relaxed and unnerved.

Anna laughed. 'How would I know how you look at me, when I'm not looking? And as for the smoking. I see what Victoria means, but that is probably just a habit you got from Jack.'

Good grief. Out of the mouths of babes as they say. Trying to make a joke of it, I lit a cigarette and smoked it, holding it between my middle and index finger and blew the smoke sideways.

'There you go, is that better?' Taking another almighty puff I put my arm around her thin little shoulders. 'Give your Uncle George a big kiss!'

She looked at me and rolled her eyes. 'Nope, and I know you're not really you!'

Anna looked exasperated. 'Stop been so juvenile Victoria and give your uncle a kiss at once!'

'No he's not Uncle George. Anyway what's juvenile mean?'

'Babyish, and that is how daft you're being. Anything else you have to say?'

'Yes.' She giggled and again put her hand across her mouth. 'I heard Daddy say to Mummy last night, that Uncle George didn't seem to be like the old George they knew. He was more like Uncle Jack as he didn't have a pretty girl on his arm all the time. And seemed to be spend most of his free time with you Anna.'

Anna looked at me and I laughed. Not very convincingly. 'My goodness, I am definitely turning into Jack then. How about giving me a kiss?'

'You don't believe me. It's true.' She stamped her little foot. 'No one ever believes what I say. I'm going to play with Mischief.' And off she went with her sister. An angry little girl, who didn't want to kiss her uncle anymore.

'Well,'said Anna. 'That was quite weird. I can't imagine what got into her. Maybe she is just mixed up like we all are in this wretched war. I know she's missing Bertie a lot, it's probably just that. Don't take any notice of her. She'll love you again tomorrow!'

'I know. I hope you don't think I am Jack in disguise. While poor old George is traipsing through mountains to get to Spain!'

She laughed, and gathering up the tea things we walked back to the Gazebo.

Chapter 42

Jack

After surgery Father and I went to see a patient of his, who had been a coma for far too long. His health had deteriorated dramatically over the last couple of days and was causing concern.

The clinic was not far from the hospital. It was a pristine building of white stone, really rather grand for a clinic. It had been donated by a rich patron, whose wife had been cured of a brain tumour by the chief surgeon,

Inside it was spotless. Everywhere was white. Long white silk curtains hung at the large windows. In the reception area a beautiful royal blue carpet covered the floor, running right up the stairs, stopping as it neared the sterile rooms. More like a hotel than a clinic I thought. There was soft music playing. Great vases of flowers stood on tall white colonnades dotted around the room.

Behind a white desk, displaying a white telephone and white Peace lilies, sat a blonde receptionist. Dressed completely in white, with a very tight skirt and frilly blouse and rather splendid legs, encased in what looked like to me nylons. - Perhaps she was a friend of Harry's too I thought bitterly - To set the whole outfit off where white high heeled shoes. She looked as though she was about to do a turn at The Windmill theatre. She smiled as father and I walked in fluttering her absurdly long eye lashes at us. Maybe she was one of George's pieces of crumpet. I smiled back, hoping a smile would do for the moment.

We walked up the stairs, the carpet's deep pile soft beneath our feet. The smell of freshly cut lavender wafted up from a small waiting room. It was a very welcoming environment for traumatised family members. I could imagine how much it would help. No smell of disinfectant. No green walls. No brown linoleum.

Father took me into the Intensive care unit. In one room a young woman laid, attached to various tubes and respirators. She had been put into an induced coma after being knocked off her bike by a lorry. There was no sound, just the rustle of the nurse's uniform as she moved quietly around her patient.

In the room next door lay a man. I guessed him to be around forty, he had been in a coma for over four months now. By his bed sat a woman and two young children. The children were drawing and seemed unperturbed by it all. The woman was pale and drawn. She smiled when we walked in, Father bent down and kissed her on the cheek. 'This is my son George, Rachel, he is doing research into brain trauma and its consequences. He will be part of William's medical team, for the time being.'

The woman acknowledged me, then looking at Father, tears filled her eyes. 'Doctor, the surgeon came around earlier. They are doing more tests on William. He said he was concerned as brain activity had lessened. I am scared he will never recover.' She looked imploringly at my Father. It was heart-rending. I knew that his brain activity had decreased and more tests had been done that morning, to check any change in the brain's pattern. There had been none.

Her husband had been a fireman, and while rescuing occupants from a bombed out house a wall had collapsed on him. Luckily the occupants had escaped, but William had suffered severe head injuries, causing a massive bleed on the brain. The surgeon who had operated was to talk with his team that evening. Father, being her GP was to be included in the discussion as I would be. In fact I was dreading it. Not being a bona-fida doctor, just a research scientist I found this side of medicine hard to cope with. But I was George and George was a good doctor, as I must be.

The next day Father and I went back to the clinic. A conclusion had been reached. William had been diagnosed as being in a vegetative state. There was no longer any brain activity. Rachel had been advised, that the best and only thing, would be to turn of the machine that was keeping her husband alive. It was a decision that I cannot imagine having to take.

There was an almighty hush in the room. The surgeon was talking quietly to Rachel. Her head was bowed. The nurse stood quietly by the window, her back turned. Father walked over to the bed and sat down next to Rachel. He took her hand, and covering it with his, kissed her cheek. She leant her head wearily against his shoulder. I could see her small body shaking with sobs. The surgeon nodded to the nurse. I watched as she disconnected the life support machine. The sound of the heart monitor slowing down was the only thing to be heard. Then it was as if someone had vacated the room. Leaving nothing behind, other than the sound of silence.

Chapter 43

Anna

Every morning Papa makes the early morning tea for us all. 'My little contribution to the household chores.' He would laugh.

Unusually, instead of leaving the tea to grow cold on my bedside table, he came and sat on the edge of the bed. Sleepily I thanked him, he leant over and kissed my forehead. 'I have some good news young lady.'

'What?' I sat bolt upright 'Jack!'

'Sadly no. But even so, the news is pretty good. The Prime Minister wants to see you. To come here to your atelier. To see the finished portrait, before it is moved for the framing and public unveiling.'

'Oh, my Lord. Here? Good grief, I will have to clean out the gazebo, it is full of rubbish, and I haven't finished painting it. When is he coming?'

I felt quite breathless at the idea of our Prime Minister, Winston Churchill, actually wanting to see me on my home ground. How exciting. How terrifying!

That morning I spring cleaned the gazebo, swept up dead flies and atrophied spiders lying in corners. I washed the windows then proceeded to finish painting, I had decided that I would do it in buttercup yellow so it would seem to be full of sunshine even on bleak days. Wrapping my hair up in an old cotton scarf and stealing one of Bertie's old shirts I got to work. The sun was shining. The birds were singing and I felt for the first time since Jack left, almost happy.

The portrait stood on an easel in the corner of the room, covered with a cloth. It no longer belonged to me. I had done my job, now it was others who, hopefully would enjoy it as much as I did when painting it.

George came over to see me as I was working. He didn't seem in the best of moods. He was so like Jack when he was in one of his black dog moods. He asked about the dance and said stupid things, like, was Harry going to steal me away? Anyone would think he was Jack. Then he got all grumpy and said he had to go. I managed to drag him back and we went and sat by the river with tea and biscuits.

I didn't mention the Prime Minister coming over. Papa said it was to be kept quiet for security reasons. I'm not sure George would be a threat somehow.

He said he had been '*in contact*' with Jack, which was brilliant news, at least he was alive and on his way home. It would be nice though to have real contact, but I guess the boys *'thought talk'* would have have to do.

Poor George he is so worried about me when I am out and about. Being in the WVS he thinks I will get blown up. As if I would. I have no fear of that. I must say when one of my co-drivers was killed last week in a gas explosion, it made me realise how fragile we all are. She was only nineteen and a sweet girl. I cried so much for her. Now she was just another statistic in this wretched war.

Victoria and Elizabeth came and joined us for tea by the river. They have been given a puppy and were so excited and wanted to show George. It is rather adorable, a little black and white spaniel. They have called her Mischief. Mother thought it would be good for the girls to have something to look after, as their outings have been very limited. She is terrified to let them out alone, which I can completely understand. Nowhere seems safe somehow. There has been a succession of air raids this last week which is exhausting. No one has really had a decent night and so we are all a bit ratty.

It was a rather strange end to the afternoon. For some reason, Victoria has got it into her silly little head that George isn't George, but is really Jack. I have no idea where she got that from. I think it upset George a bit. He did seem quite subdued when he left. Poor man. I will have to speak to Victoria and tell her to grow up, but then she is only twelve, so she is full of fanciful ideas. She reminds me of me at that age, when I was quite sure that I was really a princess. Of course no one believed me. But I knew I was.

After everyone had left I lay down in my sparkling clean gazebo. The new couch looked lovely. I am very proud of my little atelier. I looked around at my little 'house' and sighed, I was lucky. So lucky even with things the way they were, with the war and Jack and everything.

The smell of cut grass drifted through the door. The sun was setting over the hills and a pair of blackbirds were singing their farewell to the end of the day. The peace was wonderful after last night. It had been a God awful six hours of air raids. We all played cards and board games in the cellar and listened to an old wind up gramophone to try and cut out the dreadful sounds outside. Luckily the houses around us were untouched, but it is as if the sword of Damocles is hanging over us all. It is frightening times to be living in.

As I lay there, drifting towards sleep I thought of how my life was turning out. Pretty good on the work front but not sure about the rest of it. My love life is a complicated disaster, to say the least. Harry has asked me out again, to celebrate Amy and her man's engagement. But I really not sure if I want to go. I am scared it is getting too serious on Harry's part, which makes me feel uncomfortable. Also I am getting used to him being around and I do enjoy his company, but feel maybe I am stepping on dangerous ground. I often feel so guilty when I am with him. Poor Jack, there he is somewhere fleeing the enemy, while I am here in good old Blighty enjoying myself, and I feel I shouldn't be.

George is behaving more like Jack every day, being moody. I can't put my finger on it is so unlike him. Jack can be the grumpy one. George always seems to be so relaxed about everything, but not so at the moment. I will have to ask him if there is anything wrong. Maybe he's got himself involved with a girl. That used to be the story of his life, but am sure there is no one on the scene at the moment

I had a bit of a near miss the other day, when a whole wall of a house collapsed near three of us WVS girls. We had been dishing out tea to exhausted firemen, who had been fighting an inferno for the last five hours. We were covered in brick dust. It was in our eyes, hair and mouths. We were all scratched and bruised by rubble but otherwise unhurt. The firemen were amazing and made sure we sat and drunk some of our hot sweet tea. Then laughingly discussed whether or not we ought to be hosed down! There was so much camaraderie and deep affection between everyone. All drawing together and confronting this dreadful time we were living. As our Prime Minister said. *'We shall not be bowed.'* And we weren't.

The next day the same Prime Minister, Winston Churchill, with his retinue of body guards arrived. Mama greeted him with kisses -she was a great friend of Clementine, his wife - and handshakes from Papa. The bodyguards sat happily in the kitchen, drinking tea while another couple of them loitered by the front gate, looking, it seemed to me extremely obvious. But no one took the blindest bit of notice of them. The war took hold of everyone's time, therefore nothing else was of the slightest interest.

Victoria and Elizabeth in their best frocks with ribbons in their hair, giggled and curtsied when he shook their hands. They introduced him to Mischief and to their delight he asked if he could hold her for a while. Wide eyed they took in this giant of this man, with the inevitable cigar clenched between his teeth. He had us all laughing with his stories as Prime Minister while we had our tea by the river.

Mama had set up a table, covered with her best damask tablecloth, blindingly white in the sun. There were tiny cucumber sandwiches, of course with their crusts cut off. Potted shrimps, courtesy of our lovely fishmonger, who I am quite sure is falling even more madly in love with Mrs Evelyn O'Brien. Tea was poured from the best silver teapots and the china was Mama's very best. '*Saved for special occasions*' she would inform us. This definitely was one! The cups so fine to be almost translucent. A beautiful Simmel cake and brandy snaps completed the table.

Mama had hired a young girl to serve us. Who, suffused with blushes the whole time, looked every bit the part, in her black skirt and white blouse, with a little frilly apron tied around her tiny waist. I think it was all rather too much for someone so young. Her hands trembled like a leaf when she poured out the tea. But considering the state of her, she managed to do it all without dropping or spilling anything. I did feel sorry for her and gave her a couple of smiles of encouragement, which hopefully helped. All in all it was the best of afternoons. The sun shone. The ducks on the river did what ducks were supposed to do, while the swans wafted slowly up and down. It was sublime, peace, perfect peace.

I knew I had to show Churchill my portrait. I couldn't put it off any longer, so bracing myself I walked with him into my sparkling clean atelier. This to me is the hard part. Not knowing what the sitter's reaction would be. Churchill had seen his portrait only when it was in a raw state right at the start. Happily I had been allowed to take some photos of details. Such as the hands. Especially the hands. Always the artists' downfall!

Before he looked at the painting he asked to look around the gazebo. He fell in love with it - His words - And said he would commission one to be built immediately at Chequers. 'Where I will paint in solitude, away from the madding crowds.' He chuckled.

I knew he painted and was said to be very accomplished. Maybe one day he would show me *his* work. I held my breath as I took off the cloth covering the easel. He stared long and hard at the painting. Peered closely at it. Stood back, head on one side then went closer again. He grunted. An appreciative grunt I hoped. Then puffing on his cigar, he turned to me, a smile on his face. 'Young lady, it is just what I hoped it would be. I am in awe of your talent. Thank you, I cannot tell you how relieved I am. You have no idea what rubbish I have been subjected to. And I dare say there will be more atrocities to come.' And of course there was. But that was well into future, and the fate of one special painting was to go down in history.

A few days later we went '*en famille*' to the unveiling, I felt completely overawed by it all and made sure I kept well into the shadows. But I have to admit that I did feel rather proud and also extremely lucky to have had the chance to perform something, really rather special.

The next morning I was even more thrilled to read in the morning papers. *'This portrait, of our Prime Minister, was a thoughtful study of a great man, painted by a young up and coming artist Miss Anna Cooper of London. Who should be proud of her accomplished work. There is no doubt she has taken her first step on the ladder to fame.'*

Chapter 44

George. 8 weeks into his journey

The next day before it was light, in the early morning mist, Miriam and her family stood solemnly around Reuben's grave, while prayers were said and tears were shed. The beautiful sound of those prayers have stayed long in my memory and offered me then a sense of comfort on my long journey. Even though the words were spoken in a tongue that I knew nothing of.

After a bowl of coffee and bread we said our goodbyes to the owners. Normally these people would be '*ships that pass in the night,*' but this couple had gone further than their line of duty. It was in the way they accepted, without questioning, the upheaval we caused. Nothing was too much trouble. A grave was dug. A coffin made and a funeral held for an old Jewish man, who they knew nothing of and it was all done with such kindness. It was a very humbling experience.

They were middle aged and Spanish. They had lived among the mountains all of their lives, their grown up children had fled back to their native land, before the real danger reached them, and soon they too would follow, once the war was at an end and the last refugees had left.

But for now, they would stay and risk their lives, for the lives of others on their way to freedom. They were unsung heroes, like so many others. Whom without them, many people would have suffered greatly under the Nazi regime.

Miriam and Joseph embraced these dear people and kind words were spoken. The children shyly kissed them goodbye, then holding a large loaf of home baked bread and clutching little cheese-cloth parcels of Madam's fresh goat's cheese, we bade them both farewell. With a final glance over her shoulder I watched Miriam, her eyes full of tears whisper *'Adieu Papa, adieu.'* Then gathering her family around her we left, along with Remi on the next stage of our journey home.

We were a subdued little group that trudged over the mountainous terrain. It was the first wet day. The rain fell relentlessly for hours while all around us laid beauty. In the distance the snow tipped Pyrenees were barely visible. But as we walked on we saw the mountains suddenly appear out of the mist, and shine like silver in the sun that broke through the clouds. Flowers in wild profusion scattered through the rocks and grass, their perfume filling the air. The music of cow bells echoed around us, while buzzards screeched overhead, twisting and turning in the thermals, ready to fall like thunderbolts to the ground, where some poor unsuspecting creature emerged, just in time for their lunch.

We stopped to eat our bread and cheese, sitting on the warm rocks to dry out. A small stream gurgled contentedly close by. The goat's cheese, as white as snow, with its grey ash rind, spread on thick chunks of bread, was like nectar to us weary travellers. Remi somehow had managed, as usual, to fill his small leather flask with homemade brandy, along with some sweet pink pears from our Spanish hosts, it was a meal fit for a king.

The girls insisted they were allowed, '*just a sip please*,' of the brandy. Horrified by the burning taste they spat it out as being '*dégueulasse*.' Plunging their faces into the stream and taking great gulps of the sweet icy water, they emerged, their mermaid hair hanging long and loose around their shoulders. Laughing, Joseph and Miriam wrapped their arms around their daughters. Kissing their wet shiny faces, holding their little bodies close to them, Joseph said it had probably made them teetotallers for ever!

Miriam glanced over at me and smiled. Her life would soon begin anew. In a safe country, away from the terror that had faced her little family. With the warm sun and the food and drink inside us life didn't, for that short time, seem that bad after all.

This would be the most torturous part of our journey. We would spend our final night on the

French side of the border. Then from there, a Mulgari, (Basque Smuggler), would lead us through the mountains into Spain. There I would be met by British Intelligence, who would escort me home.

It was a sobering thought. I really did feel so ambivalent about the whole thing. Saying goodbye to these friends I had made. Going home. Not being able to be with Isabelle. Wondering how the hell Jack was coping with being George. It was as if the whole of my life hung by the finest thread, waiting to snap at any minute and throw my world into chaos.

Late at night, as she skies turned from brilliant blue to navy to dark purple and stars hung heavy in the night, we arrived at our final safe house. There we were greeted by a young Belgian woman called Andree de Jongh. Known to everyone as Dédée. She was a nurse who had started the Comet Line. Escorting allied pilots and refugees across the mountains, into what was known as Neutral Spain.

There were two other airmen with her, who had travelled a different route. They were bomber pilots, from the same squadron, they too had been shot down and managed to bail out as I did. They were not from my squadron, but we talked long into the night. It was good to be with others who had gone through such terrifying ordeals. To talk about our luck being here, and at last to be going home. They turned out to be brothers and I wondered if their family had had the dreaded telegram. Thinking both your sons were believed killed seemed a horrendous thought and I tried to reassure them both that the minute we got to safety they would be able to get a message home, it seemed to cheer them both up a bit, I somehow felt very responsible for them, not sure why, Just that they both seemed rather vunerable even though they were bomber pilots and reminded me of a couple of lads I had known in Scotland when I first joined up they too had had ginger hair and freckles, too young of course like most of us were.

Sitting around the table drinking cups of dark sweet coffee, Dédée told us of the Basque Mulgari who were to guide us to our final destination. She seemed so young to be doing such precarious and dangerous work. She was tiny, waif like, but with a steely look of determination in her eyes. That she had saved the lives of over 800 allies who had escaped from occupied France, was in itself amazing, but all organised by such a sweet unassuming girl, was difficult to comprehend. And now she about to save the lives of a young Jewish family, who in a short space of time, had become part of my life and would stay in my heart forever.

That night before we left, we were all given a bowl of hot milk. Discarding our everyday clothes, we were kitted out in blue workman's 'travail bleus,' and strange espadrilles made from rope and sturdy walking sticks. None of us had the slightest idea of the tortuous route we were about to take through the mountains to Endarlatsa, over the Bidasoa river and finally into Spain. The children were excited at '*dressing up*' which somehow rubbed off on us adults. It was '*an adventure*' they kept shouting. '*We're going on an adventure!*'

Then it was time to say goodbye to Miriam, Joseph and the girls. It was a very poignant moment and there was a lot of hugging and crying, exchanging addresses and promises of meeting up after the war was over. So on a moonless night, we left our last safe house and walked. Our final walk into neutral Spain

Remi was to take them to their final destination. I know they reached it, but I never heard of him again. I just hope and pray he survived. He was an extraordinarily brave young man.

I walked the final stretch of the Comet line with Dédée and the two bomber pilots. When we reached our final safe house it was only to find that no one was there. The door was open. Broken crockery lay scattered on the floor, soup bowls smashed plates, glasses and a brightly coloured tablecloth lay tangled in it all, as though someone had ripped it off the table taking everything with it. Incongruously, amongst all the mess, lay one wooden sabot and a woman's head scarf. A range stood lit, on it a large cauldron of soup simmered gently.

Suddenly through the door crashed a young girl. 'Dédée it's Mama and Papa. They took them away. They said they were going to kill them, kill them for being helpers. I was upstairs, I could hear it all. The crashing of broken dishes, someone shouting at my parents. I could hear Papa swearing and Mama shouting too. I was so frightened. I didn't know what to do, so I just hid. Oh I wish they'd taken me too.' The girl was hysterical by now and trembling all over. Tears poured down her face as she tossed her head from side to side, long fair hair covered her face as she collapsed on a chair. Hiccupping and sobbing out her words, she told us what had happened. How she knew the men who came and took her parents away. How before they'd pretended to be friends with them, when all along they were part of the Milice. - A paramilitary organization supporting the Vichy Government.- Formed to fight the French Resistance of which her parents had been part of, as a lot of the helpers were.

I must say I was somewhat surprised The Milice hadn't waited for us lot to arrive. Then they could have got rid of us all, in one fell swoop.

Dédée sat with the girl holding her hand. Calming her and whispering gentle words, until she stopped shaking and became still and quiet.

'We have to leave here immediately. We will need to climb up into the hills, there is a safe house there where we can hide out for a while. I am sure The Milice don't know of it. Hopefully we can reach there in a couple of hours or so.'

The girl said she would like to take some things with her. We saw her run up the stairs, the floorboards creaking as she walked around the room .

Coming down with a bag, she looked at us all. 'These are some things of Mama's I would like to keep.' She said between her tears.

'Also Papa's diary, where he wrote dates and names of people who would be passing through on the way to Spain. The Milice must not get hold of it whatever happens.' She sighed and hugged the bag close to her. Looking around the room, maybe for the last time, she walked with us all, out into the night.

Chapter 45

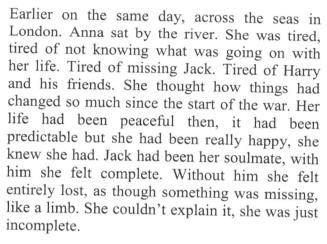

Earlier on the same day, across the seas in London. Anna sat by the river. She was tired, tired of not knowing what was going on with her life. Tired of missing Jack. Tired of Harry and his friends. She thought how things had changed so much since the start of the war. Her life had been peaceful then, it had been predictable but she had been really happy, she knew she had. Jack had been her soulmate, with him she felt complete. Without him she felt entirely lost, as though something was missing, like a limb. She couldn't explain it, she was just incomplete.

She watched as a Heron swooped down onto the river bank opposite her. Its massive wing span folding itself into what appeared to be the shape of a hunched over old man, who eyed her disdainfully. She watched as he turned his head from side to side. Her eyes pricked with tears. This beautiful creature was such a joy to behold, such innocence in a wretched world. Dipping its long beak into the water it came up with a large grey fish. Good heavens she thought I didn't know there were fish that size in there. Cheeky thing making himself at home like that. She laughed and grabbing a pencil and paper by her side, she started to draw.

Motionless, the great bird stood on one leg. Seemingly half asleep. It's almost prehistoric she thought, what a strange creature. She was pleased with her sketch, with its bold black lines. 'I will use watercolour.' She said out loud.' Just a little grey and blue would work really well.' She put her pencil down and watched as the Heron gave her one long look, then raising its gigantic wings and skimming across the river, it soared up into the blue sky and was gone. 'Come back soon.' She shouted. 'Don't forget I need you for another sitting.'

How wonderful it would to be able to fly away with her Heron. Into the nothingness of space, but then on the other hand it could all turn into a scenario like Leda and her swan. She giggled and laid back on the soft grass her feet dangling in the cool water.

The day was still. Very humid and hot. She was definitely feeling a bit sweaty, or glowing as Mama would say. 'Pigs sweat, men perspire and women glow.' Well she was definitely glowing.

She could feel the ripples of the water tickling her feet. 'Heavenly.' She sighed, lying back her arms behind her head. 'Oh how I wish I could *'thought talk'* like the twins. Maybe I could give it a try.' She knew she was telepathic and also that she had lived before. Something she had told no one. All she knew was she had been a child, maybe a baby, but definitely a boy and there was a woman crying all the time. There were memories of feeling warm as though she was being held in someone's arms, but still with a feeling of desperate unhappiness. She wished there could be more. But she knew that what she felt and saw was real. Having read a lot about reincarnation and how the Buddhist believed in it avidly, she thought that if she had been religious, Buddhism would suit her very well. Getting up she brushed the grass off herself. Picked up her sketch book and pencil and wandered into the gazebo. It was lovely and cool. She sunk down onto the sofa and closed her eyes.

Maybe she thought I could try and contact Jack, it's worth a try. She closed her eyes and concentrated. 'Jack.' She thought. 'Come and see me, I miss you.' She scrunched up her eyes, pushing her fingers into her temples, like George said, but nothing happened. She did it for about five times, but all it did was hurt. She lay like that for what to her seemed a long time, when suddenly she felt something, like a warm zephyr caressing her cheek. Then a great joy filled her heart as she heard Jack's voice. 'Jack, are you there? It's me, Anna. I miss you so much and oh I love you so much'.

Her voice broke and tears fell down her face. He was whispering words that were indistinct, then they became clearer. 'Anna, I'm here, I am really near to you, really near. I love you, tell me you love me. That you will always love me'.

'I love you Jack. I can't bear being without you. Where are you, tell me?' But there was no

answer, just a caress on her cheek and that
wonderful feeling of joy enveloped her again.
As quickly as the sensation begun it stopped.
She sat up rubbing her eyes. Jack had spoken to
her. She had actually heard him, it was amazing.
I must tell George. Jumping up from the sofa,
she kicked of her shoes and ran barefoot up the
garden, her long dark hair swinging around her
shoulders. She felt elated

Chapter 46

Surgery was over, it was time for a drink thought Jack. He poured himself a stiff scotch and took it out into the garden. It was sweltering hot and he wished they had a river like Anna's 'Oh Anna,' he thought, 'what am I to do!'

Sitting there on the old wooden bench with a very fat cat basking in the sun, he closed his eyes and thought of his girl and his wretched predicament, when suddenly he felt that strange *'thought talk'* sensation. It was George trying to reach him. He sat still and waited then he heard Anna's voice. He opened his eyes wide, it was Anna not George, what on earth…. He could see a vague outline of something, someone, but so faint it was almost indistinguishable. Then it became clearer, it was Anna blurred but it was her. How did she manage to contact him like that, it was unbelievable. Surely it was only George who could access his mind. She must have thought she was talking to him in France. So to keep up the pretence he *'thought talked'* back to her, leant out and tried to touch her cheek. Then it was all over. He opened his eyes and stared at the cat, which stared back. Now was the time to talk to Henry, try and explain, forgetting the *'Thought Talk'* that was private somehow, but he needed to get his advice about talking finally to Anna!

He thought back to last week, when he had met up with Henry,Mary and Anna at the vicarage for supper. He had decided to talk to Henry then and ask for his advice, but yet again but there was no opportunity as they spent most of the evening ensconced in the cellar while bombs fell all around them.

It had been a dreadful night, supper was over and they were just about to retire to the lounge room when the dreaded siren heralded disaster. Mary was distressed and scared 'all this' would bring on the baby, Henry was a mite twitchy too, so it wasn't the best of evenings. As for himself he drank too much, which worryingly seemed to be an ongoing habit, and flirted like mad with Anna who looked at him in disbelief and said to stop behaving like an idiot, and who did he think he was.

'Jack.' He wanted to shout. 'Bloody Jack that's who I am!' But of course he didn't.

They played cards until the early hours. Mary fell asleep as Anna did. It would have been a good time to talk to Henry then but of course he didn't.

So now walking over to the Vicarage he felt sure that this would be time to get everything off his chest to face his girl, what ever the consequences.

When he arrived Mary was resting upstairs so it seemed an opportune moment. Poor Henry, how sick he must be of him, but this was his last hurrah!

'Henry, I am going to talk to Anna'. He looked questioningly at him as if he would come up with some magical idea. 'I just thought I would let you know, what do you think I should do?'

'Jack, I don't know, it is up to you.' He said somewhat wearily. 'If you feel the time is right then do. I wish I could be more help, but as they say, the ball is in your court old chap. Look let's go and grab a pint. The sun is over the yardarm and I tell you I could do with one. All this waiting for the baby is worse than anything I have ever experienced. Worse than been ordained and that was pretty nerve wracking.'

Sitting in the pub, with the old leather seats patched and worn, the arms covered in cigarette burns, they looked around, the place was full. It was a Friday night. Pay day, end of the month. Therefore all the men, those that were left, mostly middle aged or older, were trying to enjoy themselves. He and Henry were probably the youngest of them all.

Six young men, who had been regulars had been killed at the front. There were rumours that two local boys, young airmen were missing. It was a bad time and Jack felt even worse, knowing that he was deceiving everyone. He drank too much of course and smoked too much, but at least it helped deaden everything. Henry seemed like a cat on hot bricks. Mary was a week over due. In fact he wasn't really coping terribly well with the whole thing. All in all neither of them were really having a good time at all.

While all this was going on. Mary was trying to phone the nursing home, her waters had broken. She had gone downstairs to tell Henry only to find he wasn't anywhere to be seen. She promptly burst into tears and rang Anna, who of course wasn't there either. She was on her way to see George, and not finding him anywhere had decided to go and see if he was at the vicarage.

Mary had never been so glad to see anyone as much as she did when Anna walked in the kitchen door, to find her distraught and tearful.

'Oh Anna, thank goodness you're here.' Hugging her she promptly burst into tears again. She was doing a lot of that lately. 'The phones are down. Henry has vanished. And I am having contractions.'

'I bet he's in the pub with George because I couldn't find him anywhere either. Hang on here and I will run down the road. Sit down and breathe deeply. Isn't that what they tell you to do?' Banging the kitchen door behind her, she raced towards the pub, which luckily was but a few minutes away.

Bursting into the pub, Mary grabbed Henry by the arm.

'Come on you time you took Mary to hospital.' She laughed. 'As for you George, you are just the man they need at a time like this.'

God thought Jack, I hope she doesn't have precipitated labour and I have to deliver the baby. Now that would be interesting!

That evening with Mary safely in the nursing home - run by seven day Adventist nuns, with midwives on hand for the important moments - Henry held her hand, while Jack and Anna stood at the end of the bed watching Mary, as if she was about to perform some amazing feat. Which of course she was.

'It's going to be quite a while,' smiled one of the nuns. Her white wimple nodding up and down, her round pink face beaming happily. 'I am afraid she is nowhere near the boil yet. The contractions are very weak and intermittent. I suggest you all pop out for something to eat and come back later.'

'Good idea.' Anna said. Henry really was a complete bundle of nerves. Grabbing a quick pint and a bag of crisps seemed the best scenario somehow. The pub was full. There was a serious darts match in progress. It being at such a crucial point, the three friends bought their drinks; sat and watched as the other team devoured the home team, much to the regulars' annoyance. When they were told that Mary was in labour, their faces lit up and bets were made as to the baby's weight and sex, while drinks were pressed on Henry, who sat on a bar stool looking rather bewildered by it all.

That night a baby girl was born. Born into a world of chaos. With her navy blue eyes and rosebud mouth she was a tiny spark of light in dark times. During air raids, of which there seemed to Mary far too many, all the babies slept in their cribs under their mother's beds. Quite right the women agreed that was wonderful, but what about them? They were soon to learn that mothers had to get on with it. That was just how it was, and would be for ever and ever amen.

When Mary left the nursing home, she was full of joy at her new little daughter. She named her Roberta after her father.

She loved bathing her, holding her. In fact just looking at her in amazement. To think that she and Henry had managed to make something so beautiful. Feeding her, now that was another matter. She had decided, with more than a little pressure from the nuns to breast feed. It had been awful. She cried as the milk came in. Cried when the baby wouldn't latch on. In fact she did rather a lot of crying in those early days, and realised there and then, that sleep deprivation was something she wouldn't wish on her worst enemy.

Anna fell in love with her god daughter instantly. She sketched her as a tiny infant, mostly asleep with her thumb in her mouth, yet managed to catch her wide eyed, and with her first smile. So a record was made of this little mite that bought such joy at such an unpredictable time.

Chapter 47

Jack

One evening after surgery. Two days after Roberta had been born. I walked to Anna's. Now was the time I thought. Now!

She was sitting by the river where it was cool, under the willows. 'She took hold of my hand. 'Oh George, how lovely to see you, come and sit with me.' The sound of birds and the smell of flowers made me think. Maybe it will all be okay.

We sat on the grass, Anna dangled her feet in the water and looked at me, her eyes shining. 'I have such marvellous news. I wanted to tell you the night Roberta was born but somehow it didn't seem like the right time. You won't believe it, and I couldn't really. Guess what? I *'thought talked'* Jack just now. I really did and he talked back. I had to tell you, it is incredible. I never thought I could. How do you think it was possible? With you two it's understandable but how come I could. It doesn't make sense.'

She was so excited, falling over her words as she spoke, she threw her arms around me. She was on fire. She was so beautiful with her hair streaming down her back. She stood there. My barefoot gipsy girl. How I love you, love you, love you. Now is the time. Right now. It was perfect, just perfect!

'Well.' I stuttered. 'I really don't know. Things like that are hard to understand. There is so little we do know about telepathy and the brain. I can only imagine that your love for each other broke down the barriers of the mind. We will never understand the spiritual world. You just have to accept that love can conquer, where nothing else can. Maybe that is all there is to it. I can't tell you, I don't think anyone can.'

She smiled at me and tears filled her eyes. 'Thank you George, I like that. Maybe you are right after all. I don't suppose we will ever know.'

I took a deep breath and began. 'I have to tell you something Anna, but I don't know *how* to tell you.'

'It's Jack isn't it? Something's happened to him. Tell me, what is it. Tell me George. Now.'

I actually thought she was going to stamp her foot, like a little girl!

'No, no it's nothing about Jack. Well not in a real sense. It's something I have been trying to tell you for three months. It's been like an elephant in the bloody room.'

'What do you mean?'

'Remember when Victoria was saying, I wasn't George, I was Jack?'

Yes, stupid child.'

'Well, she was right.'

'What are you talking about? What do you mean? Of course you're not Jack. What on earth is wrong with you? I don't understand. Stop it now.'

'Anna, you really have to listen to what I am about to tell you. Will you sit down with me and let me talk, please. I have to try and explain what happened.'

So I began. 'When we both joined up we decided we would change places. So we did just that. We changed places.'

'What do you mean you changed places? How could you *change* places? Jack is God knows where, and you are here, that's a fact.'

'The trouble is Anna, it's not a fact. It's a lie. God this is difficult. Will you let me talk?'

'Okay.' She put her hands up in surrender. 'Okay I won't say a word, I promise. But I know you are talking complete and utter rubbish, and you're really upsetting me George.'

'Please don't look so panic stricken. It's not the end of the world. Well not really.'

'Alright, I'm listening, I'm listening.'

So I started to tell her the whole story. From the day we decided to change places, until the day George joined up; supposedly as me. When I had finished she looked at me in complete bewilderment. She was so pale. Her eyes black in her face,

'It's all a lie. I don't believe a word of it. You are playing some silly prank on me. But why?'

'It's all true Anna, I promise.' I started to shout at her.

'Stop shouting at me.' She cried. 'What's wrong with you, you're scaring me.'

'You have to believe me. Everything I told you is the truth.'

'You can't prove it. Anyway who else have you told?'

'Henry. He promised to tell no one. Not even Mary. Other than that. No one.'

'Prove it. Show me some proof, go on.' She was angry now. She started to shout too. 'Tell me. Go on. You can't can you.'

'I *can* prove it.' I took her hands in mine. They were ice cold.

She pulled away from me her eyes flashing. 'Don't touch me. Don't you dare touch me!'

I dropped her hands and looked at her. 'When you *"thought talked"* Jack, it was me you spoke to. You told me you loved me. You missed me.

I answered and said I love you too. I said I was near to you, really near. Then I leant out and stroked your cheek. You were just a vague apparition but I could see you. I touched you and you felt it. Now tell me I'm lying'!

She was crying now, hysterically. Screaming at me.' How do you know that? You can't know that. I was talking to Jack not you. You're lying, lying. I don't understand, I don't understand. Why would you pretend to be George Why. Why? You would have told me. Jack would have told me. You would have told me. Oh God I can't think straight anymore, it's like a bad dream. I can't believe you.'

'You have to.' I said. 'What I have just told you is all true. I wish to God it wasn't. I had no intention of hurting you. Have you any idea how many times I have nearly told you? I wish now I had never done any of it.'

I was exhausted. Worn out by it all. By what I had done to my girl. I felt as though something terrible had just happened. How the hell was I to turn it round? It was too late. Far too late. The damage was done.

Anna stared at me. Tears raining down her face. 'Go away, I hate you I hate you. If what you say is true. It's unbelievable. How could you lie to me all this time? How you must have been laughing at me, when I was telling you how much I loved you. How much I missed you. And all the while you must have really been enjoying yourself. How big is your ego now! God I never want to see you again. Never. Never. Ever.' She sunk down on to the grass her head in her hands. 'Go, go. Go away.' Her voice muffled, full of anguish. I went to touch her, but drawing my hand away I walked slowly up the garden.

Chapter 48

Anna

Today I want to die.

Yesterday I was drawing by the river. It was about six in the evening. The light was perfect, laying across the river where a family if moorhens swam contentedly up and down, the chicks trying desperately to keep up with their mother. They were so adorable like little black question marks. I managed to do a quick watercolour of them and was relatively pleased with the result. Then I decided to go and lie down in the gazebo, before supper. I was tired.

Earlier, on duty, I had spent most of the day dashing here and there in the ambulance. There had been another bad raid the night before. I had spent the day dishing out tea and sympathy to people. It had been pretty awful. I was glad to get home and try and relax. That is when I decided to try and '*talk*' to Jack. And for some extraordinary reason, I actually contacted him. It was wonderful, I heard his voice and I am sure he touched my cheek. I must have slept for a while afterwards. When I woke I was so excited I had to talk to George.

He wasn't at home, so I went to the Vicarage, hoping he would be there. But no. Only Mary was there. In a state, her waters had broken!! After that everything happened at great speed. I found Henry and George in the pub. We took Mary to the nursing home. Then later that night little Roberta was born. Such an amazing night. But now I have to deal with the dreadful afternoon I had with George.

It was a couple of days later and he arrived in the garden which made me happy, until suddenly right out of the blue he dropped the biggest bombshell ever. I still can't believe it all happened. It was like a bad dream. It still is.

Now I don't know what to do. How can I go on as normal, knowing that all this time George has been Jack? It doesn't seem possible. I don't know which way to turn. No one knows other than Henry, and no way can I burden Mary with it all, while she is coping with a tiny baby. It's all too awful. I feel as though I am going slightly mad.

Tomorrow is Amy's wedding to Shane. I am maid of honour, so I have to be there. But Jack will be there. Oh God what to do? It is a complete and utter nightmare.

Chapter 49

The ceremony took place in a registry office like most war weddings. There was to be a reception afterwards, at Mary's house. It was a small wedding. Just family, plus a few friends of the young couple. A lot of eyebrows had been raised, by many of the guests. '*Fancy wanting to marry a black man and an American one too.*' Was the most usual comment, but when they met Shane he turned that on its head. He was charm personified and he obviously adored his bride. His parents and siblings had managed to fly over for the wedding, no one knew how, as most flights were banned, but his father a wealthy senator had pulled a few strings, so there they were to see their son get married. His mother was Irish, with the reddest hair Anne had ever seen. Her skin as white as milk and her eyes as blue as Amy's. Shane's two sisters were much younger and giggled a lot, they reminded Anna of Victoria and Elizabeth.

Amy looked beautiful, she wore a cream silk suit, with a pencil skirt and a tight jacket, flared at the waist. With her hair hanging lose around her shoulders, and a tiny cloche hat covered in seed pearls, she looked delightful.

Anna, dressed in a pale green silk shift dress with a matching bolero around her shoulders, her hair entwined with tiny white flowers looked exquisite. But oh how sick she felt. How on earth, she thought, can I get through the day, with Jack at my elbow most of the time. It was crazy. But for Amy's sake she had to carry it through.

Harry in his white dress suit, looked handsome as ever, and was being sweet and kind to her.

I know, she thought. I will marry Harry and disappear into the depths of America, and forget all this. She had drunk far too much champagne, and was determined to drink a lot more. She knew she was behaving like a spoilt child, but why not she thought. The idea that maybe she was going slightly mad flashed through her mind. But it would really spite Jack, and serve him right. She had overheard a guest saying, how lovely the maid of honour looked, and would she be the next GI bride? Why not? Harry was rich, handsome, kind. We would have a good life, even though it would be in a strange land. But somehow that seemed of little consequence. Things couldn't get much worse, could they? She almost laughed out loud. Deciding there and then, that she would make the day as perfect as she possibly could. Seeing a waiter walk by, with a tray of champagne glasses, she picked one up casually and knocked it back in one.

Mary and Henry were there, along with a tiny Roberta wrapped in a white shawl. Her eyes wide, with a thumb jammed into her tiny mouth. She turned out to be the star of the show, without doing anything, except being completely adorable.

As for Jack, he was glad enough to be around Anna, but didn't know how to behave after that dreadful afternoon. Every time he turned round she was hanging onto Harry for dear life. But he behaved like a gentleman and was charm personified towards the American. However, he did feet slightly sick as well. He had drunk two large whiskies before he had left home, hoping for some Dutch courage. Which even so, seemed still to be lacking.

During the reception the sirens sounded. So everyone trooped downstairs to the cellar, where tables were laid in anticipation of an air raid. The caterers were well used to having to move people to safety during celebrations. Candles were ablaze everywhere. Flowers were bought down from upstairs. Food was transported to the makeshift kitchen and the whole wedding party celebrated in style. Somehow being in the candle lit cellar romanticised it all, while everyone tried to ignore the heavy sounds echoing around outside.

Harry was more attentive than Anna had ever seen him. He danced with her almost all night. Shane butting in to dance with her said she should be the next GI bride! She laughed, but it had been such a wonderful happy occasion, and seeing Amy glowing with such joy upon her pretty face, made Anna wonder what life in America would be like, once this war was over. A little seed had been planted in her brain, which would settle there quite comfortably, for a while.

Dancing with Harry, Anna's thoughts kept flashing back to the dreadful day with Jack. She'd had far too much champagne. The evening had taken on hazy rosy glow. She cuddled up to Harry, and let the sound of the big band transport her away from it all.

She giggled. 'What's so funny?' Harry held her away from him. She looked stunning as always. Flushed and happy, her eyes, dark pools sparkled like stars

'Nothing. Just happy, too much champers I guess. I was wondering actually, what it would be like to be married to you!'

'Hang on there, honey. You don't want to marry a guy like me, anyway who mentioned marriage?'

'Just me.' She giggled again. 'I think we should be married like Amy and Shane, and you can carry me away as your GI bride!'

'I thought you were in love with Jack.'

'Not any more. That's all over. I'm all yours as they say.' And she laid her head against his chest.

'Look here Anna. I think you are a wonderful girl and all that. But marriage is not on the cards.,' he stuttered slightly. 'I-I s-s- suppose it is time to be honest with you. I am already married!'

She went cold all over and pulled away from him. 'You are joking aren't you? Tell me you are.'

'Fraid not. I just thought we were having a good time together. A little wartime romance. Nothing serious. I knew Jack was on the agenda the whole time. I guessed you thought the same.'

'How could you? Telling me you loved me. Talking of us going away for a weekend on your next leave. All this meant nothing?'

'Look Honey. You are beautiful. I love having you on my arm, making all the other guys jealous. I thought we were so good together. Anyway what's this about Jack? How come he's not in the picture anymore?'

'Too complicated.' She whispered. 'And you have made me feel a complete and utter fool.'

She tore herself away from him. And ran towards the cellar stairs.

'Anna, what the hell are you doing? Listen to the racket outside. Stay here. It is too dangerous the bombing is too near. Listen, can't you hear it?'

'I don't care. I want to die anyway. I can't bear any more. I can't'

People had stopped dancing, and were watching the little scene with interest.

Suddenly. There was an enormous explosion.

Amy's mother's hand flew to her mouth. 'Oh myGod it's the house, it's been hit.'

Her husband started towards the stairs.

Jack went to pull him back. 'There's nothing you can do. It is too dangerous to leave the cellar. Listen to it out there.'

There was another violent crashing above them. The band kept on playing, as people drifted towards the cellar steps, listening to the chaos beyond. Amy started to cry. Shane putting his arm around her led her back into the room. He sat with her, holding her hand, while the very walls shook around them.

Anna had fallen back into the shadows as the noise reigned overhead. '*I have to get out of this.*' She cried to herself. '*I can't stay here. I just can't.*' And as people moved back on to the dance floor, she started slowly to walk up the cellar steps towards the door leading into the hallway. Jack saw her. Racing up behind her he grabbed hold of her arm.

'What the hell are you doing? For Christ's sake come here.'

She shook him off.' Go away. I would rather die than stay here with you and Harry!'

'Harry. What the hell has he got to do with it?'

'Everything!' She screamed at him. And flinging open the door, she walked into hell.

Chapter 50

That night, as Anna lay unconscious in the hospital, the family stood around the bed. Evelyn and Teddy sitting either side of her, holding her hands. Jack with the surgeon, talking quietly together. Her sisters sat on a chair together. Elizabeth, her thumb in her mouth, looking bewildered, while Victoria was trying not to cry, watching her elder sister lying so white and so still. She is obviously dead, she thought. It was horrible. She hated this war. Two of her friends had been killed last week, along with their parents, when their house took a direct hit. She was frightened to death and could feel herself trembling. She took hold of Elizabeth's hand and squeezed it as tight as she could. They looked at each other. Elizabeth laid her head on her sister's shoulder.

'Well George.' The surgeon sighed.' We can do no more. We just have to hope and pray the damage to her brain is minimal. Her vital signs seem pretty good. Trouble is we won't know anything, until she wakes up.'

'If she does.' Thought Jack. 'God what a nightmare. My girl unconscious, in a coma and probably I am to blame for it all. Fucking hell. Why didn't I keep my bloody mouth shut?'

The whole scenario flashed in front of him. Every single minute embedded in his mind. The door opening. The inferno roaring in front of him. A great gaping hole where the hallway had been. The noise echoing through his head. The slow motion of Anna walking into the jaws of it all. The sound of something falling, crashing. And Anna's scream. Then there were Harry and Shane, pulling Anna clear of the beam that lay across her head.

Jack picked her up. Her clothes were singed, but otherwise she seemed to have missed the worst of the fire. Slamming the door behind him, the three men walked slowly down into the cellar, where everyone stood still and silent.

Jack laid her gently down on the floor. She was so still. Her face as white as chalk. A great gash across her forehead poured blood. There was, as in all 'shelters,' the usual first aid box. So basic, but there was Dettol and bandages and the inevitable aspirin. He poured some disinfectant over the head wound, then grabbing a large white serviette, of a table, he laid it over the gaping wound. It was imperative she got crucial medical care immediately. The whole scenario was turning into nightmare. It was up to him to sort it out.

Amy's father was watching as Anna was laid down. 'George, there is another smaller cellar which is never used. I don't know if we can even open the door. Also I have no idea where it actually leads, somewhere outside obviously but where, I don't know. There is a stretcher in the cupboard over there. I bought it in case of an emergency.' He gave a dry bitter laugh,

The door was tiny, just big enough for a man to squeeze through. The wood appeared to be rotten. A huge rusty ring hung heavily against it. Jack turned the ring. It hardly moved. It was completely corroded. He tried again and felt some movement. Then using every ounce of strength he had, he turned it and the door creaked open. By some miracle it opened onto the road, via steep stone steps. At the top he could see daylight, and hear the sound of fire engines and ambulances, and over it all the sound of bombs falling. It would be madness to go out. But there was no option.

'I'm coming with you to carry the stretcher.' It was Harry. 'I blame myself for this disaster .I said unkind things to Anna. Things I should never have said. That is why she ran away into the house.'

'Harry, I think you will find I had a lot to do with it too. We will both go, come on and be careful. She is precious cargo.'

They both looked at each other. Harry gave a wry smile. 'You bet she is.'

Everyone stood aside as the men manoeuvred the stretcher through the doorway. Crouching down they squeezed through. Out into the maelstrom of the night.

Reaching the top of the steps, they looked at each other.

'The hospital is a bit of a schlep.' Jack said. 'Best to start walking and hope we can get a lift. Keep away from the buildings, walk down the middle of the road, it will be safer and there is no traffic to speak of.'

So they walked, as the sound of chaos reigned around them. Fires burning everywhere. People standing in the streets. Firemen battling with the flames. While WVS girls dished out the inevitable tea to all and sundry. Then Jack saw an ambulance, idling by the side of the road. He banged on the driver's window. A young WVS girl lay with her head back against the seat. Smoking, with her eyes closed.

She jumped at the sound and sat up. 'Oh it's you George. I was just going off duty.' She looked at the stretcher. The girl lying motionless. 'Oh my God, it's Anna. What happened?'

Arriving at the hospital they were met with complete and utter mayhem. Ambulances were arriving. People swarming about everywhere. Walking injured were being admitted. Children were crying. Stretchers were being taken out of ambulances, while nurses ran around trying to make some sort of order out of it all.

Jack and Harry wove their way through the bedlam, to an operating room. It was empty. Lifting Anna carefully onto the table Jack bent over her she was still. So white. The horror of it all hit him. All the months he had been researching brain damage. And here maybe he had the real thing. It didn't bear thinking about.

Anna was transferred to intensive care. There she was hooked up to machines, to help her breathe, monitor her blood pressure and check all physical functions. Seeing her lying there broken and comatosed Jack could hardly bear it. He blamed himself completely. The idea of what he had done was killing him.

'George. I am afraid there is bleeding on the brain which is severe, according to the last cerebral imaging. But it is difficult to see a lot. I just wish the machines were more sophisticated. Maybe one day.' The surgeon shrugged. 'She will need to be monitored closely, a nurse will be with her all the time. Also she needs to have her family around her, as much as possible, to talk to her. But then you know all this, so I will leave her in your good hands. I think we all need to pray. She is a very sick girl. Very sick indeed.' He sighed and walked slowly out of the room.

That night, as the hours tick by, Jack sits with her, while her mother and father watch over their daughter in despair. Evelyn, with tears flooding her face, holds Anna's hand and whispers gently to her. Teddy looks completely bewildered and wretched. He chain smokes, pacing up and down like a caged animal.

He plies Jack with questions. 'Why did she run into the house? What for, there must have been a reason. It was complete madness. She would never do anything like that. Did she have an argument with someone? What about Harry. Does he have something to do with it? He seemed to monopolise her the whole afternoon. God I'll kill him for what he has done to our child.'

Jack laying his hand on his shoulder, says it was nothing to with Harry. He really didn't know what had happened. Was she really trying to kill herself he thought?

Evelyn stayed with Anna around the clock. A makeshift cot was bought in for her. Teddy went home to look after the girls, who were traumatised by it all. They had held Anna's hand, kissed her pale cheeks and cried, looking helplessly at their big sister. They seemed rather glad, when their father took them by the hand, and lead them back to the normality of their home.

Jack was with her when he wasn't at the surgery He felt urgently near to confessing to Evelyn and Teddy, the whole sordid story. But something stopped him, they had enough to cope with as it was. And what possible good could it do.

His father was with the surgeon, in deep discussion with him, while Jack listened in, hanging onto every word. Having researched coma, he felt he knew enough without being a real doctor. Another brain scan had been taken and it seemed to be much the same. There was no change.

Amy came and sat with her. She talked of the wedding and where they were going on honeymoon. She was trying to keep everything as positive and light-hearted as possible.

Mary talked to her of the baby's progress. How she had just started to smile. She played Anna's favourite Glen Miller music, on a creaky old record player, lent by one of the nurses.

Henry came and prayed by her bedside.

Anna just lay there. What could she hear, feel? Wondered Jack. Hopefully some words, some sounds would reach her. There was nothing now to do, but hope.

During the early hours of the morning, while Evelyn slept restlessly, Jack talked with the surgeon. More cerebral images had been taken, showing the bleeding had worsened. Also, there was more swelling on the brain. Anna seemed to be falling into even a deeper coma.

'George.' The surgeon talked quietly to him, as he held Anna's hand. 'This is not good. The bleeding is more severe. We may have to operate, which I do not want to do, it is really too dangerous.'

'Oh God, is there nothing we can do?' Jack looked down at his girl's white face. With tubes and wires attached to her, she seemed so alien to him. As though she was no longer the girl he knew and loved. Just an empty shell. 'She's dying.' He whispered to himself. 'She's slipping away. It can't happen. She can't die. Somehow this has to be turned around.' The sound of the respirator jangled on his nerves. He felt completely at a loss. He did not know what to do. 'Please God don't let her die. I know I don't believe in you, but if you are there, take me not her,' He felt as though he was choking. Turning away he walked over to the window. Dawn was just breaking.

All through the long night he stayed with her while Evelyn sat holding her hand. They sat together and talked to her of everything and anything. Jack needed to be careful. He knew he had to be George, so he trod carefully, not to say anything untoward. He had thought of reading a favourite book of Anna's, but he knew that George probably wouldn't know of it. So he suggested to Evelyn that they played some of her favourite music. She loved Glen Miller's *String of Pearls*, so that was played quietly. The record was a bit scratched and the needle rather blunt. Even so he thought, the familiar sound may reach her. Who knows if she can hear anything, or is her brain shutting down as we sit here. It was a terrible thing to think of. He tried to keep as cheerful as he could for Evelyn's sake, who, it seemed to Jack, was breaking down under the strain of it all.

Teddy had come in on the way to work and was horrified to see how his daughter had deteriorated. 'She is so still, so white. Shouldn't she start to come out of her coma soon?' He sounded like a lost child, frightened to death. Putting his arms around his wife, he looked helplessly at her.

Jack went outside in the corridor for a cigarette, to try and gather his senses together, to give Teddy and Evelyn some privacy. He had to seem to be less stressed about it all, Remembering, first of all that he is George, so whatever happens he mustn't show his true feelings. That, he was finding extremely hard.

The surgeon came out and joined him for a smoke. 'Well George looks like things are pretty bad. We need to have another look to see how things are. Whether or not I need to operate, I am worried that her brain activity is slowing down. It seems to me she is in a deeper comatosed state than before. Can you talk to her parents? It may be better coming from you. Just make it as positive as you can, if that is possible.' He rubbed his hands across his face, and looked at Jack. 'You know at times like this, I really wish I had chosen a different path in life. Seeing a young life slipping away, never gets any easier. Never.' He sighed, dropped his cigarette into a bucket of sand, already full of stub ends, then walked wearily back into Anna's room.

The next day another cerebral image was taken. The surgeon called Jack into his office.

'George the news is bad. I think Anna is falling into a vegetative state. There appears to be little activity in her brain. The images are not very clear, but what I and my team see, is not good. I think her parents must be told. As I think, the kindest thing to do for this young lady, is to turn off her life support. If she is brain dead then there is nothing we can do. She will be a vegetable. I hate to be crude, but that is the truth of the matter.'

'Dear God.' Jack put his head in his hands. 'Are you sure? Can't you operate?'

'No. It's too late for that. I am so very sorry. Can you speak to her parents?'

''Of course, just leave this with me for a while, I need to think how to approach them.'

'When you are ready let the nurse know, and she will page me.' Putting his hand gently on Jack's shoulder, he left him.

Jack stood there. He felt numb. 'This can't be true.' He kept thinking. 'It can't be true. What have I done?' He sat down heavily in a leather armchair. He was exhausted. How can I let this happen to Anna? The only girl I have ever, or ever will love. I have to bring her back from wherever she is. I have to.' He was too tired to think straight. He laid his head back on the chair and shut his eyes. Suddenly, he jumped up and walked over to the window. It was pouring with rain. Looking down at the car park, he saw it was almost empty. No one could afford to run cars now. Instead there seemed to be hundreds of bicycles, tied to the railings that ran around the hospital.

'I have to try and '*Talk*' to Anna, it is the last chance.' He whispered to himself. 'But will it work? She '*talked*' to me once, but that was a fluke, I am sure.' He walked around the room. Lit a cigarette and stood looking out. The rain lashed against the windows. The whole car park was awash. Turning away he sat down heavily in the chair. He closed his eyes. 'Listen to me Anna. It's Jack. I am here to bring you back, from wherever you are. You must listen. Remember us together before the war, when we were so happy, so in love. Remember the times in each other's arms? I love you so much. You can't leave now. There are too many other people who love you too. Please come back. Please.'

He sat there but there was nothing, nothing at all, he tried again and again but still nothing. He closed his eyes, it was no good, suddenly there was a stirring in the room. He opened his eyes. 'Yes, yes. There is something.' He strained to see. In the corner, by the window, was a quivering of light, with a shape in the middle,

337

like a golden star, which shimmered against the rain falling outside.

'Anna can you hear me? Please come back. I am here waiting for you. We are all waiting for you.' He could hear his voice breaking. The tears threatening to fall. 'Pease don't go away. Stay here with us. We all need you. Your little sisters, Bertie, your mother your father. You can't go you have to stay. Do you hear me? You have to stay with us.' There was a movement in the corner and he could see her face. It was just a shadow, but he could see her eyes and her long dark hair against her pale cheeks. 'Jack, Jack, is that you? What do you want, I am tired I need to sleep, please let me sleep, I am so very tired.'

'No you have to wake up, I am here waiting for you, can you see me, look hard I am here waiting for you, you have to wake now, now do you hear me, you have to wake now.' He was almost shouting.

Then there was a great gust of wind and the room was empty.

Chapter 51

Jack walked wearily back into Anna's room. Evelyn was sitting there reading her some poetry by WB Yeats. A poet she loved, often he would read his work to her when she was painting.

'His poetry makes me feel at peace somehow,' she would say and smile, that enigmatic smile of hers.

The nurse was reading on a chair in the corner, the sound of the respirator sounded in the silence. Nothing had changed. 'I suppose I expected to come back and find my darling girl was waking up,' he thought wearily. Sitting down opposite Evelyn he leant over and touched her hand. 'How are you doing? You look exhausted, why don't you try and rest while I sit with her.'

Evelyn looked up at him. 'No I am happy here, just reading her some Yeats, I thought it may help.' She reached out and took her daughter's cool hand in hers and stroked the fingers and sighed to herself. 'If only there would be some sign of life just a movement, anything that would give me hope, it is so hard just sitting, sitting and waiting.'

People were there all that day, talking to Anna, playing her music, reading to her or just telling her about everyday things, but there was no response. It was into the fifth day since the accident and Evelyn was getting desperate. She was sleeping on the cot every night and was more tired than she thought was possible.

'Please don't take her God, not like you took my babies, not again, I can't bear it, please, please bring her back to us, please.' She felt the hot tears welling up in her eyes, she brushed them away and went on reading to Anna..

Jack was there talking to the nurse who was changing a drip. Evelyn was amazed how he seemed to be there all the time, so good of him, she thought, it was almost as if it was Jack not George that sat with her. He seemed so concerned, but she realised that it was his way of standing in for Jack and being a doctor he would know exactly what was going on. There was no sound, just, the thump, thump of the respirator which felt as it was cutting right through her.

She must have dropped off when something woke her. Arching her back, she stretched, then looked down at Anna's hand. The fingers were moving, that's what must have woken me! She waited in case she had imagined it. But no, there it was again a definite movement, her fingers *were* moving, she could feel them against the palm of her hand.

'George come here hurry up, it's, her fingers, she moved her fingers I am sure of it, look they moved again, she moved her fingers!' Her eyes were wide with wonder. 'What does it mean, does it mean she's waking up? Please say it is, please.'

Bending over Jack listened to her strenuous breathing, nothing seemed to have changed. But then he watched her hands, the hand Evelyn held was still but the other one was clutching at the blanket, clutching and unclutching it. Then all at once she started to talk. Her voice was very quiet, but it wasn't Anna talking it was a childish voice and she was crying, fat tears running down the sides of her face. 'Tell Mama I don't want to go, tell her I have to, but I don't want to, I have to go with Michael.'

Evelyn looked at Jack then at Anna, 'She's waking up isn't she, isn't she?' Her eyes pleaded with him. 'What's she saying, why does she sound like that?'

'Evelyn, I don't know, let me listen.' He leant over her and watched as she started to talk again like a child. 'What is it Anna can you hear me? Who's that talking, who are you?'

Then the childlike voice again. 'William, I'm William. Mama, Michael is waiting for me I have to go too, don't cry anymore Mama, it's alright but I must go, I'm so sorry....' Her voice trailed away.

Evelyn took hold of her daughter's hand, she was ashen and her hands were trembling.

'Evelyn,' said Jack, 'do you know what she's talking about? Who's William, who's Michael?'

'I don't understand,' she whispered, 'they were my babies, they died at birth, they were twins, no one ever knew their names, not even Teddy, no one knew. I named them secretly just before they took them away from me.'

'Evelyn, do you believe in re-incarnation? Well I know Anna does, we talked of it a lot the three of us, Jack especially, I think that is what this is all about. Anna is talking and is living through your son, through his soul, I don't really know a lot about it but what I read sounds much like all this. I wish I could tell you more but I can't. If I am right it is a wonderful thing to have happened. When she wakes maybe we will learn more.'

He watched Anna's face there was a sweet smile playing around her lips, slowly her eyes opened, she looked at her mother. 'Mama? I was dreaming, I was so happy, so very happy,' she looked around her, 'I don't understand; what am I doing here, what's going on?' She tried to sit up, but was too weak and laying her head wearily on her pillow she closed her eyes, but the smile was still there.

Chapter 52

Jack

That evening, Anna finally emerged from her coma, she was disorientated, confused and very tired. Slowly and gently the surgeon talked to her and explained what had happened, but she seemed not to understand, so he patted her hand and smiled. 'You rest now and I'll come back later.'

I spoke to her quietly after he had left, she was propped up by pillows with her black hair like a dark star all around her, her eyes deep in her pale face, the wound on her head an ugly mark against the whiteness of her skin. She looked so fragile, so broken, and it was all my doing, but whatever happened I had to know what she could remember.

'Anna,' I spoke softly, 'what is the last thing you can recall? Do you remember coming to see me about '*talking*' to Jack, how excited you were?'

'Oh yes, of course, I ' *'thought talked'* him and rushed to tell you all about it but it was the night the baby was born and I had to tell you later. 'I remember how you said that love conquered all and that is why I managed to contact him, I felt so happy and so sad at the same time'

'Do you remember how I spoke to you and how upset you got?'

'No, why what happened? Why was I upset, why on earth would you upset me George, what for, tell me?'

'Oh it was nothing, just some stupid misunderstanding, not worth talking about. So you don't remember the wedding?'

'What wedding, oh, gosh, Amy's wedding of course. Oh God, she got married and I have no recollection of it all, that is terrible. What's wrong with me?'

'It's nothing, shh, don't worry about it. Amnesia is common after a head injury and you were in a coma for five days. Things will come back to you slowly, now you must rest, that is the best medicine ever, and you will be back to normal in no time at all. We have to thank God you are out of the woods, now it is just a matter of time.' I smiled at her and kissed her cool cheek, she took hold of my hand.

'Dear George, you are so kind to me, thank you for everything you have done while Jack has been away. I don't think I could have coped without you,' and closing her eyes she slept.

I closed my eyes too and sighed. 'What have I done, what have I done?'

The next day Anna was able to sit propped up in bed, the tubes had all but disappeared and she seemed more lucid, but still could remember nothing after my bloody stupid confession, God how I wish I had kept my mouth shut then none of this would have happened. All I could think of was what I had done to the only girl I had ever loved and would ever love. I felt like a criminal.

I sat with her and we talked of what had happened. She said she was frightened not being able to remember. Half of me never wanted her to, as somehow it was almost a relief that for some reason that awful afternoon had been erased from her mind. Then I wondered what would happen once it all came flooding back to her. We would both have to go through the same dreadful scenario all over again!

The neurologist came and examined Anne, he talked with her and reassured her that gradually her memory loss would return. He asked her if there had been any trauma before the accident that could have caused the amnesia but she assured him that everything had been fine. That she had been looking forward to the wedding, choosing her outfit with Amy and working on a painting of a Heron that had visited her a few days before that. Otherwise all was good. She did admit that the bombing frightened her terribly and she had nightmares about it but had always kept it to herself, feeling childish that it affected her so much. He asked her if she had

had any arguments with anyone, none she said, or if she had she couldn't remember.

So the days went on. Anna went to a convalescent home near the hospital where she rested and slept and was monitored all the time. When I went to visit her she told me of hearing Jack talking to her, telling her to come back, she said it was all a blur but she is sure it was him talking to her, or had she dreamt it all? She looked worried so I didn't say much and told her to not think too much about it. But I just thanked whoever it was for bringing my girl back from the abyss she had been falling into. It was a wonder to me that the ' *'thought talk''* had worked. It made me realise that something else was going on that we didn't understand and maybe never would. I likened it to a miracle but never mentioned it to anyone, except years later when I talked of it with Anna.

She left the home after two weeks and her life appeared to return to normal, other than the memory loss. I lived on tenterhooks, waiting for her to arrive on my doorstep and confront me with it all once again.

Harry came and visited her when she was home. Having no recollection of the wedding and their argument she was sweet and charming with him. He looked a bit sheepish I must admit and arrived with the biggest bouquet of flowers I think I have ever seen.

That evening after we had left Anna, he confessed to me that he had lied to her saying he was married. 'I panicked, like a bloody stupid guy I am, and she nearly died and it was all my fault.' He had sat there with his head in his hands. I actually felt sorry for the poor chap and was very tempted to tell him about everything but stopped as it would be just appeasing myself and would probably make things worse. I did feel sorry for the poor sod even so.

Three weeks after the accident Anna still hadn't regained her memory. The surgeon said he was somewhat surprised and was convinced that there had been some pivotal moment before the accident. That something had caused her to erase everything from her consciousness. God I felt dreadful, but what the hell was I to do? It was a torment and I lived with it and fought with it, but did nothing except to talk to Henry. Poor Henry how fed up he must have been with my 'confessions.' He sat and listened like the good priest he was and never condemned me, which I honestly deserved. However the surgeon was pleased with her progress and said there was no lasting damage to her brain. She had a lovely scar though above her left eyebrow, which bothered her more than losing her memory, or so she said.

Chapter 53

Anna

It has been just over two months since my accident and still I have no memory of it, no recollection of the wedding, which is sad because everyone said it was wonderful. Even celebrating in the cellar turned out apparently to be fun, until I spoilt it all by causing havoc. Oh how I wish I could remember. I lie in bed at night and concentrate as hard as I can but there is nothing. It is really rather scary to be quite honest, that great void in my memory. Will it ever come back? Did something awful happen like the surgeon suggested?   But if so what possibly could have occurred, if it was so dreadful surely I would remember it. I am convinced there was nothing, in fact I am a hundred percent sure.

I know that George came to see me a few days after Roberta was born that's when I told him of my ''*thought talk*'' with Jack. If there had been anything amiss I just know I would remember, anyhow what could he have possibly said to upset me?   Dear George, he has been my rock with Jack away. He is too good and kind to have a bad thought in his body, I am quite sure of that.

I do think a lot about when I was in a coma, how I thought I heard Jack telling me to come back. It is all very muddled but it was if he was pulling me away from something. I remember it being very dark where the other voice came from and where there was Jack's voice it was bright sunlight and I felt drawn towards it, as though there was a fine thread attached to me, urging me towards the light.

Also, what really I can't explain is feeling like someone else. When I got to the light I could hear another voice calling me. *'Come with me,'* it kept saying. I knew it was someone I loved as I started to walk towards the sound. Then I could hear and feel Jack willing me to follow him. It was frightening and I felt as though I was being torn apart. Then the childlike voice became quieter and more distant, then disappeared completely, while Jack's voice urged me towards the light. I will never understand what happened.

The surgeon told me I had been dying. He was completely baffled how I came out of such a deep coma where my brain activity seemed to be zero. He laughed and said he needed to re train as it was a complete mystery to him. 'Almost like a miracle,' I heard him say quietly to himself.

I have finished the painting of the Heron and am very pleased with it, I had it framed and gave it to George. He didn't want to accept it, saying it was too fine a work to just give away - which made me giggle - and that I should sell it and make a nice big killing. But I insisted. He said he would treasure it forever, he is so funny sometimes. How he reminds me of my darling Jack. Oh how I want to see my man and let him hold me again. I have to admit that sometimes I find it difficult to visualise his face and I keep seeing George's face instead, but then they are so alike, maybe that isn't surprising.

One sunny afternoon Mama came and sat with me in the garden. I must say I am frustrated at doing nothing worthwhile, not being able to work with the WVS at the moment or doing anything strenuous. Both George, his father and my neurologist have forbidden me which is very annoying, so I am painting a lot and reading. I have just discovered Flaubert's Madame Bovary, it makes me cry. I feel a bit like her sometimes; a woman in love and in a terrible muddle.

I still get very tired and seem to drop off at a moment's notice. Apparently that is par for the course and I am not to worry.

Mama and I sat on the old tartan rug by the river having tea, it was a perfect late autumn day and the river was full of activity, but no heron this time.

'Anna, do you remember, before you regained consciousness you were dreaming of being a child?'

Suddenly Mama mentioning '*my dream*' brought everything flooding back again. I had tried not to think of it too much as it made me feel so sad and I always felt like crying. I think I was a child again, maybe even a baby, I am not sure but I know a voice kept calling me. I could hear the sound of gentle crying. There were warm arms holding me. I was wrapped in something soft and the feeling of complete and utter happiness mixed with a great sadness was overwhelming. Everywhere was suffused in a golden light and there was a sound, not music, but a sensation of a gentle noise that made me feel wonderful. I can't explain really.

When I told this to Mama, she looked at me and held my hand, looking deep into my eyes. Her eyes are dark, almost navy blue. Papa always said he fell in love with her eyes before he decided that he loved the rest of her too. 'Do you remember if you were a boy or a girl, what can you remember? It is important my darling.'

'I know I was a boy, how I don't know, I can't see myself, but I am sure I had white blonde hair and my name was William and someone kept calling me to go with them. I think it was another boy called Michael but I don't know; what I do know is that it was all so wonderful. I think Paradise would be like that, feel like that, if there is such a thing.'

Mama looked at me, her eyes were full of tears. She held my hand and she started to tell me the story of how she had given birth to twins, I knew vaguely that they had died but it was never ever discussed, and she had never told anyone there names not even Papa, she had named them before they were taken from her; when she had to let them go.. She thought what had happened to me was a kind of miracle.

She said George had wondered that maybe I could perhaps be the reincarnation of William. I found this incredible but even so I sort of believed it. I have always thought I would like to follow the Buddhist's faith, it such a gentle belief and reincarnation lies at the very heart of it all, so to me it was quite feasible. I think maybe that is what did happen. I really rather hope it had. Mama said she had discussed it with George who said it sounded like a re-living. But no one can ever be sure, the spirit world is such an enigma to us all and we can't hope to explain strange happenings. We just need to accept that we are only humans and probably know very little about things that we can't explain. And probably never will.

After Mama told me about the babies, I realised that maybe that is why sometimes I would see her sitting or standing looking inwards, her eyes full of sorrow. Now I understand. Poor Mama, so long to have held such sadness inside herself for all this time. But she said my 'dream' had made her feel full of hope that her babies are at peace. Now she can be too. It was lovely to see her face light up when she talked. Holding me close we both sat with each other listening to birdsong, the gentle sound of the river; the sounds of a kind of contentment.

Chapter 54

Jack

Harry and I went to the local for a drink, something I never thought would happen again after he tried to steal my girl from me. But as he actually thought I was George, I felt I had to talk to him as the poor chap was convinced that Anna nearly died because of him, so I had to put things to rights. I don't think I will tell him about us boys and the switch as he is hardly a confidant. But even so I need to offer some explanation, and as we are both in love with the same girl we do have something, however tenuous, in common.

We met in the bar, it was quite late as surgery had gone on and on, in the end father told me to disappear as I looked exhausted.

The place was heaving, it was a Friday and pay slips were being spent in the only appropriate way for single young men at the end of the week. Cigarette and cigar smoke hung like a sea mist over us all, it was extremely noisy.

Most of the talk was of the raids that had hit London. The night of Amy's wedding was one of the worst, It had gone on from late afternoon until almost dawn. People had heard about Anna and were keen to talk to me and buy me pints, so Harry and I got happily drunk that night. I told him that Anna and I'd had a quarrel about Jack and she had got upset. That it was more than likely to be my fault, and he was probably just the tipping point that sent Anna over the edge. I said no more and he asked for no more information.

That night two rather stupid young men sat and talked of the war, America, England, Jack coming back, my research, hardly talking of Anna except Harry thinking he should tell her the truth, which I agreed would be the right thing to do. Rather hoping he wouldn't to be honest. I didn't want her falling in love with this handsome American soldier. Also I had to wait until she regained her memory then I would worry about the outcome. But now I just wanted my darling girl back.

She had been seeing a psychiatrist, Muriel, who worked alongside the neurological team. Anna had told her that she kept getting little flashes of something but nothing really. She said she felt sure that something was happening and that all would be revealed. That sent me into a panic yet again. 'I want to be able to remember the wedding George, to see Amy get married. I am so sad I seem to have missed it all somehow, so I will keep trying!' She shrugged her pretty shoulders and smiled at me. 'I will remember George, I promise, I have a feeling it won't be long now.'

I decided that I had to talk to Henry, he kept me sane somehow while all this 'stuff' was going on. I picked Anna up that Sunday afternoon and we walked along the river to the vicarage. It was a glorious sunny day, autumn was coming to an end and the trees that were were gold and red were now starting to fall. There was that lovely smell of wood smoke in the air, the scent of October, it was beautiful.

I wanted to reach out and take her hand, it was so hard not to, but after a while she slipped her arm through mine and leant her head on my shoulder. 'This is nice George, I feel so much better you know. Muriel said I was making progress and she reckons it won't be long before my memory returns. I just want to be alright when Jack comes back. I would hate him to see me like this, with a bit of myself missing.' I squeezed her arm and laughed. But I felt more like crying!

The Vicarage garden was as lovely as it had been at the wedding, yet so much had changed, the death of Robert, and the birth of Roberta. The terrible air raids and now this wretched situation with Anna, yet somehow it was all much the same, except for the large Silver Cross pram standing proudly under an old oak tree, with Mary rocking it gently, while Henry lay on a rug reading the papers. A bucolic scene of family life. I suddenly felt very envious and very sad all at the same time. Would Anna ever forgive me, would we ever be like this? Happy with everything a young couple could wish for. Please God one day it would.

We sat and had tea and homemade scones with cream and jam, where Mary had got cream from I didn't enquire. A grateful parishioner I guess! Henry looked washed out and exhausted with his hair standing on end he looked as though he had just got out of bed, poor chap. There had been nights of terrible air raids and therefore numerous funerals he had officiated at. I wondered if it would be right to burden him with my problems yet again.

When the girls took the baby to be bathed ready for bed, I broached the subject with Henry, explaining everything, how Anna and I had had a dreadful row the day before Amy's wedding and the fact she had no memory of it ever happening. He sat and listened as the good man he was, leaning on one elbow his pipe in his mouth. When I finished he stretched his arms above his head and looked at me, his eyes tired. 'What a bloody mess George, you really do get yourself into such trouble! For what it's worth, my opinion would be not to mention it ever again. Anna is obviously very fragile, physically and mentally at the moment. Leave it, let it rest. When she starts to remember it all then you can start worrying about it. But my dear chap I wouldn't want to be you when she does. And to be quite honest don't blame yourself for the accident. If you ask me that chap Harry has a lot to answer for, what a cad to behave like that, damned idiot.'

I sighed and lit another cigarette' You're right about everything, as usual, thanks for listening, again, I just needed to get it all off my chest. You are the only person who knows what is going on, forgive me burdening you with at this wretched time.' He clapped me on the back, lay down on the rug and promptly fell asleep.

Chapter 55

Anna

My mind has been full of Jack since my accident.. How I want to hold him again, for all the waiting to be over, all those long drawn out days. To be together will be complete heaven, but I feel apprehensive even so not being '*all me.*' Not remembering is awful and I so want to be perfect for him. It's as though I have bits missing, like a leg or an arm, it is a horrible feeling.

Yet, I do keep having strange flashbacks which I can't explain. Yesterday when I was drawing in the gazebo I could visualise myself shouting at George, him shouting at me. It made me feel so confused, why would we be shouting at each other, what for? Also I seem to see Harry with his arms around me, I think we must have been dancing and he started laughing a really horrid laugh that made me want to run but I couldn't. I couldn't move and then there was a lot of smoke and noise and that is all, it is so frustrating. I told Muriel my psychiatrist and she wrote everything down and said she was certain my memory was starting to return, and that I must be patient with myself.

Another strange thing is I keep having this weird feeling that I have to talk to Victoria, about the time she insisted that George was Jack. It is niggling me all the time, it is of course rubbish. But something tells me that if I do confront her with her silly statement it will help me. God knows why. I don't.

So the next afternoon, when Victoria had finished her homework, I asked her to come to the gazebo for some cake and lemonade. Mama is very strict with the girls, lessons in the morning and a few after lunch then an hour's homework. She is determined that when they return to school they will be up at the top of the form. I have huge admiration for her as she is really no teacher but has done wonders with the girls. She meets three other mothers who are home schooling their children, and I overheard them saying it was the most exhausting job in the world, after nappies and breast feeding!

I had made some homemade lemonade and cooked a cake, albeit it with horrid powdered egg, but it tasted halfway okay with lots of icing on top. Victoria sat on the couch with me in the gazebo, which looked really lovely now, I had bought new rugs with my commission money, and covers for the new sofa to protect it from me and the way I seem to chuck paint and pastel around all the time. The kittens were tumbling on the floor chasing bits of ribbon and winding themselves up in it. They were a good distraction while I tried to find out why she had made such a strange remark.

'Vicky?'

'What?'

'Remember the other day when you said George was Jack, what did you mean?'

She looked at me, she had just turned twelve and was turning into quite a beauty, with her long dark hair and beautiful smile and a sprinkling of freckles across her pretty little nose, one day she would break some man's heart.

She shrugged, annoyingly, she did a lot of shrugging lately, must be her age I thought.

'Well?'

'I just know he's Jack that's all, I can't say anything else really,' and she shrugged, again.

'Well there has to be a concrete reason, the one's you gave were all a bit vague, weren't they?'

'I don't think they were, that's what I think that's all, can't really explain. Can I have another glass of lemonade and a bit more cake?'

I sighed, irritating child that she is, but I must be patient.

'You know Jack comes home soon, maybe we should ask him if he thinks he's actually George.'

She giggled, 'I know he's George, you wait. I know he says he isn't. I just know they changed places. But why would they do that, it's a mystery Anna,' and she giggled again.

'Oh don't be so ridiculous Victoria,' she was Vicky most of the time, but Victoria when anyone was cross with her.

She frowned at me and scuffed her feet on the floor. She looked sideways at me while I was getting her lemonade. 'Well if you really want to know I saw George, who is really Jack, kiss you the other day!'

'What *are* you talking about, there's no need to be silly.'

'It's true,' she glared at me. 'He kissed you on the lips when you were asleep, here on the couch.'

'What! Anyway how could you know that if you weren't here?'

'Well I saw you, I was up the oak tree and I saw him kiss you. You were asleep and jumped up when he did. I saw it, promise, cross my heart and hope to die!'

'Victoria listen to me, do you swear you aren't making all this up, and anyway spying on me, that's awful. How often do you climb the tree and watch me, that is so naughty!'

'I swear it's true, I don't spy on you and that is the very first time I looked into the gazebo and saw Jack/George kiss you.'

'That's ridiculous, you must have imagined it, and George wouldn't do that anyway, why would he?'

'But Jack would, wouldn't he.'

'It's all too silly, I can't imagine what you actually saw, but it certainly wasn't that.'

'Okay, but I know what I saw and to me it proves that George is really Jack and Jack is really George, I think it is very romantic. Jack couldn't bear leaving you so he changed places with his brother so he could be near you forever and ever and you will live in a beautiful house and have lots of babies.'

'Don't be so ridiculous, as if he would do something like that. Let his brother go to war and nearly get killed? Never, you are so wrong.' I could hear myself getting wound up and starting to shout.

I sat down next to her on the couch and held her hand. 'Look I didn't mean to be cross, I am just a bit confused, it must be the bump on the head.' I smiled, 'who knows, I think I need to get my memory back, don't you?'

'I'm sorry you were ill, I thought you were dying, I am so glad you didn't die.' She squeezed my hand and lay her head against my arm. I kissed her on the cheek and said I was glad I didn't die too, which made us both laugh.

When Victoria had gone I went and sat down by the river, it was getting chilly, autumn was giving way to winter and the skies looked heavy with rain. The river was running fast and a few moorhens were whizzing about but otherwise it was quite empty. I wondered where the heron had gone and if I would see him again, I hoped so.

I tried to fathom out what Vicky had said. She had to be making the 'kissing' bit up to make it a bit more exciting. Or was she, I felt so muddled up inside about everything and tried to remember when and if George had kissed me, then I remembered.

One afternoon I fell asleep on the couch and I was dreaming and woke suddenly to find George standing next to me. I am sure I said, 'did you kiss me?' and he said something like 'of course not, you must have been dreaming about Jack kissing you.' If he is really Jack he wasn't actually lying, but even so I can't imagine what Victoria said is true. Just her childish imagination I am sure. Anyway, why on earth would George kiss me?' He never has, other than a brotherly kiss on the cheek. Unless, unless, the boys did change places. But why and how has Jack coped pretending to be George.

To work in the surgery, he's no GP, it's ludicrous, impossible. But is it I thought, is it?

Chapter 56

Jack

I am worrying that Anna is starting to remember the '*day of the long knives,*' yesterday I went out with her to Mario's just for a bite to eat, the raids seem to have calmed down during the last couple of days so the streets were relatively clear of any recent damage, the huge air balloons tethered to the ground were grim reminders of the fragile state this island is in. So many ruined buildings, sandbags stacked everywhere, huge queues at the shops with their empty shelves.

Everyone seemed to have a pinched frightened look about them, especially the women who with their families are trying to keep body and soul together while living on rations which can't be easy, I know mother is struggling but we seem to eat extremely well even so.

Mario served up some corn beef fritters which were delicious but the beetroot, that is a different matter, it seems the only vegetable there is a glut of, and I am trying to get to like it, with difficulty. The fritters arrived with a fried egg on top, a real treat, he said he was feeling happy as he had heard from his sweetheart in Italy, she had managed to get a message through to someone with a shortwave radio. We could hear him singing loudly in the kitchen. At least someone is happy I thought sourly.

'George,' Anna leant over the table and took my hand,' I keep having flashbacks and seeing you and me shouting at each other, did we have a row and if so what about, I can't remember anything if we did?'

'No,' I lied, 'of course not, what on earth would we row about?'

'That is just what I thought,' she smiled, 'I am so glad, it has really been worrying me, I couldn't imagine what we would be arguing about anyway.'

We carried on eating, I felt a bit sick and extremely guilty, what happens when her memory comes back? I changed the subject quickly and we talked of Jack coming home which was also worrying me, it was all a bit of a catastrophe which seemed to be gathering momentum every day.

Walking back afterwards Anna took my hand, 'George if there *was* something worrying you, something you needed to tell me you would wouldn't you?'

'Of course, why do you ask?'

'Nothing, just wondered,' and she squeezed my hand, then let it go.

Chapter 57

Anna

Tomorrow I start driving again, hurray, at last. I got the all clear so I feel life is at last returning to normal. It will be good to be back in a work environment again and to see the girls, but I have to have a co-driver with me in case. Not sure what they think will happen, but as long as I am back, that's all that matters.

Well today was a tough day, there had been a huge air raid last night and a terrace of houses had been almost raised to the ground, but what made it so appalling was that it was Molly's house. It had taken a direct hit and both she and Percy were killed. He had moved in with Molly when his wife Mavis died in an air raid as he had nowhere to live and no family left. Molly told me that they had separate bedrooms, 'it's nothing like that you know,' she tutted and blushed slightly. 'It's just nice to have someone around, to cook for and he does make me laugh.'

It was an awful day. I went to see Rose and her mother, they were heartbroken, it was so awful to see them both so distressed. Little Rose kept asking where Grandma had gone. How do you explain to a five year old that her grandmother has been killed, that she is no more. Her mother was distraught, losing her own mother while her husband was on the front line seemed to be more than she could bear. So again I watched as a family was torn apart by this dreadful war.

When I got home that night I lay on my bed and cried. I cried for Molly and Percy. For Rose and her mother. For Mary's father Robert. For my WVS girlfriends who had lost their lives in the line of duty. For all the people I knew that had died in the air raids, and then I cried for me. For my stupid mind that couldn't remember.

Muriel phoned me next morning, she had something to discuss with me. Could I pop over before lunch?

'Well Anna, I have been talking to some colleagues and the suggestion of hypnotism came up. Would you be willing to give it a try, it may work, it may not. But I feel it could well be the answer, what do you think?'

'Oh goodness I don't know. It sounds a bit scary to me but I am so fed up with myself I will try anything. Let's give it a go.'

So the next day, feeling extremely apprehensive, I cycled over to Muriel's. Her rooms were in an old Georgian terrace of houses, all slightly run down, but even so I thought, they stood there rather proudly. The whole road had been completely untouched by the air raids, everything around looked pristine and there was an air of calmness about the elegant white stone houses. Muriel's rooms were on the ground floor, with French windows looking out over a lovely old walled garden. She greeted me warmly and suggested we walked around outside as it was such a lovely morning. Putting me at ease she spoke quietly of what would happen when I was hypnotised. I must say I did feel a bit nervous about the whole thing, but decided that I would probably do almost anything to get my memory back.

Sitting in a huge leather armchair, which almost engulfed me, Muriel told me to try and relax which was harder than I realised. I closed my eyes and laying my head back I tried to breathe deeply. I wasn't really sure if she had started to hypnotise me or was just talking, I felt a bit sleepy but otherwise wide awake in a weird way.

'Think of something that makes you happy Anna. Something that brings a kind of peace, a feeling of contentment to you, and try and visualise it. Imagine it is something you want to paint, look at the colours and the light. Lie back, let yourself go and float away gently, letting all your worries and troubles disappear.'

I started to feel even sleepier. I could hear a blackbird singing outside and the sound of Muriel's easy relaxed voice. She asked if I could hear her. I nodded, well I think I did, not actually sure. I do know that her voice seemed to be coming from a long way away.

'Anna you are awakening from a deep, deep sleep. Now I am going to send you back before the time of your accident and to the last thing you can remember.'

I was in the gazebo, lying on the couch thinking of Jack and would I ever see him again, I tried to ''*thought talk*'' him, I knew it wouldn't work but I tried and it actually did. I said I loved him and missed him, he said he loved me too, I felt him touch my cheek, it was wonderful, when I woke I felt full of happiness. Shouting out loud and jumping up from the sofa I ran up the garden to tell George but he wasn't at home or at the surgery. So I went around to the Vicarage and Mary's waters had broken. The rest of that I knew. But after that nothing. But then it was all starting to come back.

George had come to see me two days after Roberta was born, I wanted to tell him about how I had ''*thought talked*' Jack and couldn't understand how I had, then he said nice things to me, how it probably really had happened and how love can conquer everything. Then came that terrible row. How I had screamed at him that he was lying. How he told me he was Jack, again and again, and how I was in complete denial and refused to believe a word he said. But then he told me of how I had '*thought talked*' him and he repeated exactly what words I had used, what I had said. That I loved him and missed him, and he had answered back that he loved me and was really near to me and how he had stroked my cheek. And then I had realised that he really was Jack and the whole wretched scenario came tumbling back into my mind.

Then it was the day of the wedding, I had felt numb from that dreadful afternoon and instead of enjoying being with Amy while we dressed all I could think about was the day before. So I was like an automaton and quite honestly wasn't quite sure what I was doing. I remember I drank a great deal too much and flirted outrageously with Harry, just to annoy Jack. Then Harry was horrid to me and I fell to pieces and wanted to run away, anywhere but where I was. The last thing I knew I was running up the cellar stairs. We had been moved there due to a massive air raid. Then the house was hit. The sound was terrifying. People were panicking while Amy's father tried to calm them all. At that minute I didn't care about anything I just needed to get away. To be anywhere but there. Wrenching open the cellar door I walked into a burning inferno, it was my Hell.

When Muriel woke me I was sobbing, exhausted and shaking, she was crouching down in front of me, her hands gripping my hands.

'It's alright Anna, it's all over.' She passed me a handkerchief and I noticed how beautifully embroidered it was with her initials and ironed so perfectly. I cried into it, feeling guilty, spoiling it with my black mascara. But the tears wouldn't stop, I felt as though I was emptying everything I held inside me. All the worry I had bottled up for so long and all the memories I thought I had lost forever.

Muriel made us some tea and we sat outside on a beautiful old Lutyens bench and we talked and talked, or rather I did, pouring out everything I had remembered, Muriel said little just nodding in assent and occasionally clasping my hands in hers.

'Well Anna, it seems you have your memories back.' She smiled at me, 'I am so pleased my dear, now I suppose you have to decide what your next move will be.'

I looked at her, 'what would you do Muriel, should I confront Jack or what?'

She looked at me, her eyes seemed to sparkle. 'Well if it was me, I think I would tell him what you told me just now and take it from there, I have a feeling he probably feels as bad as you do and is probably blaming himself for your accident.'

The next day was a Sunday so I guessed and hoped Jack would be at home. After taking a bath, washing my hair, adding more mascara that had been washed away the day before. Putting on a clean dress, one of Jack's favourites, a black and white polka dot tight fitting silk dress, with a wide scarlet belt and my favourite scarlet heels, I was ready to confront him. Confront him with everything that had happened between us. So, feeling extremely nervous -it would be like meeting Jack for the first time - How would he be with me? Probably fed up with me shouting at him. I also wondered why he hadn't tried to tell me everything again. Was he pleased I'd forgotten everything? Was the pretence to go on and on? What was going to happen when George came back? Will he tell his parents now? So many questions. I sprayed myself with a bit of Miss Dior and told Mama I was off to see George, and wouldn't be back too late.

When I arrived at George's house Nell answered the door. I wondered what she would have to say when she found out how the boys had deceived so many of us for so long. I gave her a kiss and she shouted up the stairs. 'George, Anna here to see you.' I heard a muffled acknowledgement and my man appeared on the landing, with soaking wet hair and a towel just covering him. Ah, I thought my Jack, that's just how I like you! He then disappeared into his bedroom so we went into the kitchen where Nell poured me a coffee, I felt so nervous it was awful, I could feel my heart thudding like mad, it was crazy I felt like a girl on her first date. Maybe I thought I would play along with him for a while, it would be quite amusing pretending I still had no memory. I smiled to myself a secret smile, yes I would play him at his own game, why not? Why not indeed?

We walked out into the garden, there was no gazebo to sit in but the sun was shining so we sat on the terrace and had coffee together. Nell had to go out so we were left alone. I wasn't sure if I was pleased or not, it was all a bit daunting. Could I play the innocent young girl or should I shout like a virago again? I was so relieved to have my memory back I would have forgiven him anything!

'You're looking good Anna,' Jack said admiringly, I love the dress really suits you and the shoes too, wow you look rather spectacular actually!'

'Why, thank you George. It is Jack's favourite actually, I just felt like wearing it somehow.' I smiled sweetly at him and tried to look coy, but I felt angry with him even so. With the trick he had played on me and everyone else and I could have quite easily have punched him in the face as kissed him!

I wanted to let him suffer like I had. He wasn't going to get away that easily, that was for sure. I wondered if he was relieved that I had lost my memory or was it like a torment for him, waiting for me to suddenly remember and turn on him like a woman spurned? It was all rather interesting and I wondered how it would have been if the tables had been reversed. Would I have kept it from my family? Of course I would never know. But somehow I realised how hard it must have been for him. George was far away from the daily worry of being someone else, I presume the family he stayed with all knew him as George, while poor Jack had no choice but to be George O'Brien, GP.

I must say at the start I had thought it would have been a bit of fun teasing him. But it wasn't, it was horrible to be truthful. So much had happened since George went away, how could it all be resolved in a matter of minutes.

No one even knew if George was alive anymore. There had been no news from him since he left for Spain and that was well over two months ago, which seemed far too long without any news. Jack kept saying he would know if he had died and he had no reason to believe he had. It was just the fact that every time he tried to '*thought talk*' him there was nothing, just a black void. I know that worried him more than anything. All in all it was all a damned mess.

I looked at Jack, he looked so sad, it broke my heart. How hard these last years must have been for him, pretending to be someone you're not. I had to be gentle with him, he was after all my love. But I was in a strange way enjoying teasing him.

'Any progress with Muriel?'

'Not really, nothing to talk about,' crossing my fingers under the table I asked for a cigarette.

He put two in his mouth, lit them and passed one to me. Such a Jack thing to do, something I never noticed until now. How many other things had I missed? Like the way Victoria said he held his cigarette, but now he was doing it the 'George' way. If I hadn't been so stressed about it all it would have been almost funny

We sat together in comfortable silence, it was so quiet, no sirens, just the sound of a thrush singing its heart out on top of the chestnut tree, another one joined in. We both looked at each other and laughed.

'Of course you do realise they are singing just for us!' Jack said, yawning and stretching his hands over his head. He smiled at me, his green eyes unfathomable. What now, I thought, what now?

'Jack?'

'What?'

'Oops meant to say George, sorry!'

Jack squirmed in his chair and tried to look casual, poor man, I won't tease him for too long; well maybe just for a bit longer.

'Well, what anyway?'

'Have you seen Harry at all, I haven't had a word from him, I presume he knows I was ill?'

'Of course, he came to see you when you were in a coma. There was some talk of his unit being sent to the coast, not really sure. I'll see if I can find out anything, why do you want to see him, anything important?'

I smiled innocently, 'I just wondered, I'm missing him actually, he was fun to be with while Jack was away. But never mind, it was getting a bit heated so probably a good job he has been moved away. Who knows what temptation he would have led me into?'

Poor Jack, he was definitely not liking the content of this conversation, he was smoking as though there was no tomorrow and had got up and was pacing up and down the lawn like a caged animal!

'Oh do sit down, what's wrong with you?'

He sat down and fidgeted strumming his fingers on the side of the deckchair. I could see his left leg under the table moving up and down like a piston. I giggled inwardly and wanted to throw my arms around him and tell him how much I loved him. How sorry I was for being so foul to him.

Chapter 58

Jack

Well I do wish I knew what was going on,
Mother shouted up that Anna was downstairs. I
was in the shower so came out onto the landing
with a towel barely covering me, I could see
Anna standing in the hall with the light from the
window shining on her hair like a halo. She
smiled up at me, my angel.

Mother had to go out so we went into the garden
and sat on the terrace drinking coffee. Anna
looked amazing, wearing my favourite dress
with the scarlet belt and her red high heels, all
too much for a young man to be honest.

She called me Jack by mistake and I like an
idiot responded. But I don't actually think she
noticed my reaction. Then she started going on
about Harry and how she obviously still fancied
him, she actually said she thought he may lead
her into temptation which made me very
twitchy. Just the thought of it makes me want to
hit him. But I have a feeling he may have been
posted elsewhere, rather hoping that's the case.

We didn't mention George and not having any
news for well over two months. I think we, like
the rest of us, were trying to just hope and pray

there would be news soon. Teddy has been trying to find out what he could but even he can't get any joy out MI9. All we know is that George left France for Spain and is hopefully on his way home. But it seems too long without any contact, and I am afraid that I fear for his life. Though somehow I think I would know if he had died, in fact I know I would. Even so I can't explain why there is nothing when I try to '*Talk*' to him. Maybe just a hiccup in the atmosphere or something we don't understand. Who knows? This *'thought talk'* is a tenuous thing at the best of times

Anna seemed very carefree, if I can use such a word, she is always happy and the fact that a girl like her tried to kill herself by rushing into the burning house horrifies me. And that I could have made her do something to her like that makes me feel so ashamed. I really do wish she would regain her memory so we can sort everything out. But .I have a feeling that she may not want to 'sort it out.' That is what worries me a lot. Say she doesn't love me anymore, she's okay now as she has no memory of our dreadful row, but what will happen when she starts to remember? It doesn't bear thinking about.

I was smoking like a train, my nerves were in shreds and I must say I was starting to feel somewhat uncomfortable about the whole situation, It was almost as if Anna was actually flirting with me, but can't imagine she would have been, I guess it is just my muddled mind playing tricks.

Then suddenly she jumped up and came and sat on my lap. I nearly had a heart attack, she started kissing me, what the hell was going on? She then said she loved me and forgave me for what I had done!

I stood up almost throwing the poor girl onto the ground.

'Anna, what the hell is going on?'

'Don't you know Jack? I just wanted to tell you I love you and forgive you for keeping such a secret from me for so long. And also to say I apologise for my tirade and behaving like a virago that awful afternoon.'

I looked at her in astonishment. My God she had remembered after all, she had been playing with me like a cat with a mouse, bloody hell and I went along with it, little vixen.

She stood looking at me her head on one side, her grey eyes laughing at me. Tossing her hair back she leant over and kissed me on the lips.

'How long have you known?'

She smiled, 'Since yesterday, Muriel hypnotised me and everything came flooding back .I remembered how awful I was screaming at you, telling you I hated you. I couldn't believe I had behaved like that, I feel quite ashamed of myself. I realise now that you boys did what you did because it felt like the right thing to do at the time. I just wish you had taken me into your confidence. I felt so hurt that you didn't trust me enough to keep it quiet.' She looked at me under her eyelashes, 'do you forgive me Jack?'

I looked at this girl. My girl, who stood before me looking beautiful and for a minute, very vulnerable. I felt tears starting and blinked them away. 'I love you Anna, I have never stopped loving you, it has been a complete nightmare keeping this from you. How many times I nearly told you, you have no idea, and yes of course I should have taken you into my confidence. I realise now it was wrong to keep it just between us boys. Will you forgive me too?'

She moved towards me her eyes bright with unshed tears. 'Oh Jack, yes, yes, yes, I love you too and I am so glad you are Jack and not George. Oh dear, that sounds awful, but you know what I mean.' Putting her arms around me she lifted her face towards me and smiled, her little girl smile. So I kissed her.

Chapter 59

Well that seems to be that I suppose! End of the story? I think not, let's go and see what is happening in the Cooper house.

It is the evening of the next day. Anna is helping her mother Evelyn to lay the table in the dining room, it is set for ten people. The best china is laid out on a beautiful white damask tablecloth, the cut glasses glint in the candlelight. It is reminiscent of Isabelle's birthday party but there will be different people sitting around the table this time. There will be Evelyn, Teddy, Anna, Bertie – home on unexpected leave -Victoria and Elizabeth, also Nell, Ernest and Jack as well as Mary and Henry and of course baby Roberta, who will sleep peacefully upstairs and no nothing whatsoever of what is happening.

Evelyn had decided that as Bertie was home and the fact that he had been made a commissioned officer, was just the best reason to have a celebration. So there was to be a dinner party that Saturday night.

The evening before when Anna had said goodbye to Jack, they had decided that tomorrow would be *'The day of the big secret!'* What better time to tell everyone; the only undercurrent was the fact there had been no word from George for so long. He was so conspicuous by his absence, it was palpable. Nell was very down and trying to think positively, while Ernest too was trying to be optimistic about the whole wretched scenario.

Meanwhile Teddy was convinced that something had gone terribly wrong. What had happened to Jack he didn't know, but hopefully nothing too terrible. He was sure if there was bad news they would have received it by now. No news is good news he kept telling everyone, therefore a party might do everyone's morale some good.

So a little after seven o'clock that evening ten people were gathered on the lawn. The evening was balmy and it was good to be enjoying the last of the autumn evenings. Even baby Roberta was enjoying the sunshine, being passed from arms to arms, kissed, cuddled and goo-ed at.

Champagne was handed around and canapes made by Anna, with limited ingredients, were consumed happily.

Everyone agreed that it was the best of ideas to celebrate Bertie's commission and the return of Jack, hopefully soon. And of course the recovery of Anna, who seemed almost to be back to her normal self. Just waiting for her to get her memory back, which everyone assured everyone else, that it wouldn't be long.

Toasts were made to Bertie who hadn't stopped smiling since he arrived, Evelyn too was happy to have her boy back even though for such a short while. Teddy was happy too, proud of his son and having three girls and only one boy it was nice to have a bit of masculine company for a change. It had been a very feminine environment since he left.

As the sky darkened everyone moved inside, there was the smell of rain in the air, the feeling of a storm impending, the sky had turned a strange lemon yellow, bathing everyone in a golden glow.

'How beautiful us girls look,' Evelyn said, 'beautiful golden girls.'

Everyone laughed and the worries of Jack missing were lost for a fraction of time. It was as if everyone was waiting for something, as if time stood still for those few seconds. Anna felt it and squeezed Jack's hand.

The smell emanating from the kitchen was divine, Teddy had been given a large side of beef from a grateful patient who had just had his gall stones removed. Luckily he also happened to be the local butcher.

'When shall we tell them?' Anna whispered.

'I don't know, maybe once we are all sitting down?' Jack answered, looking slightly unsure about the whole thing. 'I am a bit worried if we should bring all this up while George is still missing, maybe we should wait until there is some news, may it be good or bad. Also maybe you should have told your parents about you regaining your memory.'

'I know, I think you are right, I will tell everyone at the same time. It will all be fine. I think everyone needs a boost especially *your* parents, your mother looks exhausted. Maybe just being around everyone who loves her will help. I do think it is the right thing to do. We'll tell them before I bring in the entrée, it's cold so it can hang around for a bit; just make sure everyone's glass is full. Who's going to start? I think you should if you are happy with that?'

Jack glanced at her and swallowed. 'I suppose so, I do feel a bit nervous though, think I'll have a sneaky scotch in the kitchen first.'

Anna kissed him on the cheek, they were still outside while everyone had gone into the dining room. 'You'll be fine, I will be right next to you.'

Kissing her hard on the lips Jack held her hand briefly and they walked slowly back into the house.

Chapter 60

George

Well this has been one hell of a time. I thought I was nearly home. But we have taken great strides. Backwards.

When we left the house, Dédée, the girl Florence, myself and the other two pilots trudged for what seemed hours up into the hills. There we were taken in and fed and watered by kind people, who were horrified to hear of the Milice attack. They told us that these men were everywhere, crawling over the mountains looking for anyone involved in the French Resistance, taking them away and torturing or shooting as the will took them. It was a nightmare for these good people, who were risking their own lives to save other innocents caught in a maelstrom of fear.

Dédée told us how the Milice worked alongside the Nazis, rounding up any Jews ready to be deported to the east. They were violent cruel people, with no compassion for men women or even children. The majority of them were men who had been out of work for a while. That the Milice promised regular wages and good food rations was one huge factor that swayed these men into joining. The other, that they would be exempt from being forced labourers in Nazi Germany. So it was a battle waiting to be won, but by whom?

That evening we sat around the table long into the early hours deciding what to do for the best.

I think we all slept fitfully during the last hours of the night. Waking in the morning to torrential rain and thunder we drank our bitter black coffee in silence, each wrapped in their own thoughts. The girl Florence, was very subdued and pale. She wept as she talked of her parents, whether she would ever see them again. She wept as she talked of her grandparents who lived in the valley. How they would be in a panic when they found out what had happened to their daughter and her family. She told us she had been a junior nurse at her local hospital and was worried if she would ever be able to find work again. The poor girl was in great distress. Dédée assured her that she would help her and she was not to worry. Being a nurse herself she promised to do anything she could. It seemed to relax the girl and holding Dedée's hand she smiled for the first time.

The rain persisted for most of the morning and when it started to lessen we went outside to see how the land laid. We were at the top of the mountains, far from civilisation it seemed of any kind. Goats and sheep wandered around and dark eyed cream cows, lowed gently their bells echoing around the hills. It all looked so bucolic and so perfect, it was hard to believe so much horror was all around us.

Dédée decided that we should stay put for a while, she was going to see what, if anything, was happening. So the four of us played cards and smoked strong French cigarettes and drank black bitter coffee while listening to the rain once more beating against the windows. Thunder rumbled in the distance as flashes of forked lightening lit up the heavy skies.

As I sat there I thought of Isabelle and how I wished I was with her. I thought of Jack too and wondered why I couldn't ''thought talk'' him. Every time I tried there was nothing. I was worried something had happened to him. But inside I knew that if something was wrong there would have been some sign. Brushing the worry away I concentrated on my Poker game which I was losing badly, fortunately we were playing for matchsticks.

Our 'helpers,' an elderly couple, served us hot soup and home baked bread for supper and tried to reassure us that we were safe with them and if anyone could keep them that way it was Dédée.

Late that evening Dédée returned. 'I have spoken with some 'helpers' and they say three other houses were raided and the occupants taken away by the Milice. They are everywhere, like ants over ant- hills. You have to go up higher into the mountains and cross into Spain that way, there is no other choice. I can't lead you as I need to help others who are also hiding out from the Milice. The son of one of the helpers who is part of the Basque Mulgari will guide you across the mountains, he is a very experienced mountaineer so you will be in good hands.'

'I want to come with you and help,' it was Florence. She went over to Dédée and held her hand. 'Will you take me with you, I don't want to leave with the others, this is my country. I need to be here and to do what I can in the name of my mother and father, please let me. As I am a nurse, I can be of some use I think.'

Dédée smiled at her and putting her hands on her shoulders looked her straight in the eye. 'Florence, if that is what you want it is fine with me, it will be dangerous you know that, if they catch us......' She didn't need to go on.

The boy that was to guide us looked to be far too young to take us on such a hazardous journey. He was well built with a shock of black hair, very tall for a Frenchman, his name was Romain and like Remi before him he had the inevitable Gitane hanging from his lip. He was part of the Resistance as well as a Mulgari and hated the Milice, so he told us how pleased he was to help us over the mountains.

He called it *The Freedom Trail*. There were several other routes that started off in Belgium and different areas of France, they all headed for the border into Spain and to freedom. He told us that most of the escapees were Jewish, fleeing for their lives. We would probably pick up several of them on our way, when we were to leave the next day at the crack of dawn.

Florence and Dédée left that evening, it was a sad farewell, especially saying au revoir to Dédée who had been with us for a short while but had made a huge impression on me. Florence was quite composed and had seemed to have grown from a frightened girl into someone with confidence and determination. Her parents would have been very proud of her and I hoped and prayed that maybe they would return. But somehow I thought not.

We stood and watched them both as they walked down the hill, one tall slim figure, carrying over her arm the bag with her prized possessions while the other arm was wrapped around the waist of a smaller slighter figure. I watched them as they disappeared into the twilight and out of my life.

The next morning, while it was still dark the four of us left the safe house, hoping and praying these kind people would stay safe themselves.

We climbed high into the mountains, it was hazardous and extremely tiring as the terrain was rough and steep. The weather had changed and it was warm again, the rain had ceased for the time being. We stopped overnight in a deserted shack and slept on old sacking and straw. Gone were the comfortable beds and home baked bread, we had some bitter coffee that Romain had with him in a thermos, it was lukewarm and pretty disgusting, and a loaf of stale bread went with it.

The next day the route got rougher and steeper, but there were beautiful waterfalls cascading down the mountains with sweet crystal clear water and a few intrepid mountain goats grazing on the steep slopes.

As we climbed it started to feel a lot cooler. Romain said we would reach the snow line soon. As we neared the top of the mountain the views were extraordinarily beautiful, quite awe inspiring. The whole range of the Pyrenees was laid out in front of us, the tops covered in thick snow. As we trudged upwards, the snow line began, it was shallow and slippery, then the snow became a lot deeper. Our espadrilles were useless and our feet were frozen, but there was nothing else to do but carry on.

We had to hide out when Romain, using his binoculars, spotted a group of men below us in the distance. 'There are caves just a bit higher up, some will be full of bedding and supplies left by other escapees, if we can reach there we will safe, hopefully. I have a horrid suspicion that it is The Milice I can see. We can't take the risk so we must find a hiding place immediately. I don't think they will bother to climb as high as this but I daren't take that chance.'

Finally we reached what seemed to be just another part of the mountain, but Romain pulled aside plants growing in abundance amongst the thick stone, to reveal a huge gaping hole.

Turning on his torch we followed him into the cavern, the air was freezing, worse than outside, we were all shivering, but inside was to us a palace, there was a burnt out fire with a hole in the roof of the cave to let out the smoke, an old camping stove, oil lamps and tins of food, the snow was our drink. We got the fire going with twigs we found lying around. Taking off our espadrilles, that were falling apart, we warmed our feet and sat on the old rugs and blankets that were piled up everywhere, gradually we started to feel warm. Romain opened three of the tins with a rusty old tin opener, one was full of some kind of stew the others held some peaches in syrup and some kind of meat in jelly. We were starving so anything would have done, it actually wasn't too bad. Romain reckoned it tasted of dog food, I did wonder how he knew! The best find was a large bottle of brandy, covered in dust but it tasted sublime, so drinking it out of old tin cups we toasted each other and prayed for a safe journey.

Chapter 61

While everyone was working out where to sit' baby Roberta was kissed goodnight by everyone then taken upstairs, where she lay snug and warm in a large drawer lined with her baby blanket. She was fast asleep, her thumb jammed into her mouth, before Mary had even closed the door. She would miss all the excitement, but would be told and re told the story long into her childhood.

Well here they are, all eleven of them sitting around the table. Candlelight playing softly against the crystal wine glasses while a coal fire crackled gently in the grate, not really necessary as it was still relatively warm for the end of autumn but it gave out a warm golden glow that added to the ambience in the room. The women all looking elegant in their long evening dresses, the dark silks and velvets contrasting with the whiteness of their shoulders while the candlelight cast a soft light across their faces. The men smart in their dinner jackets, smoking and laughing and enjoying the intimacy of their families and friends.

When Jack stood up and nervously tapped his glass with a fork, cleared his throat and began, his audience looked with expectation at this young man who turned towards his sweetheart and smiled down at her.

'Anna and I have something to tell you,' he reached down and put his arm around her bare shoulders. There was a gasp and everyone turned to each other, a murmur went around. 'Oh God they've fallen in love' and a great deal more muttering in the same vein.

Jack laughed at their faces. 'Don't look so worried all of you, it's not what you think. George hasn't fallen in love with Anna. I have!'

Anna giggled and stood up next to Jack.'What George is trying to say is he isn't actually who you think he is, he is Jack. My Jack.'

'Good grief, I knew it.' It was Nell her hand clasping her throat, she turned to Ernest. 'I told you something was strange, oh my God and all this time it has been George in danger. Why on earth would he chose to go to war when his heart is so fragile? And Jack why did you let him?'

Everyone started talking at once, it was chaos. Suddenly Nell stood up and was almost shouting. 'How could you deceive us like that, telling lies, pretending the whole time, while your brother is fighting for his life? Oh my God, I am so angry, you have no idea!' And she promptly sat town and burst into tears. Ernest put his arm around her.

'Shh, Nell, it is alright, you have had a shock, we all have, I must say I feel rather upset too. Living with you Jack and never knowing, you must be a very good actor young man. But quite honestly this is not the time for recriminations it is a time for forgiveness, so come here.' And taking hold of his son's shoulders he kissed him on both cheeks then threw his arms around him while everyone clapped.

Poor Nell, she looked so confused, so upset. Everyone fussed around her and Jack held her close and told her he loved her and hadn't meant to upset her, saying that both her sons had behaved irresponsibly and he was sorry. It had just seemed the perfect solution at the time. He looked like a young boy again, in trouble for some silly misdemeanour.

Evelyn looked completely bemused and a little stunned. Henry held his head in his hands. Mary looked across at Anna and shaking her head smiled questioningly at her friend. Teddy looked around the table in amazement while Victoria jumped up and down in her seat. 'Told you so, told you so, I knew Uncle George was really Uncle Jack.' Elizabeth watching her sister giggled and jumped up and down with her. You could hardly hear yourself talk, it was complete mayhem.

So '*the secret*' was out.

Ernest stood up, 'Shh, let's hear what it's all about from my son, which one I am not sure.'

There was a ripple of laughter, more cigarettes were lit, more wine poured and everyone sat back and waited.

Jack with the support of his girl relayed the story of '*The switch.*' You could hear a pin drop as he talked, a few gasps, someone sniffed and blew their nose. The little girls, wide eyed stared at their uncle, this was the most exciting thing ever, they decided later, that had ever happened to them.

When Jack had finished he looked across at his family he spoke softly, his voice trembling slightly. 'Mother and Father, I want you to know again that if I have caused you any hurt by all this deception I apologise from the bottom of my heart. George and I had no intention of upsetting anyone and I realise now that neither of us had thought it through 'til the end. I hope you will forgive us both.'

There was an audible sigh then everyone got up, the men clapped Jack on the back and shook his hand. Nell held him tight and said he should be ashamed of himself then telling him she loved him dearly kissed him and burst into tears again; saying she just wanted George back then she would be happy. No one said anything, as most felt as though George was lost to them. But of course it was not even hinted at it.

Evelyn held Anna's hand and kissing her whispered, 'you are such a naughty girl letting me still think you had no memory. But oh how glad I am you are back my darling from such a dark place.' Looking at Jack she shook her head and hugged him.

Mary kissed him too and hugging Anna looked at her 'You okay?'

'Oh yes, I'll tell you all about everything later.'

Victoria jumped up and threw her arms around Jack's waist. 'You see I knew all the time, I was right, I was right!'

Jack picked her up and gave her a resounding kiss on her cheek, 'you little monster, that's what you are a little monster.'

Somehow Evelyn had persuaded her fishmonger to beg steal or borrow some prawns, she knew quite well that he was a bit 'soft on her' as everyone said so she smiled sweetly and of course he delivered, so with the small amount she had and with a lot of shredded lettuce and salad cream she managed to make a passable prawn cocktail. There were sighs of satisfaction as the prawns were eaten, and toasts to Evelyn for managing to produce something so delicious even with the wretched rationing.

There was laughter and repartee and copious amounts of Teddy's best claret was consumed. All in all, everyone was enjoying themselves immensely.

'Anna?'

'What?'

'Fancy coming outside for a fag?'

'Have one here, everyone else is.'

'I need to have you to myself, do you have any idea how desirable you look tonight. It has been nearly two years being near you, watching you, seeing you out with another man. Not allowed to touch you. It has been a nightmare!'

She smiled 'Oh well, in that case…..'

Outside it was pitch black. Voices from across the road could be heard indistinctly, a car door slammed, an engine started up, the sound of a front door shutting, then silence. Light peeping through blackout curtains broke the blackness of the night, the moon was but a blur in the sky. An owl hooted somewhere in the distance. It was very still; the smell of rain was in the air.

The young lovers stood under the porch, the girl's head on the man's shoulder his arm around her waist. Their cigarettes glowed in the dark.

'Well that seemed to go down alright, you have no idea how bloody glad I am it is all over. I do wonder what Father really thinks though, finding out his son is a pacifist. I don't suppose I will every really know. I just pray he and Mother don't think too badly of me.'

Anna put her two fingers against his lips. 'Shh, all will be okay just kiss me.' He could feel her hair brushing his cheek, her mouth was slightly open her lips soft against his.

'You know,' she whispered, 'I have had such a strange feeling all day I'm not sure why, it's as though I am waiting for something to happen. I hate it when I feel like this, it's a horrible sensation predicting something yet not knowing quite what it is. Say it is something dreadful like a bomb falling on us all. Oh God how I wish all this war was over and everything could be back to normal. Knowing you are Jack helps but George missing is such a helpless feeling. Do you feel anything? You said you did when he was in trouble.'

'No I don't feel anything that is why I am sure he is safe, that there will be a good reason for him not contacting us. Please don't worry, everyone else can worry for you, especially me.'

They stayed locked together in each other's arms, the silent night like a cloak around them. 'Don't you think we should go back in?'

'Five more minutes, let's just walk down to the gate and see if there is anything exciting happening.'

Anna giggled, 'I don't think there will be somehow.'

Arms around each other they leant over the wrought iron gate, they could feel the first spots of rain and a distant rumble of thunder. There was nothing to be seen, just a lone figure and a cigarette glowing in the dark, all was quiet.

Walking slowly back towards the house, they heard the latch on the front gate click. They both turned around.

Chapter 62

George

We hid out in the cave for two days. When we thought the men who had been hanging around had disappeared, we left and walked higher and higher. We were on a narrow path through the mountain with a huge drop one side, we all kept as close as we could to the mountain side as it was one hell of a way down.

The younger pilot seemed very nervous and panicky and said he daren't look down as he got vertigo. 'Not the right thing for a bomber pilot to have', he laughed. 'But somehow flying doesn't bother me it's just when I am on terra firma it gets to me.'

The further up we climbed the colder and more treacherous it became, everywhere there were huge ridges in the mountains with deep gorges, it was a perilous trail.

I watched the younger brother as he seemed to be looking upwards rather than where he was going which seemed a dangerous game to play as the terrain was very uneven and rocky and everywhere were crevices and deep gulfs in the mountains. Suddenly and without warning there was a peircing scream as he slipped and fell, his brother ran towards him and reached out to stop him falling but it was too late, the young boy had disappeared, all I could see was his one hand clenched tightly around a clump of dead grass. Throwing himself to the ground his brother grabbed hold of his hand trying to pull him back up. I watched in horror as they both began to slip into what appeared a bottomless pit. I stretched out to seize his other hand as he struggled desperately to keep hold of his younger brother, but it was too late, suddenly their hands separated and in a deathly hush we watched as the young boy hurtled downwards into blackness, it was terrible. His brother looked in horror as he watched him disappear into the void. He threw himself down on the ground and sobbed. He looked at me in desperation. 'I couldn't hold him, our hands were so cold, he just let go, oh God I should have looked after him, watched him, I knew he was terrified of heights, what have I done, what have I done'.

'You haven't done anything, it was no one's fault.' I leant down to comfort him and he jerked away from me as if in pain, I looked at his arm and realised it must have broken when he had thrown himself on the ground. I held him against me as he shuddered and cried, it was a dreadful time for the poor kid.

Romain, leant over and touched the shaking shoulder, then he bent his head and said a prayer, it was a simple French prayer that I had heard before, and it made me think of Reuben's funeral, the gentle way he went into the dark night, the beautiful words said over his body, the tender way he was laid to rest. This time there had been nothing, just a violent end to a young man's life. Is that all there is I thought? Just that, nothing else, but somehow I felt there must be something that we don't understand and maybe never would. Being able to *"thought talk"* with Jack was beyond both out comprehension, but I knew there was something out there that at the moment none of us understood., I will have to wait until it is my time I thought, to find out.

I turned away and tended to the boy's broken arm Hopefully I could set it well enough but there was no way I could do it without causing him agony. I cursed that I had nothing to relieve his pain, Romain had a flask of brandy so he gave him a slug from that. It was a horrendous time for the young airman but he seemed too much in shock to notice a lot. The crack of the bone as I reset it seemed to echo around the mountains, causing him promptly to pass out, much to my relief, so I worked quickly. The break was clean there were no fragments of bone which was good. Romain found a piece of wood to make some sort of splint and tearing off a bit of my shirt I managed to support the arm as best as I could.

It was a subdued threesome that night who rested in a goat's man's shack, where the elderly owner kindly fed and watered us. He told us how he hated the Milice and that his son and family, lower down in the valley had fled after being hunted by them. Knowing that his son was part of the Resistance they were intent on catching him, but with his wife and two young children he managed to get out into neutral Spain, before they were caught. The old man said he had no idea where they were only that he had heard on the grapevine they were safe. He said he would stay put, herding his goats. He had no real fear of the Milice, he was pretty harmless and anyway as it was too high for many to reach so near the snow line. And definitely far too treacherous for the cowardly Milice - his words.

He fed us homemade soft white cheese from his goats that roamed the mountains. There were great wedges of crusty bread and as usual the rough red wine to drink while we listened to this brave old man telling us fascinating tales of the Resistance and their fight with the Milice and the Nazis. I watched as the young airman knocked back a fair amount of wine which bought some colour back into his pale cheeks, but there was not enough to bring oblivion which I guessed is all he wanted just then.

Romain had a Morse code transmitter, which he used religiously morning and night, keeping in touch with safe houses and other guides. The next morning he told us he had heard that there were a group of Jews who were being hunted by the Milice - after a few of them, while been rounded up ready to be deported to the east - had managed somehow to escape and were hiding higher up the mountains, we hoped to reach them that evening and lead them, along with us to safety.

Just as dawn broke we trudged further and further up the mountains, well past the snow line, the views from the top were magnificent. And what was even more magnificent to us escapées were the distant lights of Spain. The snow got thicker and our feet got wetter, but seeing the lights made the adrenalin kick in and we were almost running up the steep slopes. The small group of Jews were hiding out in a cave, a bit like ours but with no food or bedding. They looked wretched, grey and thin, their clothes in shreds, their eyes blank with suffering, it was hard to look at them without feeling such anger against their perpertraotors There were seven of them all men. No one spoke as we all walked up and up and up.

That night we all slept in another safe house, this one was a small farm where a very large lady and even larger man welcomed us in, their accent was singsong, it sounded beautiful, more Spanish than French, they were generous and kind, yet again. We were fed a great spicy stew with hunks of crispy bread and of course the inevitable coarse red wine.

The group of Jewish men were ravenous and when we had all eaten they started to talk. The wine had loosened their tongues and the hot food had bought colour to their faces. They said they had been travelling for nearly a month with the Milice hot on their heels. Where their families were they had no idea. They had been separated from them while they were being deported. One of the men cried as he talked of his small children and wife being wrenched from his arms. It was a terrible tale to witness and something I will never forget as long as I live. The hatred of man against man would never change, it is something that is beyond my comprehension.

Three days later

Now we were on the very edge of Spain. Looking across at the lights that were twinkling in the dark. Romain told us we were a mere hundred metres from safety. As we walked over the border we were all exhausted and instead of shouting with joy which we must have all felt like doing, the Jewish men kissed the ground and hugged each other while us two weary airmen shook hands with each other and seemed surprised at the very idea that we had actually made it. Romain was slapped on the back and everyone clapped loudly, it was a wonderful moment as we walked slowly towards freedom.

At last we were out of danger; we had missed being picked up by Franco's Guardia Civil and maybe being swapped for some other poor enemy, or even worse, thrown into prison or some concentration camp. It was all due to

Romain, he had been warned the Guardia were in the area and managed to sneak us away and out of danger.

That night we slept in a ramshackle old farmhouse where the Spanish couple kissed each of us on both cheeks and treated us like unsung heroes, we were offered great mugs of red wine and toasted for our 'bravery.' The next morning we were all given rusty old bicycles, to cycle into San Sebastian a few kilometres away.

We must have been a rare sight in our filthy clothes and tattered espadrilles. Two of the Jewish men had never ridden a bike before, so with them holding onto the bikes in front we cycled towards freedom. This time it was a day of rejoicing, and now we *did* all roar with the sheer joy of finally being free, but I felt it must have been a very ambivilant time for the Jewish men knowing they would never see their families again and of the airman who had suffered too much for one so young.

The seven men were escorted by Romain to a holding area where they were given clean clothes and fed while awaiting their departure to safety and a new life in a new country. They seemed almost sad to say goodbye to us and hugged us like old friends. Again, another part of life that would stay in my memory for ever.

We two airmen were escorted by officials from MI9. We would be de-briefed then taken to Gibraltar.

I said goodbye to the young airman and wished him well, making sure that he was able to send a message home, it would be a sad time for his family, maybe not as bad as thinking both your boys were dead but I couldn't imagine there would be much rejoicing when he returned. It was a hard time for this young man and to this day I often wonder what became of him.

One of the men from MI9 promised to relay a message home to say I was on my way, as I was not allowed, for security reasons I suppose, to use any form of communication. So I wrote out a message to be sent to Father, making the chap promise it would be sent as it was of vital importance. I must say I did feel a sense of relief knowing that everyone at home would know I was alive and kicking. I will surprise them by not contacting them again I thought. I liked the idea of that just turning up, seemed a good idea somehow. A bit of a wheeze as Henry would say.

Chapter 63

George

Well here I am in Gibraltar and I have no idea what the hell **is** going on, over the last five days I have been moved from A to B and back again. The young airman was whisked away never to be seen again, he was probably by now, drinking tea out of his own cup, in his own house, sleeping in his own bed, surrounded by his own family and here I am stuck, why, I need to know, why? All I got from the Intelligence chaps was that we had to wait until a ship was available, as finding one at the moment that would get us safely back to Blighty was a dodgy process.

I was free to walk around do what I wanted as long as I returned to the barracks at night. It is a real British fortress here with a huge naval base and a sprinkling of the army and air force. Now that Franco has decided he is definitely aligned with Hitler and they are the best of friends, he wants nothing to do with America or Britain. It is a dangerous game he is playing, but here in Gibraltar we are safe. Being on British soil is a little paradise, in the middle of chaos.

Well at last a glimmer of hope on the horizon, a private yacht, the Malahne having been commissioned by the Navy, will be coming into Gibraltar in the next day or two and if all goes well I will be on my way home. There are about twenty other airmen waiting to leave along with me, so we are all keeping everything crossed while playing endless games of Poker, with minute amounts of money - our paltry allowance while waiting - watching dreadful old films and drinking too much, thanks to the generosity of our hosts. The sun shines relentlessly which keeps up our morale, but everyone is getting slightly twitchy.

Today, finally is the day I leave for home. The Malahne, a beautiful piece of nautical engineering sailed gracefully into the harbour two days ago. It has been converted into a warship but outwardly looked like the luxury yacht it had been, spending its days swanning around enjoying itself.

The inside of the boat is beautiful, all wood and brass. Even kitted out like a warship, one can see what it must have been like when it was just a wonderful plaything, for some rich chap, but now it was to take some rather weary airman back to dear old Blighty.

As it left, the quayside was swarming with spectators, waving union jacks and singing God Save the King , making me feel very patriotic and a little bit proud to be British! While we all joined in with the singing, the boat slipped majestically out of the harbour and I felt a sense of happiness of going home, but a huge sadness of drifting even further away from my beautiful girl.

After what seemed forever the yacht Malahne sailed into Southampton waters. It had been an uneventful voyage all in all, except when a few shots were fired from enemy ships, more to scare than injure as they were too far away to cause any damage but even so it was with a sigh of relief that we all sat down that evening toasting with Pink Gins our journey back to Blighty.

We had arrived at the docks late that evening with the rain pouring down, everywhere in darkness and the distant drone of enemy aircraft overhead. 'Off to do London again, poor sods,' one of the crew remarked. 'Surprised there's anything else to bomb.' My heart turned over at his words, I knew it was bad there and prayed all my loved ones were safe.

We stayed overnight on board, it was strange to be still with no movement to lull me to sleep. The bunks were hard, not the luxurious beds that the Malahne were fitted out with before the war.

I had got to know two men on my journey home, one the navigator Johnnie, who I celebrated with one night when he had received a message that his wife had just given birth to his first child, a little girl. The Captain, Norrington was to be her godfather. I never found out Johnnie's last name or Norrington's first name but that seemed of little consequence, they were kindness themselves, and were again two people that I will never forget. That night I heard the story behind the Malahne before she was commissioned, it all sounded amazing and I was thankful for such a beautiful vessel bringing me home.

The next afternoon after a brief chat with some chaps from intelligence I was put on a train to London. It was full of other military personnel, some walking injured accompanied by nurses, young men, a bit like me, that looked far too young to have actually being in the war. We were on our way home!

I walked the five miles to home, it was just getting dark. I had a torch but was loathe to use it, not sure why. I was in London not Normandy! The whole of the city seemed torn apart, it was horrendous. Obviously last night had been a bad one, the smell of smoke hung in the air, some fires were still smouldering while firemen were dousing the flames and helping families to dig through the rubble of their homes. The nearer I got to home the more fearful I felt, what if they had been bombed? What if everyone was dead? I shook myself, *'shut up, and don't be so bloody morbid.'* I walked quickly just wanting to be home. To surprise everyone.

I was wearing a new uniform and this time my hat actually fitted me. The last hat I had burnt at the chaumière, along with my uniform.

Somehow the familiarity of it all felt good after so long in civvies. I put my wallet into my top jacket pocket making sure Isabelle's photo was safe and sound. In my trouser pocket I could feel the cold metal of Anna's locket against my fingers. My lucky charm I thought. How good it will be to give back to her, which made me wonder if she had found out about *'the switch,'* if anyone else had and if so how had it gone down? Was I going to walk into a web of secrets or not?

At last I reached our house, it was in darkness, not even a peek of light showed through the blackout curtains. I went around to the back, the door was locked, I went to the front door, banged on it, no answer, shouted through the letter box, but the house was empty. So much for the surprise! Shit oh shit, where would they all be? I knew there was a spare key under one of the flower pots, so letting myself in and turning on the kitchen light I looked at Mother's wall diary, there it was, 'Dinner at Evelyn's.' Super, even a better surprise with everyone there, so locking the door, returning the key to its rather obvious place I started to walk towards Anna's house.

It had just started to rain and I could hear a distance rumble of thunder. The Cooper's house was just around the corner so lighting a cigarette I walked quickly down the road. I could see another couple of cigarette ends glowing near the porch. I started to run. Opening the little iron gate I walked up the path where I could just about make out two people standing by the front door. They turned when they heard me.

Standing on the porch Jack looked at Anna, then looked at George. Anna looked at George then looked at Jack. George looked at them both and laughed. 'If you could see your faces!'

'Oh God, we thought you were dead!' Anna burst into tears and flung her arms around him.

'Why no word George? Everyone has been so worried. I tried *'thought talk'* but there was nothing, but oh thank the Lord you are safe.' And hugging his brother close to him he held onto him for dear life.

'What do you mean you didn't you get the message that I was on my way home? I asked one of the MI9 men to contact Father and he promised he would. I wasn't allowed to phone or anything, all the phone lines were down or whatever. I was told that someone in authority would contact home, so I trusted this official chap to give you a message which I wrote out religiously for him. God I'm so sorry. How on earth are Mother and Father? Bloody hell, someone will swing for this. That's why I didn't contact you again once we left Gibraltar, as I wanted it to be a surprise. I had no idea you hadn't heard anything, I feel dreadful putting you all through this.

'How ridiculous,' said Jack, 'what is wrong with people, one message would have eased our minds I must say. But, you are here and your timing is perfect!'

'Why is it perfect, what's going on?'

'It just is,' laughed Anna, 'you couldn't have timed it better. Everyone is in the dining room. We are celebrating Bertie being here and ostensibly to celebrate him being made a commissioned officer. The advent of your return, me getting my memory back, - I will tell you all about that later, it is a long, long story - but it was really so we could tell everyone about the secret of you boys changing places.'

'How did it go down? It has been a nightmare not knowing anything.'

'Come inside and find out.' Opening the front door quietly as possible, closing it carefully behind them, the three creep in, then drawing the heavy blue velvet curtain across the door to cut out any light, they walk into the hallway, the black and white tiles lit by a large standard lamp throws a golden glow across the room.

Out of the kitchen door comes Evelyn holding aloft a large blue and white platter on which an extremely large piece of beef lay proudly, it seemed almost too heavy for her to hold as she walked out backwards, pushing the door open with her foot.

'Mama, let me take that,'

George mouthed at her, 'let me,' and as Evelyn turned around George took the plate from her. Her hand flew to her mouth. Anna put her finger against her own lips, 'shh!'

'Oh my goodness, George,' she whispered. 'I can't believe, what are you doing here? We all thought...' she stopped herself. Oh but it is so wonderful and what timing.'

Anna stifled a giggle,' just what we said.'

So holding her mother's hand she walked into the dining room with Jack following. Behind with the platter held high came George.

Everyone turned, 'Oh look at that, heavens above, what a delicious smell, Evelyn where on earth did you get hold of that? How wonderful.'

'Here's something far more wonderful!' Anna said as George put the platter down in front of Ernest and Nell.

'Oh my God. It's you Jack, I mean George, oh dear I don't know what I mean I thought.... We thought you were dead and we would never see you again, oh come here, just come here.' And Nell holding onto her son sobbed and sobbed.

Ernest looked at George, his eyes full of tears 'Well, well young man why didn't you let us know you were alright?'

'I explained to Anna and Jack that I had asked for a message to be sent but it obviously never was. I presumed you all knew I was on my way home, I just wanted to turn up out of the blue and surprise you and mother. But obviously I got all that wrong I am so sorry.'

Ernest hugging his son said. 'My dear boy, having you home is all that matters. I am not sure if I can take any more surprises, and I am sure your mother can't.'

He smiled at Nell and putting his arm around her kissed her on the cheek, she leant against him and smiled.

Before we sit down and eat,' said Anna , 'I just want to tell you all that I cannot think of anywhere else I would rather be at this moment, surrounded by those I love and cherish.'

'Hear, hear.' The words went around and glasses were clinked.

George turned to Anna. 'Here, this belongs to you I think,' and putting the locket in her hand he kissed her on the cheek, 'I think this maybe have saved my life. Now it is time to be returned to you, maybe the 'real' Jack should put it on.'

Anna smiled. 'Oh George I had forgotten all about it, how wonderful to have it back and you along with it.' Everyone laughed while Jack fastened the little gold locket around his sweetheart's neck, where it nestled against her pearls.'

'Also, I would like to tell you all that I am married to a wonderful girl called Isabelle, I will fill you in with all the details later. I have a photo of her that I managed to 'steal' before I left.'

The photo was passed around the table with words of admiration. 'Goodness' someone said, 'she looks just like Anna'.

Of course, she does, George smiled to himself, of course she does.

Epilogue

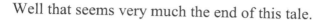

Well that seems very much the end of this tale.

Let us leave everyone to their happiness, their lives at this moment in time, are pretty good, considering the chaos that lies all around them

The war will rage for a few more years, then lives will return to normal. But the story of the twins '*switch*' will go down in the history of the O'Brien's and the Coopers for decades to come.

If we look a few years ahead to the end of the war we can see how some of our characters evolved.

Anna, of course married Jack and had a tribe of children but she still paints famous faces which hang in galleries all over the world. Jack became a renowned pathologist, working alongside Florey, until he branched off on his own, working with a team researching brain damage in young children.

Nell and Ernest still live in the same house, Ernest has retired and now George runs the surgery.

Evelyn and Teddy also live in their house with the black and white tiled hallway. Teddy has retired from government and is writing his memoirs, of slight concern to some of his colleagues!

Isabelle left France and came with her twin boys to live with her new husband, where they bought a house near the surgery. Her parents stayed in St. Samson looking after Regis, who suffered severe shell shock after the war, but is slowly recovering

Joseph, Miriam and their girls moved back to France, but there were too many memories in their old house so they now live in the Chaumière. And, there is a rumour in the village that Regis and one of the girls are walking out, but maybe that is just hearsay.

Amy lives with Shane in Washington and there is talk of him becoming President and Amy First Lady, but that probably is just hearsay too!

Harry deciding that research was not for him, trained as a defence lawyer, working for the under-priviliged in the ghettos of New York.

Remember Sologne who fell in love with a German officer? Well she had a very sad end to her life. Her father found out about her liaison with the young German officer, whom he then shot and killed. He was arrested, taken into the town by the German Military, where he was executed by firing squad in front of the villagers. *'To teach him a lesson'* apparently. Sologne distraught, threw herself into the Seine, while the marée was in full force. Her body was found four miles upriver a day later. She was given a full catholic mass and burial and a plaque was placed in the church after the war, celebrating a young girl's life.

The town of St. Samson was bombed by the American's and British to get the Germans out. It was almost flattened, but parts still remain of the old town and the beautiful church still stands, albeit with damage to some of the exterior.

The Brocante still stands but the fat Madame has long gone as has the cat. The Café Du Sport still exists with the same owners, who never quite got over the death of their little waitress. When the German's left, fireworks were let off on 'the bac' as it chugged across the river; the old couple who ran the ferry having long gone too. There is even talk of building a bridge over The Seine, much to everyone's dismay.

Mario from the café is still there, still singing to his clients. He has acquired a rather large Italian lady as his wife, who cooks, according to the customers, the best lasagne ever.

Andrée de Jongh, aka Dédée, who guided George for some of his journey across the Comet Line, was awarded the George Medal in 1946. She had saved over 700 men, women and children taking them to safety and freedom. In 1943 she was captured on her 33rd journey into Spain, where she was sent to Ravensbruck concentration camp, but luckily survived. She died at the age of ninety in Brussels, Belgium.

Florence stayed with Dedée working with her on the Comet Line but happily she too survived Ravensbruck and went to work as a nurse in Belgium, until after the war when she gave up her life as a young girl and became a Sister of Mercy in an enclosed order on the French border with Spain.

As for Victoria, who probably threw everything into disarray, she turned into quite a beauty and became a famous music hall star.

Her sister Elizabeth eloped with a penniless musician and went to live in the Hebrides, where she became a shepherdess. Teddy bought them a smallholding, where they now raise rare breeds of Highland cattle, her husband has just sold his first piece of music that was actually chosen by someone on Desert Island Discs.

As for Bertie, well he went from strength to strength and spent his life at sea, with, as they say, a girl in every port.

A Message from the Author

I live in France, in La Mayenne, with my husband and various animals; we have an old, rather draughty farmhouse in the middle of nowhere. I have five children all married with children of their own.

By profession I am a portrait artist. But I have enjoyed writing since I was very young. I have written three children's books; really so I could illustrate them but hope one day to get them published. But this book seemed to write itself and so I decided now was the time to take the plunge and get it out there!

When we were in our early thirties we moved with our children to Normandie and the Chaumière was where we bought them up and where they attended the local school. The 'big house' behind us belonged to a family who we became firm friends with. During the occupation of France it was the headquarters of German soldiers.

The town of St. Samson is real, but the name has been changed. Most of the shops and Le Café Du Sport are still there. We visit there frequently as it has so many memories of years gone by.

Printed in Great Britain
by Amazon